JUDICIAL APPLICATION OF EUROPEAN UNION LAW IN POST-COMMUNIST COUNTRIES

Studies in Modern Law and Policy

Series Editor: Ralf Rogowski,
Professor of Law, University of Warwick

Also in the series

Constitutional Evolution in Central and Eastern Europe
Expansion and Integration in the EU
Edited by Kyriaki Topidi and Alexander H.E. Morawa
ISBN: 978-1-4094-0327-2

Central and Eastern Europe After Transition
Towards a New Socio-legal Semantics
Edited by Alberto Febbrajo and Wojciech Sadurski
ISBN: 978-1-4094-0390-6

Democracy, Law and Governance
Jacques Lenoble and Marc Maesschalck
ISBN: 978-1-4094-0395-1

Judicial Accountabilities in New Europe
From Rule of Law to Quality of Justice
Daniela Piana
ISBN: 978-0-7546-7758-1

The European Social Model and Transitional Labour Markets
Law and Policy
Edited by Ralf Rogowski
ISBN: 978-0-7546-4958-8

The Changing Law of the Employment Relationship
Comparative Analyses in the European Context
Nicola Countouris
ISBN: 978-0-7546-4800-0

Property in Work
The Employment Relationship in the Anglo-American Firm
Wanjiru Njoya
ISBN: 978-0-7546-4587-0

Judicial Application of European Union Law in post-Communist Countries

The Cases of Estonia and Latvia

TATJANA EVAS

University of Bremen, Germany

Routledge
Taylor & Francis Group
LONDON AND NEW YORK

First published 2012 by Ashgate Publishing

Published 2016 by Routledge
2 Park Square, Milton Park, Abingdon, Oxfordshire OX14 4RN
711 Third Avenue, New York, NY 10017, USA

First issued in paperback 2016

Routledge is an imprint of the Taylor & Francis Group, an informa business

British Library Cataloguing in Publication Data
Evas, Tatjana.
Judicial application of European Union law in post-communist countries : the cases of Estonia and Latvia. – (Studies in modern law and policy)
1. Judicial process—Latvia. 2. Judicial process—Estonia. 3. International and municipal law—Latvia. 4. International and municipal law—Estonia. 5. Jurisprudence—Latvia. 6. Jurisprudence—Estonia. 7. European Union—Latvia. 8. European Union—Estonia.
I. Title II. Series

Library of Congress Cataloging-in-Publication Data
Evas, Tatjana.
Judicial application of European Union law in post-communist countries : the cases of Estonia and Latvia / by Tatjana Evas.
p. cm. — (Studies in modern law and policy)
Includes bibliographical references and index.
ISBN 978-1-4094-4369-8 (hardback : alk. paper)
1. International and municipal law—Baltic States. 2. Law—Baltic countries. 3. Law—Estonia. 4. Law—Latvia. 5. Law—European Union countries. 6. Post-communism—Former Soviet republics. 7. Judicial process. 8. Law—Interpretation and construction. I. Title.
KJC5057.E93 2012
349.24094796–dc23

2012015710

ISBN 13: 978-1-138-27911-7 (pbk)
ISBN 13: 978-1-4094-4369-8 (hbk)

Contents

For Anna Katarina and my Family

List of Tables and Figures

Tables

Figures

List of Cases

European Court of Justice

106/77 Administrazione delle Finanze dello Stato v Simmenthal SpA. [1978] ECR 629

11/70 Internationale Handelsgesellschaft mbH v Einfuhr- und Vorratsstelle für Getreide und Futtermittel [1970] ECR 1125

283/81 Srl CILFIT and Lanificio di Gavardo SpA v Ministry of Health [1982] ECR 3415

33/76 Rewe-Zentralfinanz eG and Rewe-Zentral AG v Landwirtschaftskammer für das Saarland ECR [1976] ECR 1979

39/72 Commission v Italy [1973] ECR 101

50/76 Amsterdam Bulb BV v Produktschap voor Siergewassen [1977] ECR 137

8/81 Ursula Becker v Finanzamt Münster-Innenstadt [1982] ECR 53

C- 558/08 Portakabin Ltd and Portakabin BV v Primakabin BV [2010] ECR I-0000

C-1/05 Yunying Jia v Migrationsverket [2007] ECR I-1

C-106/89 Marleasing SA v La Comercial Internacional de Alimentacion SA [1991] 1 ECR 4135

C-110/94 Intercommunale voor zeewaterontzilting (INZO) v Belgium [1996] ECR I-857

C-118/00 Gervais Larsy v INASTI [2001] ECR I-5063

C-127/07 Société Arcelor Atlantique et Lorraine and Others v Premier ministre, Ministre de l'Écologie et du Développement durable and Ministre de l'Économie, des Finances et de l'Industrie, [2008] ECR I-09895

C-127/08 Metock et al. v Minister for Justice [2008] ECR I-6241

C-140/08 Rakvere Lihakombinaat AS v Põllumajandusministeerium and Maksu- ja Tolliameti Ida maksu- ja tollikeskus [2009] ECR I-10533

C-143/88 and C-92/89, Zuckerfabrik Süderdithmarschen AG v Hauptzollamt Itzehoe and Zuckerfabrik Soest GmbH v Hauptzollamt Paderborn [1991] ECR-415

C-144/04 Werner Mangold v Rüdiger Helm [2005] ECR I-9981

C-161/06 Skoma-Lux sro v Celní ředitelství Olomouc [2007] ECR I-10841

C-168/05 Elisa v Centro Movil Milenium [2006] ECR I-10421

C-198/01 CIF v Autorita Garante della Concorrenza del Mercato [2003] ECR I-8055

C-213/89 R v Secretary of State for Transport, ex parte Factortame Ltd [1990] ECR I-2433

C-218/01 Henkel KGaA [2004] ECR I-1725

C-232/09 Dita Danosa v LKB Līzings SIA [2010] ECR I – 0000

C-234/04 Kapferer v Schlank & Schink [2006] ECR I-2585
C-241/07 JK Otsa Talu v PRIA [2009] ECR-I 4323
C-255/02 Halifax plc, Leeds Permanent Development Services Ltd, County Wide Property Investments Ltd and Commissioners of Customs & Excise [2006] ECR I-1609
C-268/06 Impact v Minister for Agriculture and Food [2008] ECR I-2483
C-314/08 Krzysztof Filipiak v Dyrektor Izby Skarbowej w Poznaniu [2009] ECR I-11049
C-337/97 Parfums Christian Dior SA and Parfums Christian Dior BV v Evora BV [1997] ECR I-6013
C-354/03, C-355/03 & C-484/03 (Optigen Ltd (C-354/03), Fulcrum Electronics Ltd (C-355/03) and Bond House Systems Ltd (C-484/03) v. Commissioners of Customs & Excise [2006] ECR I-483
C-355/97 Beck Landesgrundverkehrsreferent der Tiroler Landesregierung v Beck Liegenschaftsverwaltungsgesellschaft mbH and Bergdorf Wohnbau GmbH [1999] ECR I-4977
C-397-403/01 Pffeifer v Deutsches Rotes Kreuz, Kreisverband Waldshut eV [2004] ECR I-8835
C-403/98 Azienda Agricola Monte Arcosu v Regione Autonoma della Sardegna [2001] ECR I -103
C-409/06 Winner Wetten GmbH v Bürgermeisterin der Stadt Bergheim [2010] ECR 0000
C-432/05 Unibet (London) Ltd and Unibet (International) Ltd v Justitiekanslern [2007] ECR I-2271
C-445/06 Danske Slagterier v Bundesrepublik Deutschland [2009] ECR I-2119
C-471/07 and C-472/07 Association générale de l'industrie du médicament (AGIM) ASBL and Others (C-471/07 and C-472/07), Janssen Cilag SA (C-471/07) and Sanofi-Aventis Belgium SA (C-472/07) v Belgian State [2010] ECR I-0000
C-472/08, Alstom Power Hydro v Valsts ieņēmumu dienests [2010] ECR I-0000
C-513/99 Concordia Bus Finland Oy Ab, formerly Stagecoach Finland Oy Ab v Helsingin kaupunki and HKL-Bussiliikenne [2002] ECR I-7213
C-555/07 Seda Kücükdeveci v Swedex GmbH & Co. KG [2010] ECR I-0000
C-560/07 Balbiino AS v Põllumajandusminister and Maksu- ja Tolliameti Põhja maksu- ja tollikeskus [2009] ECR I- I-04447
C-6/64 Flaminio Costa v ENEL [1964] ECR 585
C-6/90 and C-9/90 Francovich and Others v Italian Republic [1991] ECR I-5357
C-9/92 Commission of the European Communities v Hellenic Republic [1993] ECR I-4467
Case 14/83 Von Colson und Kamann v Land Nordrhein-Westfalen [1984] ECR 1891
Case 148/78 Pubblico Ministero v Tullio Ratti [1979] ECR 1629
Case 268/83, Rompelman v Netherlands [1985] ECR 655
Case 41/74 Van Duyn v Home Office [1974] ECR 1337

T-324/05 Republic of Estonia v Commission of the European Communities [2009] ECR II-03681

Constitutional Court of Latvia

2000-03-01 of 30 August 2000 On Compliance of Article 5 (Items 5 and 6) of the Saeima Election Law and Article 9 (Items 5 and 6) of the City Dome, Region Dome and Rural Council Election Law with Articles 89 and 101 of the Satversme (Constitution), Article 14 of the Convention for the Protection of Human Rights and Fundamental Freedoms and Article 25 of the International Covenant on Civil and Political Rights

2001-08-01 of 17 January 2002 On Conformity of Article 348 (the seventh part) of the Civil Proceedings Law with Article 92 of the Republic of Latvia Satversme (Constitution)

2001-12-01 of 19 March 2002 On Compliance of Paragraph 26 of the State Pension Law Transitional Provisions with Articles 91 and 109 of the Satversme (Constitution)

2002-21-01 of 20 May 2003 On the Compliance of Article 27 (the Fourth Part) and the Text of Article 28 (the Second Part) "for the Time Period until the Age of 65 Years" of the Higher School Law and Article 29 (the Fifth Part) of the Law "On Scientific Activity" with Articles 91 and 106 of the Republic of Latvia Satversme
2004-18-0106 of 13 May 2005 On the Compliance of Section 9, Paragraph 3 of the Education Law Transitional Provisions with Articles 1, 91 and 114 of the Republic of Latvia Satversme, Article 2 of the First Protocol of the European Convention for the Protection of Human Rights and Fundamental Freedoms as well as its Article 14 (linked with Article 2 of the First Protocol), Articles 26 and 27 of the International Covenant on Civil and Political Rights, Article 5 of the International Convention on Elimination of any Form of Race Discrimination, Articles 2 and 30 of the Convention on the Rights of a Child as well as Article 18 of the Vienna Convention on the International Agreement Rights

2006-03-0106 of 23 November 2006 On the Compliance of the Words "or other attributes" and "separate voiced slogans or speeches held", Included in Section 1, Paragraph 4 of the Law "On Meetings, Processions and Pickets"; the First Paragraph of Section 9; the Words "keepers of public order", Included in Section 12, Paragraph 3, Item 1; the Words "and pedestrians", Incorporated in the Second Paragraph of Section 13; the Second Sentence of Section 14, Paragraph 6; the Words "not earlier than 10 days", Included in Section 15, Paragraph 4 as well as Section 16 and Section 18, Paragraph 4 with Section 103 of the Republic of Latvia Satversme, Section 11 of the European Convention for the Protection of Human

Rights and Fundamental Freedoms as well as with Section 21 of the International Covenant on Civil and Political Rights.

2007-03-01 of 18 October 2007 On Compliance of the Words "Without Restriction on the Term of Office" of Part 1 of Section 7 of the Constitutional Court Law with Article 83, Part 1 of Article 91 and Part 1 of Article 101 of the Satversme (Constitution) of the Republic of Latvia.

2007-11-03 of 17 January 2008 On Compliance of the Part of Riga Spatial Plan 2006–2018 Related to the Territory of the Freeport of Riga with Article 115 of the Satversme (Constitution) of the Republic of Latvia.

2008-09-0106 of 16 December 2008 On Compliance of the First Part of Section 230.1 of the Criminal Law with the First Sentence of the First Part of Article 7 of the European Convention on Human Rights and Fundamental Freedoms and Article 64 and 65 and the Second Sentence of Article 92 of the Satversme (Constitution) of the Republic of Latvia.

2008-35-01 of 7 April 2009 On compliance of the Law "On Lisbon Agreement Amending the Treaty on European Union and the Treaty Establishing the European Community" with Article 101 of the Satversme (Constitution) of the Republic of Latvia.

2009-11-01 of 18 January 2010 on Compliance of the Second Sentence of Para 7 of the Transitional Provisions of the Law "On Judicial Power" (wording of 14 November 2008) with Article 1, Article 83 and Article 107 of the Satversme (Constitution) of the Republic of Latvia.

2009-111-01 of 22 June 2010 on Compliance of the Second Sentence of Paragraph 7 and the second sentence of Paragraph 20 (in the wording of 16 June 2009) and the third sentence of Paragraph 20 of the Transitional Provisions of the Law "On Judicial Power" with Articles 1, 83 and 107 of the Satversme of the Republic of Latvia.

Case No 2008-35-01 of 7 April 2009 On compliance of the Law "On Lisbon Agreement Amending the Treaty on European Union and the Treaty Establishing the European Community" with Article 101 of the Satversme (Constitution) of the Republic of Latvia.

Case No. 2007-10-0102, of 29 November 2007, On Compliance of the Law "On Authorisation to the Cabinet of Ministers to Sign the Draft Agreement between the Republic of Latvia and the Russian Federation on the State Border between Latvia and Russia Initialled on August 7, 1997" and the Words "Observing the Principle of Inviolability of Borders Adopted by the Organization of Security and

Supreme Court of Estonia

3-3-1-68-07
3-3-1-75-08
3-3-1-79-08
3-3-1-80
3-3-1-80-06
3-3-1-80-08
3-3-1-81-08
3-3-1-85-07
3-3-1-86-07
3-3-1-87-07
3-3-1-87-08
3-3-1-88-07
3-3-1-90-06
3-3-1-95-06
3-3-1-96-06
3-4-1-1-03
3-4-1-1-05
3-4-1-25-09
3-4-1-4-98
3-4-4-1-96

Supreme Court of Latvia

SKA-175/2009
SKA-46/2008
SKA-46/2008
SKA-496/2008
SKA-1/2006
SKA-397/2007
SKA-46/2008
SKA-0096-08
SKA-0136-08
SKA-0144-08
SKA-0276-08
SKA-0284-07
SKA-0308-07
SKA-0363-07
SKA-0397/2007
SKA-0397-07
SKA-0422-06
SKA-0441-06
SKA-0496/2008
SKA-1/2006

Estonia: Ordinary Courts

Latvia: Ordinary Courts

List of EU Secondary Legislation

Regulations

Regulation (EEC) No 2988/74 of the Council of 26 November 1974 concerning limitation periods in proceedings and the enforcement of sanctions under the rules of the European Economic Community relating to transport and competition OJ L 319

Council Regulation (EC) No 1257/1999 of 17 May 1999 on support for rural development from the European Agricultural Guidance and Guarantee Fund (EAGGF) and amending and repealing certain Regulations OJ L 160

Council Regulation (EC) No 1260/1999 of 21 June 1999 laying down general provisions on the Structural Funds OJ L 161

Council Regulation (EC) No 1346/2000 of 29 May 2000 on insolvency proceedings OJ L 160

Council Regulation (EC) No 1/2003 of 16 December 2002 on the implementation of the rules on competition laid down in Articles 81 and 82 of the Treaty (Text with EEA relevance) OJ L 1

Council Regulation (EC) No 1782/2003 of 29 September 2003 establishing common rules for direct support schemes under the common agricultural policy and establishing certain support schemes for farmers and amending Regulations (EEC) No 2019/93, (EC) No 1452/2001, (EC) No 1453/2001, (EC) No 1454/2001, (EC) No 1868/94, (EC) No 1251/1999, (EC) No 1254/1999, (EC) No 1673/2000, (EEC) No 2358/71 and (EC) No 2529/2001 OJ L 270

Commission Regulation (EC) No 1972/2003 of 10 November 2003 on transitional measures to be adopted in respect of trade in agricultural products on account of the accession of the Czech Republic, Estonia, Cyprus, Latvia, Lithuania, Hungary, Malta, Poland, Slovenia and Slovakia OJ L 293

Council Regulation (EC) No 40/94 of 20 December 1993 on the Community trade mark OJ L 11

Commission Regulation (EC) No 60/2004 of 14 January 2004 laying down transitional measures in the sugar sector by reason of the accession of the Czech

Republic, Estonia, Cyprus, Latvia, Lithuania, Hungary, Malta, Poland, Slovenia and Slovakia OJ L 9

Commission Regulation (EC) No 796/2004 of 21 April 2004 laying down detailed rules for the implementation of cross-compliance, modulation and the integrated administration and control system provided for in Council Regulation (EC) No 1782/2003 establishing common rules for direct support schemes under the common agricultural policy and establishing certain support schemes for farmers OJ L 141

Commission Regulation (EC) No 817/2005 of 27 May 2005 fixing the minimum selling price for skimmed-milk powder for the 19th individual invitation to tender issued under the standing invitation to tender referred to in Regulation (EC) No 214/2001 OJ L 135

Commission Regulation (EC) No 832/2005 of 31 May 2005 on the determination of surplus quantities of sugar, isoglucose and fructose for the Czech Republic, Estonia, Cyprus, Latvia, Lithuania, Hungary, Malta, Poland, Slovenia and Slovakia OJ L 138

Commission Regulation (EC) No 1628/2006 of 24 October 2006 on the application of Articles 87 and 88 of the Treaty to national regional investment aid (Text with EEA relevance) OJ L 302.

Directives

Council Directive 68/360/EEC of 15 October 1968 on the abolition of restrictions on movement and residence within the Community for workers of Member States and their families OJ L 257

Council Directive 73/148/EEC of 21 May 1973 on the abolition of restrictions on movement and residence within the Community for nationals of Member States with regard to establishment and the provision of services OJ L 172

Council Directive 77/249/EEC of 22 March 1977 to facilitate the effective exercise by lawyers of freedom to provide services OJ L 78

Sixth Council Directive 77/388/EEC of 17 May 1977 on the harmonization of the laws of the Member States relating to turnover taxes – Common system of value added tax: uniform basis of assessment OJ L 145

Council Directive 79/409/EEC of 2 April 1979 on the conservation of wild birds OJ L 103

Second Council Directive 84/5/EEC of 30 December 1983 on the approximation of the laws of the Member States relating to insurance against civil liability in respect of the use of motor vehicles OJ L 8

Directive 98/5/EC of the European Parliament and of the Council of 16 February 1998 to facilitate practice of the profession of lawyer on a permanent basis in a Member State other than that in which the qualification was obtained OJ L 77

First Council Directive 89/104/EEC of 21 December 1988 to approximate the laws of the Member States relating to trade marks OJ L 40

Council Directive 92/43/EEC of 21 May 1992 on the conservation of natural habitats and of wild fauna and flora OJ L 206

Council Directive 93/13/EEC of 5 April 1993 on unfair terms in consumer contracts OJ L 95

Directive 98/27/EC of the European Parliament and of the Council of 19 May 1998 on injunctions for the protection of consumers' interests OJ L 166

Directive 2000/26/EC of the European Parliament and of the Council of 16 May 2000 on the approximation of the laws of the Member States relating to insurance against civil liability in respect of the use of motor vehicles and amending Council Directives 73/239/EEC and 88/357/EEC (Fourth motor insurance Directive) OJ L 181

Council Directive 2000/43/EC of 29 June 2000 implementing the principle of equal treatment between persons irrespective of racial or ethnic origin OJ L 180

Directive 2000/35/EC of the European Parliament and of the Council of 29 June 2000 on combating late payment in commercial transactions OJ L 200

Council Directive 2000/78/EC of 27 November 2000 establishing a general framework for equal treatment in employment and occupation OJ L 303

Directive 2001/42/EC of the European Parliament and of the Council of 27 June 2001 on the assessment of the effects of certain plans and programmes on the environment OJ L 197

Council Directive 2001/51/EC of 28 June 2001 supplementing the provisions of Article 26 of the Convention implementing the Schengen Agreement of 14 June 1985 OJ L 187

Council Directive 2003/86/EC of 22 September 2003 on the right to family reunification OJ L 251

Council Directive 2003/109/EC of 25 November 2003 concerning the status of third-country nationals who are long-term residents OJ L 16

Directive 2004/38/EC of the European Parliament and of the Council of 29 April 2004 on the right of citizens of the Union and their family members to move and reside freely within the territory of the Member States amending Regulation (EEC) No 1612/68 and repealing Directives 64/221/EEC, 68/360/EEC, 72/194/EEC, 73/148/EEC, 75/34/EEC, 75/35/EEC, 90/364/EEC, 90/365/EEC and 93/96/EEC (Text with EEA relevance) OJ L 158

Directive 2005/29/EC of the European Parliament and of the Council of 11 May 2005 concerning unfair business-to-consumer commercial practices in the internal market and amending Council Directive 84/450/EEC, Directives 97/7/EC, 98/27/EC and 2002/65/EC of the European Parliament and of the Council and Regulation (EC) No 2006/2004 of the European Parliament and of the Council ('Unfair Commercial Practices Directive') (Text with EEA relevance) OJ L 149

Council Directive 2006/69/EC of 24 July 2006 amending Directive 77/388/EEC as regards certain measures to simplify the procedure for charging value added tax and to assist in countering tax evasion or avoidance, and repealing certain Decisions granting derogations OJ L 221

Council Directive 2006/112/EC of 28 November 2006 on the common system of value added tax OJ L 347

List of Abbreviations

CAA	Estonian Constitutional Amendment Act
CEE	Central and Eastern European
CFI	The General Court (ex Court of First Instance)
ECJ	The Court of Justice (ex European Court of Justice)
ESC	Estonian Supreme Court
EU courts	The Court of Justice of the European Union
LAPA	Latvian Administrative Procedure Act
LCC	Latvian Constitutional Court
LCCA	Latvian Civil Procedure Act
LCPA	Latvian Criminal Procedure Act
LSC	Latvian Supreme Court
LTR	Long Term Residence
MSs	Member States
OCMA	The Office of Citizenship and Migration Affairs, Latvia
PRIA	Estonian Agricultural Registers and Information Board
SRS	Latvian State Revenue Service, Latvian Tax Office
TCB	Estonian Tax and Customs Board
TEC, EC Treaty	The Treaty Establishing the European Community
TFEU	The Treaty on the Functioning of the European Union

Foreword

Prof. Dr. Ulrike Liebert and Prof. Dr. H.C. Norbert Reich

The seminal enlargement of the EU in 2004–2007 – the accession of twelve new members, ten out of which were from the former East Central European 'socialist states', and among these three post-Soviet states in the Baltic regional – has faced the Union as much as the states themselves with considerable political, economic and legal problems. One of the key issues – the development of the rule of law – is typically at stake in any new democracy. But, arguably, resolving it proves even more difficult in post-Communist or post-Soviet countries, such as the Baltic states. The present book – fruit of the author's productive cooperation in two multi-annual interdisciplinary research projects[1] – provides surprising information and valuable insights that promise to reshape the terms of important debates, in law as well as in the social sciences.

Legal debates are centred around the concept of '*coherence*' in the three dimensions as 'substantive', 'institutional' and 'argumentative' in applying EU law in the context of national litigation in the new Member countries of Estonia and Latvia. The first relates to the fundamental EU law concepts of 'supremacy', 'direct effect' and 'harmonious interpretation', and their effect on the legal development in these two post-Soviet jurisdictions. The second is concerned with the role of courts and their dramatic transformation as instruments of the 'ruling class' (that is, the Communist Party) to independent and responsive Community/Union courts in cooperation with the European Court of Justice, both on the central constitutional level and on the everyday working of the judiciary. The third explores the 'argumentative dimension' which implies a departure from the Soviet style of formal and positivistic legal thinking to a more purpose-oriented application and interpretation of EU law to litigation submitted to national courts which were completely new to them.

The analysis is based on very detailed, careful studies of the Constitutional Judiciaries of Estonia (the Supreme Court which also fulfils the function as constitutional court) and the Latvian Constitutional Court which reveal certain differences in the detailed coherence analysis of the author, though these are, however, being gradually overcome. The adjudication of EU law by ordinary courts on rather complex litigation having a direct link with EU law – which the author describes with admirable understanding of the underlying legal and political issues – shows again a very nuanced picture where Estonian courts seemingly had less problems that Latvian courts, even though some 'grey areas' remain, in

1 ConstEPS, RECON.

particular concerning the status of third-country nationals of Russian citizenry. Notwithstanding, the author comes to the quite positive conclusion that 'the negative predictions related to the ability of lower courts to apply EU law beyond the textual positivist approach in general are not conformed in the Estonian or Latvian courts. The overall conclusion on jurisprudence of Estonian and Latvian courts is rather positive.'

Comparative political scientists will welcome *Judicial Application of European Union Law in post-Communist Countries* as an important interdisciplinary contribution to better understanding of the transformative impacts of EU enlargement in empirical, theoretical and comparative terms. First of all, this book provides systematic evidence that the conversion of the judicial systems of Eastern European post-Communist Member States has neither been slow and short of capabilities nor excessively conflictive but astonishingly successful. Thus, it helps correct the conventional wisdom that the triple transitions from communist single-party regimes to capitalist democratic states ruled by law suffered from weak prospects for consolidation. Secondly, to account for this surprising finding, the author draws on comparative Europeanization approaches without limiting herself to the simplistic 'fit' – 'misfit' terminology. Instead, she elaborates a sophisticated theoretical framework that allows her to advance an original argument about the pivotal role of national court litigation and adjudication, where the performance of the latter was measured by the degree of coherence of how European Union law was applied. In other words, she proposes to pursue a bottom-up view, where litigants are working hand-in-hand with national and European judiciaries, thus replacing communist legacies of legal positivism by the willingness and ability of judges to make use of EU law for mediating conflict in a large variety of economic, social and political fields. Evas's meticulous empirical examination, finally, rests on her careful case selection: for substantiating the positive record of new Member States she could have selected the more favourable cases – post-socialist Member States from East Central Europe that have been better researched. Instead, she chose to pioneer two more challenging examples – namely the 'post-soviet' Eastern European states in the Baltic region, Estonia and Latvia, both still *terra incognita* to large extents. Certainly, findings from these cases cannot be generalized, as they cannot count as typical or representative for other new member or candidate states. But they help correct established assumptions and develop new propositions. Although similar on most accounts, the two cases show some significant variation as regards the weaker performance of the Latvian compared to the Estonian judiciaries, suggesting that institutional factors might account for these differences, such as the relatively lower autonomy of the judiciary in the former case.

Bremen, May 2012

Preface and Acknowledgements

In the world renowned folktale 'The Bremen Town Musicians', by the Brothers Grimm, four animals leave their homes to go to Bremen, famous for its freedom. Despite the title of the fairy tale, apparently the animals did not reach Bremen and settled happily elsewhere. However, I did reach this 'small but brave' Hanseatic city to complete this book in an environment of academic freedom. This journey through the Hanseatic region, Reval, Riga and Bremen, is a somewhat unexpected but most interesting and challenging experience that ultimately informs my academic perspective and topic of this book, not to mention professional collaboration and friendships for which I am extremely grateful.

First and foremost, I would like to express deepest gratitude to Prof. Dr. Ulrike Liebert and Prof. Dr. h.c. Norbert Reich. Professors Reich and Liebert have always found time and interest to comment on my work and engage in continuous academic exchange. Their intellectual sharpness combined with an open-minded attitude, a sense of humour and great personal qualities combined to facilitate and contribute to my professional and personal learning. Professor Liebert with her warm devotion helped me to develop good taste and understanding on comparative methodologies, theories of political science, Europeanization literature, the craft of data collection, and interviewing techniques. Professor Reich with his precision for detail, deep knowledge and excellence in EU law helped me to navigate in the fast-developing field of EU law.

On this note I also want thank our great ConstEPS team Petra Rakusanova-Guasti, Ewelina Pawlak, Aleksandra Maatsch, Kathrin Packham, Sönke Maatsch, Janna Wolff, Alexander Gattig and Sandra Kröger at the Jean Monnet Centre for European Studies for invaluable discussions and joint activities through work on this book. A special word of appreciation is due to my colleague and friend Shazia Wülbers who fuelled the writing process with optimism on so many occasions.

Also I would like to express special gratitude to Ms. Sarmīte Inberga, a chief judge at Sigulda City court, for her profound interest in my research. Without her support this work would have been significantly less insightful. I would like to acknowledge ZERP colleagues Professors Andreas Fischer Lescano and Josef Falke and Olga Batura as well as colleagues in the Reconstituting Democracy in Europe (RECON) Project for commenting on and discussing my work, Christopher Goddard for his friendship and patience with editing and proofreading the manuscript and Edgars Koskins for his assistance in collecting Latvian data. My gratitude to the series editor Ralf Rogowski and anonymous reviewers, to Bethan Dixon, Jeanne Brady and Sarah Horsley from Ashgate for supporting and navigating me through publication process. Volkswagen Stiftung and RECON project kindly provided financial support throughout my research. Without this financial support this journey would be much more difficult. I am grateful to the vivid numerous scientific discussions of the RECON project that significantly contributed to my theoretical framework.

While I cannot recognize everyone individually I would like to thank all my colleagues and friends who made this book possible. Last but not least, words of deep gratitude go to my family, my parents and my sister. I dedicate this book to my daughter and my parents for their love, patience and understanding through the years.

Bremen, March 2012

Introduction
National Adjudication and the Coherence of the EU Legal System

"Where there is law, there is order, where there is order, there is security, but security means peace and harmony."

Hermanis Apsītis 1938[1]

Analysis of national adjudication of European Union law is by now a classical play of EU legal scholarship.[2] To put it simply, the main scenes in the script are well known: the principle of supremacy, direct effect, national remedies and preliminary reference. Equally, the leading actors are easily identified: national courts and the Court of Justice of the European Union.[3] Even the twofold nature of the arena where this play is staged – the autonomous nature of Community law and the decentralized system of EU law enforcement – is by now taken for granted. However, as political science scholarship on European legal integration indicates, just consider 27 Member States, each of whose performance of this classical play is somewhat different. Not only because the scripts are continuously fine-tuned through reforms of primary and secondary law but also because the leading actors (national and EU courts) are of different characters and temperaments, let alone the impact of individual constraints, interests and preferences among leading institutional and also other actors (for example, national political elites, the European Commission). As a result, adjudication of EU law by national courts is always a dynamic performance

1 Hermanis Apsītis, the last Minister of Justice of the First Sovereign Latvia, 1938 as cited by Latvian Ministry of Justice available at www.tm.gov.lv.

2 Continuous scholarly focus on the performance of national courts and their interplay with European Courts is justified by the importance assigned to national courts in the EU legal system. The effectiveness and legitimacy of decentralized EU law enforcement in contrast with traditional international law practice is considerably more intimately linked to the performance of national courts. National courts drive the project of European legal integration further by referring sensitive questions of interpretation of Community law to, and subsequently applying the decisions of, the European Courts. Most recently, on a policy level, the role of national courts in implementing Community law is, for example, highlighted in the Communication from the European Commission 'A Europe of Results – Applying Community Law' COM (2007) 502 final.

3 'The Court of Justice of the European Union' refers collectively to the Court of Justice (ex European Court of Justice), the General Court (ex Court of First Instance) and the EU Civil Service Panel (together also referred to as 'EU courts').

that on the one hand is defined by common EU legal norms and principles, and that on the other hand always has a unique national flavour.

This book is a theoretically inspired and empirically grounded interdisciplinary contribution to the study of the complex relationship between the idea of coherence and the European Union legal order, with a focus on national adjudication in post-Soviet, recent 2004 entrants to the European Union. I confine myself to the *national judicial perspective*[4] and discuss how the idea of coherence is played out by national EU law jurisprudence in two new Eastern European Member States.[5] Focusing on coherence in the application of EU law within national legal systems, I assess and compare how Estonian and Latvian national courts understand and apply EU law, explicitly or implicitly considering appeal to coherence of the EU institutional legal order.

Considering the European Union as an institutional normative system defined by different interlocking local, national, and supranational legal orders, with none being privileged (Bankowski and Scott 2000: 17–30), the most evident but also the most difficult question is through what mechanisms should this plurality be balanced to produce a functioning, sustainable, and legitimate legal system(s)?[6] Legal theory (for example, MacCormick 1978: 152–94, Aarnio 1998: 28–40, Aarnio 1997, Aarnio, Alexy and Peczenik 1981, Hage 2004, Peczenik 1989, Bankowski and MacCormick 1992) has highlighted the importance of coherence as an ideal feature of law and as a regulative rationality criterion of judicial argumentation. Ken Kress (1999: 536) suggests that coherence theories of law have a special claim on us:

> The idea that law is a seamless web, that it is holistic, that precedents have a gravitational force throughout the law, that argument by analogy has a special significance in law, and the principle that all are equal under the law, provide strong *prima facie* support for a coherence theory of law.

---

4 'National courts apply Community law on a daily basis and must uphold Community law when it contravenes national laws. In this sense, the national judge is traditionally seen as the first judge of European law, to whom parties may refer litigation and requests based on EU law', European Parliament (2007).

5 For a discussion on the idea of coherence as applied in this book, please refer to Chapter 1 'Conceptual Framework' below.

6 For discussion on the nature of the EU legal order, see for example, de Witte (2010), who points that 'the autonomy of EU law is not absolute but relative; it does not mean that EU law has ceased to depend, for its validity and effective application, on the national law of its member states, nor that it has ceased to belong to international law.' On the autonomy of EU law from national member states see for example, Barents 2004, Schilling 1996 and Weiler and Haltern 1996.

Is it plausible and desirable to translate theoretical appeals to coherence to the supranational context of the European Union?[7] Neil Walker (2005b: 8) notes

> … the degree of interpenetration of national and European legal orders implied by supranationalism means that the ways in which we normally conceive of the relationship between adjacent but presumptively separate legal orders are inadequate to grasp the dense complexity of the relevant ties.[8]

Competing understandings offered by legal theorists on the extent of interpenetration of legal orders within the EU legal system and mechanisms for inter-system conflict settlements concentrate on the relationship between authority and coherence (Walker 2005a). The main challenge to this relationship is the *sui generis* nature of the European Community. As Stefano Bertea (2005: 154–72) succinctly puts it, 'The European order seems to require an appeal to coherence at the same time as it makes this appeal problematic.' The EU's contested constitutionality and debates on the notions of sovereignty, the European polity and legitimacy lead to extremely divergent positions on what the EU legal system is or should be, and how the relationship between authority and coherence should be reconciled (for example, Walker 2005a, Fossum and Menendez 2010a).

The guiding rational and scientific contribution of this book is twofold. First, it proposes a conceptual framework for assessing and comparing transformations of national judicial systems in the context of EU membership. Thus, it contributes to the EU legal theoretical debate on the relationship between 'authority' and 'coherence'. Secondly, by applying this conceptual framework to the case law of the Estonian and Latvian courts, the book analyses the involvement of post-Communist Member State courts in decentralized enforcement of EU law and the constitutional, institutional and structural adjustments that accompany acceptance of the EU mandate by national courts.[9]

I understand coherence in functional terms and as a matter of degree. In other words, I refer to coherence as an empirical instrument to assess comparatively the extent to which national legal systems have voluntarily abandoned traditional international conflict of laws rules in order to secure functioning of the EU legal

---

7 For more practical treatment of the notion of coherence see for example, Prechal and van Roermund 2008 and Bertea 2005; for theoretical accounts see for example, Richmond 1997, Kumm 1999, La Torre 1999, Walker 2003 and Lindahl 2003.

8 By normal means, by which we conceive the relationship between legal orders, Walker suggests either 'episodic "conflicts" of private international law or the competing singular formulae for linking public international law to national law (monism versus dualism)'.

9 The notion of the 'Community mandate' is used to encompass all the tasks of the courts related to the application of EU law in national jurisdictions including if necessary setting aside the 'national constitutional mandate', that is, obligation to apply national constitutional norms when in conflict with Community law. For theoretical and conceptual understanding of the term 'Community mandate', see for example, Claes 2006.

system. The system of application of EU law by national courts is coherent if it is able to resolve inconsistencies between legal norms without either infringing principles of EU law or undermining national legal doctrine.

Against this background, the central research question that this book investigates is whether and how national 'specialties' informed, *inter alia*, by post-Communist legacies, are reconciled by national courts with the requirements of uniform and effective application of EU law. What types of legal conflicts emerge in national courts in enforcing EU law? Will courts justify enforcement of EU legal norms and rights for citizens, in particular, and how will courts contribute to making the EU legal order more understandable and accessible to ordinary people? And what do these national CEE 'judicial flavours' bring to the project of European legal integration and ultimately to our understanding of the evolving European legal order?

A starting-point that inspires this research and informs the choice of its theoretical framework and methodology are insights from three strands of literature: first, legal theory; second, political science literature on the Europeanization of national legal systems and judicial discourses, and third, interdisciplinary 'enlargement' literature focusing on the transformative potential and institutional and substantive (legal doctrinal) adaptation of legal institutions (especially Supreme and Constitutional courts) to accession and post-accession challenges. Through critical analysis of existing scholarship on the application of EU law by national courts, I refine central concepts to capture factors considered in the literature to impact application of EU law by national courts.

A voluminous political science literature on judicial politics in the European legal system (for example, Cappeletti, Seccombe and Weiler 1985, Haltern 2004 and Vauchez 2008) is strongly biased towards multiple accounts of the role and jurisprudence of the Court of Justice of the European Union (ECJ)[10] in the process of European legal integration and thus framed in terms of inter-systemic coherence.[11] The literature provides significantly less evidence of the impact of Europeanization on national legal systems or an intra-systemic account of coherence.[12]

In developing a theoretical-analytical framework of intra-systemic coherence, the debates in the Europeanization literature suggest that time, scope and procedure for accepting fundamental EU law principles as well as the institutional

10 Under TFEU renamed 'the Court of Justice', here referred to as the ECJ.

11 The so-called 'Integration through law' approach. See in particular the 'Florence Integration Project' started in 1981 at the European University Institute that resulted in a series of publications entitled *Integration Through Law.*

12 This research lacuna is highlighted by Stone Sweet (2004: 23), who argues that the focus of existing political science literature on judicial discourses is on the 'impact of adjudicating EU law on the institutional evolution of the EU, rather than on the impact of EU law on (or Europeanization of) national legal systems'; see also Stone Sweet 2007. To overcome this challenge a number of recent articles, although yet rather limited, are emerging with an attempt to evaluate the domestic impact of EU law on courts and institutions both substantively and empirically, see for example, Connant 2001, Nyikos 2007, Jupille and Caporaso 2009, Ketelhut 2010.

dimension of the legal system are central. The application of main EU law principles in the practice of national courts is neither automatic nor without difficulties.[13] Conditional acceptance of EU principles by national courts may lead to delayed and partial application of EU law in national legal systems. Weak judicial institutions could also become a hindrance to intra-systemic coherence. Considering post-Communist legacies, strong scepticism has been voiced in the Europeanization literature to suggest slow and selective application of EU law in new MS. Consequently, an assessment of application of EU law at the level of the national judicial system requires examining acceptance of main EU law principles in practice as well as 'inter-court' (national courts-ECJ) and 'intra-court' cooperation and cooperation between courts and other political actors. Those variables are discussed under substantive and institutional coherence dimensions.

Intriguingly, analyses by legal scholars (cf. Ginter 2008, Narits 2008, Albi 2005b, 2010, Laffranque 2009) of the jurisprudence and doctrinal legal developments of CEE supreme and constitutional courts with a focus on fundamental cases rebuts the scepticism of institutional and structural approaches. Constitutional legal scholarship holds that, with varying degrees of intensity and commitment, the highest national courts of CEE countries show the legal craft and ability to overcome traditional orthodoxy on sovereignty and to accept the main legal doctrines of EU law (for example, Ginter 2008, Albi 2002, Sadurski, Ziller and Zurek 2006, Febbrajo and Sadurski 2010, Albi 2005a, Albi and Ziller 2007) as well as to resolve often very challenging constitutional legal issues related to accession and Union constitutional reforms.[14]

Finally, the third strain of research that this book builds on is legal theory. It draws heavily on the institutional theory of law (MacCormick 2007) and the idea of coherence. The analytical framework of coherence that I develop and apply to the case law is elaborated in detail in Part I of the book. Here I limit myself to the methodological question of how the analytical-theoretical framework of coherence can be used for analysis of case law and how it can help to bring together insights from doctrinal legal scholarship and Europeanization studies to assess application of EU law in the national legal systems of the new Member States and its implications for European legal integration. Apart from the notorious ECJ *Laval* case[15] involving Latvia, and to a lesser degree perhaps the Lisbon judgment of the Latvian Constitutional Court (Reich 2009),[16] the national legal systems, not to mention jurisprudence of the Estonian and Latvian *ordinary*

13 Burley and Mattli 1993; Claes 2006.

14 For example, judgments of the Czech Constitutional Court on the Lisbon Treaty Pl. US 19/08 judgment of 26 November 2008; Pl. US 29/09 judgment of 3 November 2009; judgment of the Latvian Constitutional Court on the Lisbon Treaty Case No 2008-35-01of 7 April 2009.

15 Case C-341/05 Laval un Partneri Ltd v Svenska Byggnadsarbetareförbundet [2007] ECR I-11767.

16 The Constitutional Court of the Republic of Latvia Case 2008-35-01 of 7 April 2009.

courts, remain largely *terra incognita* for international European legal integration scholarship.[17] Even scholars of CEE transformation tend to concentrate mostly on the central European states of Poland and the Czech Republic to draw overarching conclusions for the whole CEE region (for example, Kühn 2005).

According to Neil MacCormick, an appeal to coherence in adjudication

> ... requires an identification of the deeper values embodied in the rules and principles in force with the system. Coherence is exhibited precisely in the interpretation and maintenance of the system so that it secures a relatively ordered and structured scheme of political, social and human values. (MacCormick and Summers 1991: 536)

As this quote suggests, a systemic analysis of adjudication requires a 'grander' overview of the legal system that goes beyond the classic 'black letter' doctrinal legal approach.[18]

The task of producing a rationally coherent view of systemic values requires the structured ordering of material from court rulings justified by judges through legal reasoning and argumentation. Therefore, structured analysis of legal reasoning, argumentation and justification structures advanced by the courts helps to yield a deeper understanding of the normative legal order envisaged as valid and in force within a given jurisdiction.[19] Drawing on MacCormick's institutional theory, law (enacted by the legislator) becomes alive and meaningful for a concrete person (legal or physical) either through authoritative interpretive decisions (of courts and administrative agencies), or through the possibility to rely on these authoritative interpretations (and their enforcement) if enacted law is violated by state organs or other persons. In that sense, courts (and case law) are defining features of a polity based on the rule of law where interpretive decisions of courts are key to understanding the most prominent characteristics of the relevant legal landscape. The methodological tool for capturing law in its socio-institutional context that this book adopts is the method of *rational reconstruction.*

The method of 'rational reconstruction' assumes that the episodic and fragmentary character of legal materials forms part of a complex, well-ordered and rationally explainable larger whole (Alexy 2010). Thus, as has been argued by legal theorists including MacCormick, Wroblewski and Alexy, court judgments are rationally grounded and explained by national institutional, constitutional and cultural contexts within which courts operate as well as by the wider international legal context. As Maduro and Azoulai (2010: xiii) argue, 'A court's jurisprudence cannot be

17 Studies on national constitutional/higher courts see for example, Ginter 2008, Laffranque 2009, Albi 2002, Narits 2008.

18 On competing legal-theoretical approaches see for example, Buckel, Christensen and Fischer-Lescano 2009.

19 On the system theory of law in context of the constitutional pluralism in Europe see for example, Fischer-Lescano and Teubner 2006, Teubner and Fischer-Lescano 2004.

immediately ascertained by looking at individual cases. It is also the product of a broader community of actors than courts themselves. It is woven by judges interacting with lawyers and legal scholars, all acting in a particular social context.'

The method of 'rational reconstruction' contrasts with the 'classical' legal method in so far as it helps to view court judgments not only as mere legal *dicta* but as part of a wider normative system which is shaped by factors such as political ideas, institutional structures, legal cultural norms, as well as cognitive frameworks, professional training and the social background of judicial personnel. This methodological approach, *inter alia*, through analysis of the jurisprudence of ordinary courts in the broader socio-legal context, allows us to connect research into legal practices with people's needs and real-life problems, as well as with analysis of institutional structures, to capture the dynamics of 'simultaneity' of law and politics in the transformation of judicial systems.[20]

Table I.1 Expectations informing analysis of national adjudication based on review of the literature

Literature	Expectations	Focus of analysis
Legal scholarship	POSITIVE: High degree of normative coherence/convergence with EU law	Legal norms
Enlargement literature/ Europeanization	NEGATIVE: slow transformation of judicial institutions; 'culture of dependency';	Institutions
Legal theory/ communication studies	NEGATIVE: legal positivism/ formalism; legal culture – lack of methodological argumentative skills of judges	Legal argumentation and justification

Existing scholarly accounts of application of EU law by the judiciaries of CEE Member States are limited due to their (1) predominant focus on the larger Central European states[21] and (2) narrow focus on key cases of the highest courts. Below I discuss those shortcomings and suggest how the research design chosen by this book helps overcome these limitations.

Considering the historical, political and social differences between Central European and post-Soviet Baltic countries, the dynamics and difficulties of application of EU law by national courts will not necessarily follow the same pattern. To offer a more differentiated account of the Europeanization of legal systems

20 Not regarding its normative claims but rather its general approach, this methodology of rational reconstitution also resonates with the legal theory of 'new legal realism', see for example, Nourse and Shaffer 2009.

21 Most scholarly attention is directed to the larger Central European MSs – Poland and Czech Republic.

in the CEE region, this book concentrates on a comparative analysis of the two Baltic Member States, Estonia and Latvia. These two countries provide interesting cases for a most similar case comparison in terms of historical experience and institutional structures. In the socio-political context, both countries (a) share very similar historical, social and normative experiences under Communism; (b) were part of and gained independence from the Soviet Union at the same time; (d) share a similar geopolitical position, and (c) applied for EU membership and acceded to the EU around the same time. At the level of formal structures and legal systems, both countries had acceded to the main international treaties, adopted a monist approach to international law and transposed the *acquis communautaire* relatively well, prior to formal EU accession. However, as analysis of Estonian and Latvian case law from 2004 through 2009 will reveal, there are marked differences on how their judicial systems have taken up the European mandate.

Existing analyses of the judicial systems of CEE countries (for example, Sadurski 2005) mostly focus on the jurisprudence of national constitutional and supreme courts.[22] Emphasis on performance and doctrine setting by the highest courts and analysis of 'key' cases may be justified and sufficient for a classical legal method account. However, in the light of the rational reconstruction method adopted in this book, this is insufficient to assess the application of EU law in national legal systems. Margit Vutt (2009) rightly stated that 'through a small part of cases considered on appeal in the Supreme Court one can see only general tendencies, but it does not give an adequate picture of the legal conflicts that have taken place in society.'

Only a small fraction of all cases reaches the highest courts, and not in all countries do individuals have direct access to the constitutional courts (for example, in Estonia) for protection of their rights.[23] Thus, adopting the perspective of an individual facing a legal dispute, the accessibility, effectiveness and practice of ordinary courts are crucial. As correctly noted by Annus and Tavits (2004) in their study on the judiciary in countries undergoing democratic transition, 'ordinary courts may play a much greater role … than supreme or constitutional courts, especially because they are closer to the citizens and influence public perception about the fairness and acceptability of the new regime.'

---

22 National higher courts have been credited with playing an important role in the consolidation of new post-Communist democracies, *inter alia*, through judicial activism on matters of social policies, politically sensitive matters of the historical past and individual citizenship rights.

23 According to statistical data (Ministry of Justice 2010), the Estonian Supreme Court from 2004 to 2009 on average adjudicated 412 cases yearly (2009 shows the highest number: 472 cases); this is on average 20 per cent of all cases submitted through the appeal procedure (in 2009, 20 per cent administrative cases, 29 per cent civil cases, 25 per cent criminal cases and 38 per cent misdemeanour cases), www.nc.ee/?id=79 compared with over 53,000 law disputes submitted yearly to the first level courts (25,000 civil, 2,700 administrative, 13,500 misdemeanour and 12,000 criminal).

Very few articles specifically analyse EU law jurisprudence of Estonian and Latvian ordinary courts. Available research on Czech and Polish ordinary courts acknowledges alarming variation in the reception of EU law between supreme and ordinary courts (Kühn 2005, Ginter 2008). For example, a study by Kühn (2005) provides rather cautious findings from the Czech Republic and Poland identifying a large gap between EU-friendly application of EU law by the highest courts and slow, conflicting and limited application by national lower courts. Thus, the substantive coherence dimension concerned with coherence of the legal system in application of EU law also contributes to a more nuanced understanding of application of EU law by lower courts that is lacking in existing scholarship. Therefore, the present study on Estonia and Latvia will test findings from analysis of the highest level against those from the lower level.

To do so and to overcome those shortcomings in the current state of the art, this book examines the 2004–09 jurisprudence of Estonian and Latvian national courts of all instances.[24] To avoid a selection bias and grasp all possible instances of reference to EU law by national jurisprudence (even those that might be insignificant from internal lawyers' perspective) the dataset includes cases that in their full-text judgments mention EU law provisions or practice of EU courts: in total over 1,800 cases.

The national jurisprudence dataset is composed as follows. National full-text electronic databases (Estonian: KIS and Supreme Court[25] databases; Latvian: Lursoft, Constitutional Court and Supreme Court databases) of judicial decisions in national languages have been searched with the keywords 'European Union', 'European Community', 'ECJ', 'directive', 'European Parliament' and 'European Council'.[26] This search in the selected period resulted in (N=531) cases for Estonia and (N=1281) cases for Latvia [=total dataset]. The total dataset was analysed quantitatively[27] and qualitatively.

---

24 Coverage: Supreme Court and Constitutional Court 01.05.2004–31.12.2009; jurisprudence of ordinary courts 01.05.2004–31.12.2008. In Latvia it was possible only to collect cases of the Riga City Court (court of first instance) due to extreme difficulties in electronic access to full text court judgments of other courts of the first instance.

25 The Supreme Court of Estonia (SC) database includes court judgments and regulations from all chambers including the constitutional review chamber. Estonia does not have a Constitutional Court. The constitutional review function is covered by the Constitutional Chamber of the Supreme Court of Estonia.

26 The Estonian KOLA and KIS database and Latvian Lursoft database cover judgments of the courts of first instance including *county courts* that have general jurisdiction on all civil, criminal and misdemeanour matters, and *administrative courts* with jurisdiction on administrative matters. The databases also cover courts of second instance including *courts of appeal*.

27 Data on the date of the national judgment, court reference number, court issuing the judgment and name of the judge(s) are collected on all judgments in the dataset (the general dataset).

Table I.2 Total dataset of cases (number of cases)

Supreme/Constitutional Courts (third level)		Appeal Courts (second level)		County/City courts (first level)	
Supreme Court of Estonia	121	Administrative Regional Court (LV)	273	Estonian courts of first level (all courts)	154
Supreme Court of Latvia*	227	Latvian Regional Courts	681	Riga City Court	297
Constitutional Court of Latvia	46				

*Refers both to cases of the Senate of the Supreme Court (cassation cases) and cases of the Supreme Court Chambers (acting as a court of appeal).

Based on qualitative assessment of full-text judgments, cases in which European Union-related search terms appear but are not discussed in substance were eliminated [= substantive dataset].[28] The substantive dataset is composed of national court-level judgments where EU law was invoked as a legal argument or where the court substantively discussed application of EU law. The substantive dataset covers national case law of all levels subject to two caveats. First, due to technical access limitations to Latvian jurisprudence, the Latvian substantive dataset covers only Riga City Court as a court of first level. Secondly, the substantive dataset focuses on areas of law where possible inconsistencies between the EU and national law were argued. The substantive dataset of Estonian and Latvian judgments forms the centre of the legal analysis that follows.[29] Considering the number of judgments, the qualitative analysis of the substantive database in Part III of the book is focused on the largest (in terms of number of cases generated) groups of cases.

28 For example, cases that mention that a car had a European Union registration plate, or that a person had a European Union insurance card.

29 The analysis includes the type of court; the type of litigant (private individual, company/organization, national institutions and authorities), lawyers involved in the litigation, the type of subject matter of the litigation, the EU law provision involved, how a EU law provision or case law is invoked in the litigation, whether a preliminary reference has been requested either by the litigating party or the court, the outcome of the case and whether the case has been appealed to a court of higher instance.

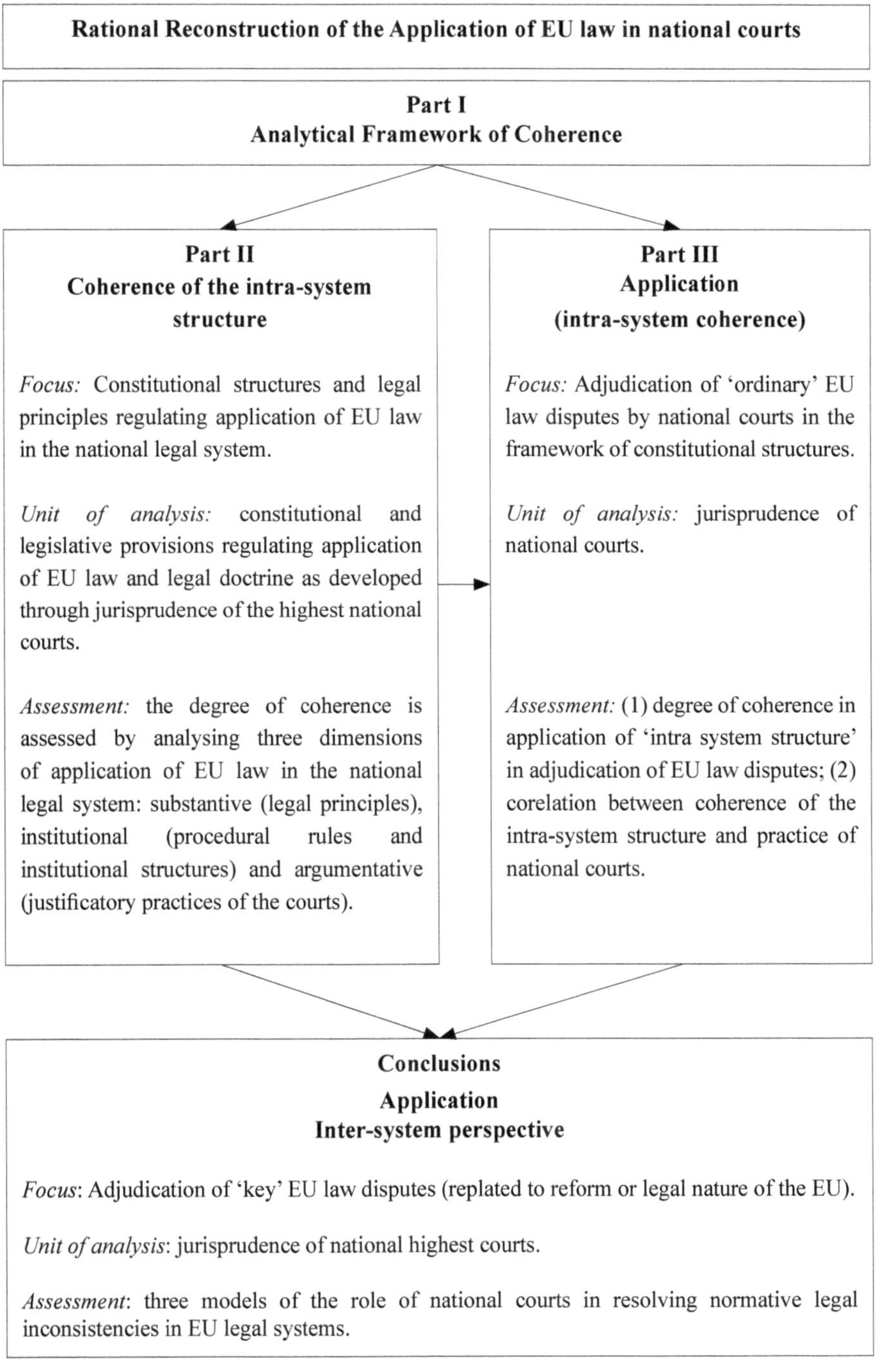

Figure I.1 Logical structure of analysis

The analysis and main argument of the book develops in four steps. In Part I, first I propose a framework based on the notion of coherence. Secondly, I explain how the idea of coherence is applied to assess the application of EU law by courts of both national legal systems. And finally the divergent expectations of the literature will be examined through a framework of coherence. I suggest conceptualizing 'coherence' through three analytically different but interconnected dimensions of EU law adjudication, namely the substantive, the institutional and the argumentative.

In Part II, working through Estonian and Latvian constitutional structures and judicial practice of higher courts, I account for what contributes to and what threatens coherent application of EU law in national legal systems. First, through analysis of constitutional provisions and jurisprudence of national courts on the doctrine of supremacy, direct effect and harmonious interpretation, I examine the substantive dimension of coherence. Secondly, I investigate institutional judicial structures as well as intra-court and inter-court cooperation and relations between national courts and political actors to assess the institutional dimension of coherence. Finally, under the argumentative dimension, I focus on the legal methodological tools that courts apply to adjudicate legal disputes and communicate their decision.

Part III discusses application of EU law in the daily judicial practices of Estonian and Latvian ordinary courts. Against the coherence approach, I assess how national ordinary courts relying on constitutional structures and jurisprudence of higher courts resolve legal conflicts related to application of EU law. First, I examine legal conflicts emerging in national courts applying EU law, as well as legal principles applied to resolve incoherencies between norms. Secondly, I discuss whether in interpreting EU law divergent positions emerged between levels of national courts *and/or* national courts and EU courts. Third, I analyse through what types of arguments (linguistic, systemic, teleological) national courts resolve substantive incoherencies between national and EU legal norms.

The last part of the book, 'Synthesis and Conclusions', brings together the findings from these analyses with theoretical discussions. I summarize and then develop further conclusions from my findings on the performance of 'newcomer' courts in the context of competing understandings of the project of European legal integration.[30] I will contend, perhaps to the surprise of sceptics of post-Communist transformation, that both jurisdictions are neither slow nor unable to effectively apply EU law in national legal systems. The judicial systems of Estonia and Latvia have in a short time successfully trumped Soviet law legacies and have well adapted to the new legal challenges of adjudicating EU law. Moreover, both

30 On competing theories on the reconstitution of democracy in the EU and theory of constitutional synthesis, see Reconstituting Democracy in Europe (RECON) Project. For theoretical foundation of the RECON Project see for example, Eriksen 2007, Eriksen and Fossum 2009, Fossum and Menendez 2010b. For the discussion on the European democracy and identity construction see Liebert 2012a, 2012b.

cases through their own unique institutional and methodological style bring new dynamics and fresh air to the project of European legal integration.

The case of Estonia is less complex in terms of EU legal disputes adjudicated by national courts (structural funds, surplus stock and ethnic discrimination cases), while Latvian courts have been tested through complex cases related to VAT and competition rules. On many accounts, the Estonian case (albeit with some shortcomings indicated by discrimination cases) presents an example of legal conceptual and methodological modernity (through its understanding of the supremacy and accessibility of legal and judicial materials through e-technologies).

The Latvian case is an interesting example of where international and EU law norms and principles are successfully synthesized by national courts to resolve complex legal issues. Although legal principles behind the application of EU law are not always extensively explained by national courts, which may quickly lead to a negative conclusion on the application of EU law in Latvia, a more careful analysis of jurisprudence reveals the opposite. National courts accept the EU law mandate 'naturally' following from the Latvian legal system consistently developing a 'primacy of international law' approach.

Based on analysis of national jurisprudence from 2004 to 2009 I argue that the Estonian judicial system – through the pro-active legal-communicative role of the Supreme Court, the dynamic role of lower courts, open access to legal information and jurisprudence, intra-institutional judicial organization and training as well as intensive use of modern e-technologies – has developed a relatively coherent legal *modus operandi* in that it has proved a strong capacity to generate well argued, justified and reason-based rules of conflict solutions. Thus, concerning 'economic' cases, the Estonian system is an extremely positive example of the intra-system coherence of application of EU law that resolves inconsistencies between legal norms without either undermining EU or national norms and principles. Notably, this coherent 'operation system' appears to be relatively less developed in non-economic 'citizenship' cases of ethnic discrimination on pension and residence entitlements.

The Latvian judicial system and adjudication is more complex and less coherent in terms of institutional arrangements and argumentative patterns. However, it is more coherent in terms of substantive adjudication of both strictly economic and non-economic cases. Essential normative-constitutional and institutional conditions for the application of EU law exist. National courts do explain and apply fundamental principles of EU law as well as resolving complex EU law-related matters coherently and remarkably well. However, recent problems related to the Latvian judicial system triggering public outrage, as well as a tendency for national courts to be not always comfortable with an understanding of law and jurisprudence as a normative system of communication, contribute to institutional and argumentative incoherencies of the system. Moreover, a publicly accessible database of Latvian jurisprudence is lacking. Finally, intra-institutional judicial organization and training, as well as limited professional academic scholarship, constitute further impediments to the coherence and ultimately the effective application of EU law.

Thus, assessment of the application of EU law in these relatively similar cases by 'newcomers' reveals strikingly different 'ways' contrasting both cases with each other as well as comparing them to the Central East European accession countries.

PART I
The Three-Dimensional Coherence Approach

Chapter 1
Conceptual Framework

> ... discussing problems of law or legal theory in terms of narrative coherence gets on lawyers' nerves. They become impatient when someone tries to convince them of the quite received opinion that law should be and is presumed to be coherent. They become suspicious when they are asked to learn still another fashionable word for what – if anyone knows – *they* know about coherence in law ... They even become slightly aggressive, at least in my country, when they hear coherence in law epitomized as 'narrative': for 'nar' in Dutch means 'fool' or 'jester'; and should not law at least be taken seriously?
>
> Bert C. van Roermund 1990: 310[1]

In addressing the main research questions, the defining approach of this book departs from the state of the art. Before developing the conceptual framework in more detail and defining the central research hypothesis of this book, I will review major approaches from the political science and law literature.

State of the Art – Literature Review

A starting-point that inspires this research and informs the choice of theoretical framework and methodology is insights from three strands of literature: first, legal theory; secondly, political science literature on the Europeanization of national legal systems and judicial discourses (Stone Sweet 2004, Slaughter, Stone Sweet and Weiler 1998, Slaughter 1995, 2003, Weiler 1994, Jupille and Caporaso 2009, Connant 2001, 2002, Nyikos 2007; Golub 1996, Carrubba and Murrah 2005, Alter 1996, 1998, 2000, 2001, 2009, Burley and Mattli 1993, Claes 2006), and third, interdisciplinary 'enlargement' literature focusing on the transformative potential and institutional and substantive (legal doctrinal) adaptation of legal institutions (especially Supreme and Constitutional courts) to accession and post-accession challenges (Kellermann et al. 2006, Zemanek 2006, Kühn 2005, Albi 2005a, Sadurski 2006, Albi and Ziller 2007). Through critical analysis of existing scholarship on the application of EU law by national courts, I refine central concepts to capture factors that are considered in the literature to impact the application of EU law by national courts.

---

1 Bert C. van Roermund, 'Narrative Coherence and the Guises of Legalism', in Nerhot, P (ed.), *Law, Interpretation and Reality* (Springer and Kluwer Academic Publishers, 1990) p. 310, with kind permission from Springer Science+Business Media B.V.

A voluminous political science literature on the relationship between national and European courts is dominated by multiple accounts of the role and jurisprudence of the ECJ and thus framed in terms of *inter-systemic* coherence (Stone Sweet 2004, Connant 2001). The literature provides significantly less evidence on the impact of Europeanization on national legal systems or the *intra-systemic* account of coherence. Most recently, a notable contribution to the study of Europeanization of national judicial systems has been made by Jupille and Caporaso (2009). They developed and tested two analytical models of the impact of European law on the domestic judicial field. The study by Jupille and Caporaso does not specifically address the issue of coherence; however, the analytical models that this study develops also contribute to understanding of mechanisms and principles that contribute to coherence of the application of EU law in national legal systems.

Jupille and Caporaso suggest two models. First, the 'statist' model, based on the idea of the traditional Westphalian international legal order and reasoning, presumes that EU law enters domestic judicial discourse primarily through direct inter-court communication – the preliminary reference procedure – and will be heavily influenced by conscious and continuous control by state actors.[2] Secondly, the 'indigenization' model, which goes beyond reliance mainly on the preliminary reference procedure, provides for politically less predictable and less controllable 'spill over' effects of EU law concepts on domestic judicial discourses in unforeseen and constitutionally important ways (Jupille and Caporaso 2009: 206).

Testing these two models against the jurisprudence of the UK courts, Jupille and Caporaso found that even in the 'special' jurisdiction of the UK with its long-standing and strong common law judicial tradition, there is overwhelming evidence in support of the indigenization model. Based on empirical evidence from UK cases 1970–2005 (N=4389), they identify an overall trend in case law so that 'an initial logic of conscious, intended and controlled "compromises" of Westphalia gives way, over time, to an alternative logic in which legal concepts and discourses cross-fertilize each other' (Jupille and Caporaso 2009: 220). The breaking point of logic change depends on domestic mechanisms for legal incorporation (imitation, socialization of the legal community) (Burley and Mattli 1993, Slaughter 1995) and the set of institutional and doctrinal factors of the domestic legal order (Vink et al. 2009). Referring to Table 1.1. below, the 'statist' model closely resembles the 'Westphalian' Model 1 with legalistic mechanisms for cooperation between national and European legal systems. The 'indigenization' model resembles a shift from legalistic/mechanical 'Westphalian' to discursive/persuasive characteristics of the 'post-sovereign' discursive/persuasive system.

The analysis by Jupille and Caporaso is a notable empirical contribution to the study of the impact of EU law on national judicial systems. However, their

2 Under the Westphalian international system, the sovereignty of the state is centre stage. On critical analysis of the Westphalian international legal order, see for example, Cutler 2001, Beaulac 2000, 2004.

methodology cannot be directly applied to new Member States (MSs). To trace the process of domestification and logic of change in the UK legal system, Jupille and Caporaso quantitatively assess reliance by national courts on EU legal concepts that were originally foreign to the national jurisdiction. This method of analysis of change presupposes a mature legal system and a strong judiciary as preconditions for the reach of EU law into a national legal system such as the UK's. Notably, this precondition is missing in the new MSs where legal doctrines and legal cultures are in a state of continuous flux and readjustment from the Soviet legal system to the new realities of the European Union.

The analytical categories developed by Jupille and Caporaso are nevertheless useful tools to assess mechanisms and principles contributing to the transformation of legal systems resulting from application of EU law. Applying insights from Jupille and Caporaso to develop a framework for intra-system coherence, legal principles (substantive coherence) and institutional mechanisms for cooperation (institutional coherence) between national courts and the ECJ are key variables.

In terms of inter-system coherence, that is, the relationship between 'coherence' and 'authority', the 'statist' model with a strong institutional dimension and political control ultimately means that divergent normative claims are settled primarily through authority-based solutions where national institutional actors are decisive. By contrast, the 'indigenization' model, with its emphasis on legal principles, points to mechanisms for settling normative inconsistencies through reason-based solutions. Thus the locus of authority in the application of EU law shifts from a traditional international-law approach conditioned on the explicit permission of political actors (and thus subject to the externalities of the political process) to a national-law approach where national courts have the authority to resolve normative inconsistencies based on valid legal rules and principles without direct political interference.

Considering the historical-legal background of the new MSs, it is not possible to differentiate between the 'statist' vs 'indigenization' logic based on penetration of EU legal concepts that were originally foreign to the national legal systems.[3] Instead, I propose to distinguish a logic of application of EU law in national judicial systems by analysing the normative position of EU law within the hierarchy of national legal norms and based on the legal reasoning and justifications of the courts. This 'statist' model would be characterized by 'conditional acceptance' of the main EU law-structuring doctrines of supremacy and direct effect, combined with a tendency towards predominantly legalistic-mechanical[4] application of EU legal norms. Both characteristics combined point towards the national institutional (politically controlled) authority as the final arbiter in conflicts between national

3 The legal systems of new Member States do not have a long uninterrupted history of legal doctrine.

4 Legal-mechanical application of EU law is defined here as a predominant interpretation of legal norms based on a narrow linguistic, formal understanding of law that does not rely on legal principles and considerations of fairness and justice in a deeper sense.

and EU levels. On the other hand, the unconditional acceptance of doctrines accompanied by analytical-persuasive reasoning[5] of courts would correspond with the 'indigenization' model.

The two models, 'statist' vs 'indigenization' not only suggest different logics but also generate divergent expectations about the pace of application of EU law in national legal systems.[6] In the immediate post-accession period, the statist logic would heavily rely on direct references to the ECJ and result in a slow take-up of the new and daunting task of applying EU law in national systems. The process of domestication of EU law is conditioned on the willingness and ability of national courts to apply and cross-reference EU law, principles and ECJ judgments and thus gradually learn to craft the naturalization of EU law as part of the domestic legal order.[7]

Shifting the focus from the political science literature on the underlying logics and temporal expectations regarding application of EU law in national legal systems, the enlargement literature has concentrated on the institutional capacities of the judicial system and the jurisprudence of the national highest courts (Sadurski 2006, Galligan and Matczak 2007). Sceptical voices from the post-Soviet transformation and enlargement literature have suggested that, considering the relatively short period during which transformation has taken place (discussed in Kühn 2004, Capeta 2005) and the warning that the Soviet legal legacy is in the 'fibre of those societies and will live on for generations' (Hendley 1996: 17), national courts will be unable to effectively participate in the decentralized system of EU law enforcement. This criticism has focused on the lack of deeper institutional adaptations of the legal and judicial institutions (Bobek 2008, Kühn 2004, Emmert 2003); on differences between legal cultures (Rodin 2005); on unsettled intra-court power struggles and instability; on the heritage of the 'socialist' judicial tradition based on strong textual positivism

5 Consideration of EU law as not only authoritative but also as a persuasive authority, through application of systemic and teleological-evaluative arguments.

6 Historical analysis of acceptance of EU law in the original six MSs suggests that national courts tend to take up the new task slowly. 'Indigenization' in Western EU Member States did not occur immediately after joining the European Community as national judges and other state institutions (for example, legislatures or parliaments) were hesitant to give away overnight their deeply enshrined national constitutional traditions and practices; it took time until national courts found convincing reasons to apply EU law in national jurisdictions more intensively. On legal historical analysis of acceptance of main EC law legal doctrines in domestic legal structures of the six original EU MSs, see for example, Claes 2006, Mattli and Slaughter in Slaughter et al. 1998.

7 It has been argued in the literature that the temporal process of accepting EU law in national jurisdictions is hindered by the existence of a strong constitutional court and federalism (Alter 2009: 293). Factors (identified in the literature) that facilitate the pace of acceptance of EU law include (1) national political interests, (2) self-interest of litigants and judges, and inter-court competition, (see for example Slaughter et al. 1998); (3) inter-state trade and intensive application of EU law by neighbours (Stone Sweet 1998).

(Kühn 2006), and inadequate training of national judges especially in the lower courts (Bobek 2007, Kerikmäe 2009). In fact, even the European Commission (2003a, 2003b) in its latest 2003 pre-accession report stressed that although in CEE there are functioning judicial systems in place that generally meet accession criteria, a further effort was still necessary to train the national judges of Estonia and Latvia on issues of EU law. At the extreme end of this line of argumentation, some commentators feared that the accession of post-Communist Central and European MSs had the potential to endanger the functioning of the EU legal order as a whole (Capeta 2005).

Other cautionary arguments were put forward in relation to new MSs to suggest that the application of EU law, even after formal accession, would follow the logic of 'path dependency' (at least for some time) and thus exhibit patterns of 'external Europeanization' characterized by 'transplantation' logic (Amichai 2006).[8] Thereby, EU law provisions would be treated by national courts not as part of domestic legal discourse but rather as an international legal 'transplant' that under certain circumstances of authority must be referred to or applied. Therefore, 'transplantation' logic would result in a rather restrained participation of national courts in EU constitutional discourse.

Intriguingly, analyses by legal scholars of the jurisprudence and doctrinal legal developments of CEE supreme and constitutional courts with the focus on fundamental cases rebuts the scepticism of institutional and structural approaches. Constitutional legal scholarship holds that with varying degrees of intensity and commitment, the highest national courts of the CEE countries have shown the legal craft and ability to overcome traditional orthodoxy on sovereignty and to accept the main legal doctrines of EU law (Ginter 2008, Albi 2002, 2005a, Sadurski, Ziller and Zurek 2006, Febbrajo and Sadurski 2010, Albi and Ziller 2007) as well as to resolve often very challenging constitutional legal issues related to accession and constitutional reforms of the Union.

Framework of Coherence

The conceptual framework is premised on the assumption that courts, in applying EU norms in the national context and thus undertaking a reconciling exercise, must safeguard, *inter alia*, the principle of coherence that is a core value of both national and EU constitutional law. I conceptualize coherence as an analytical concept that helps to assess the institutional normative order as a system. *Coherence is defined here as a dynamic principle of action, organization and functioning of the legal system encompassing conflict avoidance rules and procedures that secure legal certainty, stability, predictability, justice and legitimacy of the normative legal order.*

8 The notion 'legal transplant' was introduced by Watson in his seminal book *Legal Transplants*, 1974 and further developed in Watson (1995, 1996). In relation to Eastern Europe see Ajani (1995: 93–117).

The idea of coherence as employed here is not identical to its ordinary or most common meaning. Traditionally, theories of coherence can be broadly distinguished into (1) accounts based on the theory of truth that are concerned with the question of whether a given line of reasoning or a normative system lead to a correct or right answer (constitutive coherence), and (2) theories of knowledge that investigate whether an argumentation or a normative system cohere with other justified beliefs (epistemic coherence) (Raz 1994, Rodriguez-Blanco 2001: 212–32). I will not explicitly deal with philosophical issues of the validity and truth of law or alternatively with theories of justified beliefs. My account of coherence is more legal practice oriented and concerned with the notion of coherence in the application of EU law in national legal systems.[9]

In a nutshell, in the context of the European Union, three main approaches can be distinguished in the relationship between coherence and authority: (1) pluralist-sovereignty, (2) complex unity and (3) post-sovereignty (Walker 2005a: 11–12). The pluralist approach builds on the logic of sovereignty and respect for plurality of sovereign authorities (Richmond 1997, Kumm 1999). Coherence between legal orders is not a normative value but rather a derivative achievement of institutional mechanisms that attempt to resolve the (inevitable) clash of final authorities. The complex unity approach (von Bogdandy 2000) emphasises EU-wide legal unity that is to be secured by 'sovereign independent' devices such as that suggested by Ingolf Pernice: 'multilevel constitutionalism' (Pernice 2002). Finally, the post-sovereign approach (MacCormick 1999, Maduro 2003, Gerstenberg and Sabel 2002) suggests that a focus on sovereignty (in a strong sense as suggested by sovereign-pluralist approaches or in a weak sense as suggested by complex unity approaches) is not necessary and should be replaced by a heterarchical system of authority that goes beyond state-centred understandings.[10]

How can these competing approaches be translated into national judicial perspectives? In other words, what role should national courts adjudicating EU law disputes play under each of the alternative approaches to the relationship between authority and coherence? The pluralist-sovereignty approach is closest to the international law understanding of the relationship between competing legal orders. National courts, especially constitutional courts, are central players with a strong normative claim to final authority. Justificatory discourses about competing norms are structured around the normatively most valid claim to authority, that is, more legalistic rather than deliberative 'best reason' or 'common good' discourses. The system is strongly hierarchical and references to the ECJ will be very limited.

9 This is not to suggest that my understanding of coherence and its application to analysis of jurisprudence is completely detached from legal-philosophical theories, but rather to emphasise that my aim is not to provide a legal philosophical argument but to apply this principle to legal practice.

10 Most recently, see also theory of constitutional synthesis developed by Fossum and Menendez (2010b).

The complex unity approach shifts the emphasis from the national level as a final authority to the European level. The hierarchical structure is organized so that in judicial disputes the ECJ claims final authority. National courts are important but normatively in EU law matters they are 'subordinated' to the EU level for reasons of unity of the European order. This approach suggests intensive referencing from national courts to the ECJ.

The post-sovereignty approach relocates the locus of authority from hierarchical-legalistic to discursive-persuasive points of authority. Thus, it is not institutional-based authority but rather reason-based authority that takes centre stage. An intensive, ongoing dialogue and cooperation between national and EU courts is a pre-requisite for coherence of the European legal order through 'best reason' persuasion and the 'common good'.

The system of application of EU law by national courts is coherent if it is able to guarantee the legality and legitimacy of the use of power and to resolve inconsistencies between legal norms without infringing either principles of EU law or undermining national legal doctrine through (1) norms and legal principles that are clearly set and consistently applied without discrimination by (2) independent, competent and professional judicial institutions with (3) rational and persuasive justifications that are credible to other legal practitioners and the general public.

This book understands intra-system coherence as developed by institutional theory of law. It builds on legal theoretical accounts of judicial legal reasoning (Dworkin 1986, Hart 1994, Kelsen 1967, MacCormick 1978, 1984) (that is, internal legal perspectives concerned with the nature and rationality of law itself) combined with the theory of constitutional pluralism (that is, informed external observer perspective on the conditions and mechanisms of voluntary non-hierarchical convergence of legal orders) (MacCormick 1993, Kumm 1999). Thus, analytically, coherence is not a static legal norm but rather an organizing principle for bundling constitutional norms, institutional structures and legal argumentation that sustains legal orders and contributes to the legitimacy of judicial institutions.

In legal theoretical literature, coherence is conceptualized in two different but interrelated ways, focusing on systemic or argumentative aspects. First, the *theory of coherence of legal systems* focuses on explaining how different judicial decisions fit within the legal system, in other words, how judges in resolving particular cases reconcile complex (and at times contradictory) legislative materials issued by different legislative bodies (that is, national and EU legislature) and then how those individual judgments are connected with the constitutional, political and moral structures of society (Dworkin 1986). Against this background, I do not reduce understanding of coherence to uniformity or monism. Rather, I take the same line as Moral (2003: 302), who argues that

> … a base-dependent and pluralistic notion of coherence, unlike competing notions, deals with the diversity of law without distorting it: It is possible to make sense of the law and legal reasoning, without giving up its complexity, and without attempting to make the law a tensionless normative system.

Secondly, the *theory of coherence of legal argumentation* is concerned with analysis of the rationality of arguments and justifications within a judgment (Alexy 2010). The understanding of coherence adopted by this book addresses and combines both conceptualizations of coherence. I propose to apply the insights of the theory of coherence of legal systems to analyse application and understanding of principles of EU law aiming to reduce conflicts between national and EU law (for example, supremacy, direct effect) by national courts. Additionally, at an institutional level, I analyse the procedural mechanisms available to national courts for cooperation with the ECJ (that is, preliminary reference procedure). Furthermore, in accordance with the theory of coherence of legal argumentation, I propose not only to analyse coherence of the legal system but also to analyse the argumentation of the courts. However, differently from theorists of legal argumentation, I do not use the strict notion of coherence that aims to analyse the logical rationality and correctness (truth) of a legal decision adopted by the court. Rather, I analyse arguments distinguishing two broad types of legal reasoning: legal-mechanical and analytical-persuasive. Consequently, what matters is not the rationality of the legal structure of the specific decision but rather aggregate justificatory patterns and reasons adopted by the court in reaching decisions. This 'simplified' approach aims to identify specific post-Soviet legacies that include criticism of textual positivism, among other factors.[11]

In applying this analytical framework of coherence to the jurisprudence of national courts (intra-system coherence) in EU law adjudication, I propose to distinguish three dimensions of the *principle of coherence:* substantive, institutional, and argumentative.[12] These three dimensions are neither necessary pre-conditions nor outcomes of coherence but rather factors that in the context of EU law adjudication contribute to or threaten the legal certainty, effectiveness, and legitimacy of the legal system.

Substantive dimension of coherence

The focus of the '*substantive*' dimension of coherence is (1) on the norms and (2) on the legal principles available to courts in resolving potential conflicts between national and EU law. The guiding principles here are those of supremacy, direct effect and harmonious interpretation. In analysis of jurisprudence, substantive incoherence arises for instance from a clash between substantive norms, a clash of understandings of interpretations, or if courts resist or fail to refer to and to apply EU norms. A clash of substantive norms need not necessarily lead to incoherence

11 I do not claim that a more fundamental and nuanced analysis of the coherence of legal argumentation is not important. However, considering the research questions of this book it is neither possible nor necessary to undertake analysis of the logical rationality and correctness of the legal decisions.

12 Inter-system coherence arguments, discussed in the Introduction, see Table 1.1 and in Chapter 8.

but it does when courts fail to recognise or resolve this clash through principles of supremacy, direct effect and harmonious interpretation. To give an example: in situations where EU law provisions are not (or are not correctly) transposed into national law or which expose a clear divergence between understandings of certain legal concepts between EU and national law, national courts either fail to acknowledge existence of the conflict between national and EU law or fail to resolve this conflict through EU law principles. This dimension of coherence is central to legal theory and to doctrinal legal analysis as it includes the consistency of norms within the internal legal hierarchy of the legal system.

Institutional dimension of coherence

Secondly, the '*institutional*' dimension of coherence is central to the understanding of institutional values, interactions between national and European courts, between different levels of national courts, national courts and political actors. Here the assumption is that institutional incoherence may emerge from conflicting institutional competency claims resulting from divergent interests and expectations of various actors on how EU law-related conflicts should be institutionally adjudicated and settled. The best-case scenario in terms of institutional coherence is then national legislation or legal doctrine that provides clearly defined and uncontested competences and procedures on how EU law-related disputes should be adjudicated and how and when a preliminary reference from the ECJ should be requested. This dimension of coherence is central to institutionalist political science and law-in-context perspectives.

Argumentative dimension of coherence

Finally, the dimension of '*argumentative*' coherence includes analysis of legal argumentation. As argued above, I define coherence of legal argumentation in terms of two broad categories: 'legal-mechanical' and 'analytical-persuasive'. I conceive of legal-mechanical application of EU law as a predominant interpretation of legal norms based on a narrowly linguistic, formal understanding of law that does not rely on legal principles or considerations of fairness or justice. Although 'legal-mechanical' justifications of the reasoning of the court may satisfy minimal conditions of coherence, modern legal understanding of the role of courts and legal reasoning suggests that courts have a duty to citizens to justify and communicate legal decisions (Habermas 1997, Palazzo 2002, Menendez 2000, Closa and Fossum 2005, van Hoecke 2001). In this context, coherence of the legal system requires analytically persuasive justifications. Especially in the context of post-Soviet states, where courts have been notable for their textual positivist legal culture and reliance on the narrow linguistic interpretation of legal norms, a shift towards a communicative legal methodology would signal an important change towards normative argumentative jurisprudence and hence a modern understanding of the law.

Table 1.1 Inter-system models of conflict solution by national courts in the EU legal system[13]

Locus of final authority/ mechanism of justification	**Hierarchical**		**Non-hierarchical**
	'Westphalian' (sovereign-pluralist)	'Regulatory' (complex unity)	Post-sovereign (synthesis)
Legalistic/ mechanical	Classical international conflict of laws approach characterized by predominant reliance on national constitutional doctrines and linguistic arguments. National Constitutional Courts are final arbiters in the legal conflicts of competing norms. References to the ECJ are rare.	Multilevel conflict of laws solutions where the EU is the final normative authority and EU-wide legal unity is a leading structuring element supported by predominantly technical, linguistic arguments. The ECJ is the final arbiter. The role of the ECJ is central.	
	High proportion of legalistic, technical and bureaucratic language in the court opinions. The predominant style of court opinions is magisterial and authoritative. High proportion of formal rather than substantive reasons. Implicit logic of rationality is logico-deductive, that is, syllogistic subsumptions.		
Discursive/ persuasive	As above but national courts in addition to linguistic arguments also refer to systemic and evaluative arguments, although preserving national sovereignty rights as a final criterion in resolving conflicts.	As above but the ECJ in addition to linguistic arguments also refers to systemic and evaluative arguments preserving unity of EU law as a final criterion in resolving conflicts.	Best reason 'common good' solutions of competing normative claims. National sovereignty/authority based arguments replaced by main reliance on 'reason based' systemic, evaluative and transcategorical arguments based on universal and common values.
	Lower proportion of legalistic and technical language in court opinions. Court opinions are extended and elaborate. Lower proportion of formal rather than substantive reasons. Implicit model of rationality is not deductive but discursive – open choice supported by arguments.		

13 The criteria to distinguish categories of justifications are adopted from MacCormick and Summers (1991).

Research Hypothesis

To adopt this analytical framework allows us not only to assess the degree of coherence of application of EU law in national legal systems but also to test divergent expectations following from the literature. Based on the literature review I test three hypotheses. First, the 'Slow Starter' hypothesis is structure and process oriented and presupposes that EU law enters domestic judicial discourse slowly, that the level of activity of courts in applying EU law is slow, and that application of EU law is controlled by other state actors. The claim is that traditional 'lack of impartiality' and 'culture of dependency' still constrain the jurisprudence of the courts and thus ultimately hinder their full participation in exercise of the EU mandate. In testing the 'Slow Starter' hypothesis, I rely on and develop further the analytical propositions advanced by Jupille and Caporaso (2009) as well as political science literature that perceive courts as political institutions. This hypothesis resonates primarily with the institutional coherence dimension and, if confirmed, would mean that national legal systems are characterized by substantive institutional incoherencies in application of EU law due to their political dependency.

Unlike the 'Slow Starter' hypothesis that focuses on the formal institutional structures and procedures that enable national courts to carry the EU mandate, the '(Dis)ability' hypothesis aims at outputs of the courts in the shape of jurisprudence. This hypothesis is substance oriented and examines doctrinal developments and argumentative or justificatory patterns in the jurisprudence of national courts. This hypothesis considers two sets of conditions. The first relates to whether the doctrinal developments and constitutional or legislative adjustments that are necessary for the courts to fully accept the EU mandate are in place. The second set of conditions relates to the 'legal techniques' that courts use to resolve controversies at hand. Therefore, the 'ability hypothesis' claims that these conditions are not in place, while the 'disability hypothesis' expects that they are. Accordingly, I will examine whether and how national courts accept the fundamental doctrines of EU law, what national legal issues arise and how judges reason in legal controversies related to applying EU law.

One of the central research questions is what legal constitutional issues national courts were confronted with. How did courts reason acceptance of EU law? How did courts justify application of EU law in daily practice? The aim is thus to analyse whether and how in the given national institutional structures and legal conceptual framework within which courts operate they are able fully to participate in the decentralized application of EU law. In testing the '(Dis) ability' hypothesis, I utilize insights from legal culture and legal theory literature regarding legal reasoning, argumentation and justification structures in court practices. Specifically, I adopt the framework and methodology developed by MacCormick and Summers (1991). This hypothesis corresponds to the substantive and argumentative dimensions of coherence. If courts fail to apply EU law as a result of clashes between national and EU norms that they cannot or are unwilling to resolve through EU law-structuring principles, then this would indicate substantive incoherencies. Failures to justify application of EU law would be indicators of argumentative incoherence.

Finally, the 'Conflict' hypothesis refers to the relationship between (a) national highest courts and ordinary courts, and (b) national courts and EU courts. It claims that the traditional culture of dependency and passivity as well as limited training and background in EU law of national judges in post-Soviet new EU Member States contribute to passivity or resistance of national courts in applying EU law (Mattli and Slaughter 1998). This hypothesis corresponds to the institutional dimension and tests the coherence of intra-court and inter-court cooperation.

Table 1.2 below summarizes the analytical framework of coherence that I apply to empirical analysis of national jurisprudence and hypothesis.

Table 1.2 Intra-system coherence: analytical framework

Coherence	Main focus of analysis	Dimensions	Literature	Hypothesis
Substantive	Norms and legal principles	Constitutional adaptations Doctrine of supremacy Doctrine of direct effect Principle of harmonious interpretation	Doctrinal legal analysis	H.2. (Dis)ability
Institutional	Institutions, actors, interactions	Preliminary reference procedure Access to information Court system N. Courts – ECJ N. Courts – other political actors	Political science research Historical Institutional Economic Social Behavioural	H.1. Slow-Starter H.3. Conflict
Argumentative	Values, discursive-argumentative perspectives	Legal Culture Argumentation and interpretation methodology	Legal theory Political Theory Communication studies	H.2. (Dis)ability

PART II
Intra-System Coherence: Constitutional Structures and Adjudication of EU Law by the Highest National Courts

Chapter 2
Substantive Coherence: Constitutional Structures and Principles

Six years of membership in the EU provide rich evidence and a solid empirical basis to test how national courts from post-Communist MSs deal with the increased post-accession complexity of national legal systems and accompanying intra-system incoherencies. In Part II, I start with analysis of the constitutional principles and institutional mechanisms that structure national systems of application of EU law. The aim is to assess what normative, institutional, or argumentative factors contribute to and endanger coherent application of EU law in national legal systems. In discussing EU law's main structuring principles of supremacy, direct effect and harmonious interpretation, I adopt a national judicial perspective, emphasising application and understanding of those principles by national courts and not on historical-legal developments of the ECJ.[1]

In Part II, applying the three-dimensional analytical framework of coherence I explore the following questions: how are changes in national constitutional structures tailored to EU membership and main EU legal principles that aim to resolve incoherencies between EU and national legal norms conceptualized and applied by national highest courts? In other words, how are structuring legal principles of EU law understood and applied by national courts to resolve instances of substantive incoherencies between national and EU norms (Chapter 2, substantive coherence dimension)? How do institutional and procedural arrangements regulating intra-court (between national courts), inter-court (between national courts and EU courts) and between courts and other political actors structure and impact resolution of EU law-related disputes in national courts (Chapter 3, institutional coherence dimension), and finally, how are legal culture and self-understanding of the judicial role by judges reflected in the interpretation techniques and justification patterns of the highest courts in EU law adjudication (Chapter 4, argumentative coherence dimension)?

In Chapter 2, focusing on substantive coherence, I discuss constitutional structures and principles that define application of EU law in national jurisdictions. Rather than defining and investigating substantive normative conflicts in the jurisprudence of ordinary courts (see Part III), here I concentrate on the national constitutional structures and EU legal principles of supremacy, direct effect and

1 Instead of discussing all the details of each relevant principle, each subsection after introducing the legal principle will focus on the relevant aspects that are most important and pertinent to the new MS.

Table 2.1 Factors contributing to and endangering intra-system coherence in application of EU law in the national legal system

	Factors	Impact on coherence	
		+	–
I	**Substantive Coherence**		
1	Set of norms and rules that regulate application of EU law	Regulated at the constitutional level and explained by the highest courts	Unclear
2	Doctrine of supremacy	Full acceptance	Conditional acceptance
3	Doctrine of direct effect	Full acceptance	Conditional acceptance
4	Doctrine of harmonious interpretation	Full acceptance	Conditional acceptance
II	**Institutional Coherence**		
5	Preliminary reference (procedure)	Clearly regulated through procedural codes and explained by highest courts	Unclear
6	Court system	Independent	Politically dependent
7	Information (e.g. access to court judgments, legislation) use of e-technologies	Full and easy access	Partial and difficult
8	Inter-court cooperation	Trust (liberty)	Distrust (coercion)
9	Intra-court cooperation	Trust (harmonious)	Distrust (conflicting)
III	**Argumentative**		
10	Legal culture (openness to supranational norms)	Open	Restrictive
11	Legal interpretation	Persuasive – communicative	Technical-authoritative

harmonious interpretation that guide national courts in settling possible substantive incoherencies. The purpose is to assess the application and boundaries of legal principles that are available to national courts in resolving conflicts between substantive norms. Legal principles are tools that national courts can use to resolve conflicts between national and EU law. Therefore, the analysis of application of legal principles that follows below is central to understanding the mechanisms that help to sustain substantive coherence between EU and national legal norms.

EU Law in National Constitutional Doctrine

Constitutional provisions defining the position of EU law *vis-à-vis* national constitutional arrangements structure and explain the overall national legal dynamics of application of EU law. A legal system that precisely defines the place of EU law in the hierarchy of legal norms and procedural parameters of regulation of conflicts contributes to a more coherent system of application of EU law. In this case, national courts have clear guidance on the relationship between national and EU law, so that incoherencies based on misunderstandings or divergent understandings of the guiding principles are less likely.

At the beginning of the 1990s,[2] inclusion of strong sovereignty provisions in the text of national constitutions (Vallikivi 1999a, Ziemele 2005, Määlksoo 2003, Romans 2001)[3] was supported by a massive public movement (Lieven 1993) and associated in the collective mind with fundamental changes from the Soviet system (Müllerson, Fitzmaurice and Andenas 1998).[4] The amendment of sovereignty provisions even by the mid-90s (amid EU membership preparations) became an extremely sensitive and unpopular political and legal issue (Laffranque 2001, Albi 2002).[5] Unable to reach political compromise and fearing public sentiment, the scope of EU-related constitutional amendments in Estonia and Latvia is minimal even as compared to other new MSs.[6]

Estonia, following the positive results of its public referendum on EU accession, had simultaneously adopted the Constitutional Amendment Act (CAA), containing two substantive and two procedural paragraphs. Latvia also held a public referendum on the fact of accession, although EU-related amendments to two sections of the Constitution were adopted through Parliament. The succinct wording of the constitutional amendments, tailored for joining the EU, secured a publicly acceptable political compromise but did not conceptually resolve the

2 Adopted by public referendum in Estonia on 28 June 1992 and re-adoption of the 1922 Constitution by the Latvian Parliament in 1990.

3 Estonia and Latvia claimed restoration of independence based on the contested principle of 'continuity of the state'. Thus, the Baltic States claimed and succeeded that under international law they are *de jure* not new states but continuations of the statehood interrupted by occupation by the Soviet Union.

4 See also recently a judgment by the Latvian Constitutional Court discussing the issue of the principle of state continuity case 2007-10-0102 of 29 November 2007 and case 2009-94-01 of 13 May 2010.

5 To resolve this legal dilemma, both countries created expert groups, which included national and foreign experts, to advise on how to overcome this constitutional challenge.

6 Albi (2005b: 405–13) has suggested classifying 2004 accession countries, according to the scope of EU-related constitutional amendments, into three groups: the first group that have adopted a *wide* package of EU-related amendments (Slovakia, what was then Czechoslovakia and Slovenia); the second group with a *medium* range of EU amendments including Poland and Hungary; and finally the last group with *minimal* constitutional amendments includes the three Baltic countries of Estonia, Latvia and Lithuania.

issue of sovereignty either in the public mind or in national legal doctrine (Pettai and Veebel 2005, Laffranque 2002, 2003, Albi 2002, 2005b).[7]

The constitutional textual 'veil' on the scope of the adopted amendments preconditioned further legal debate, *inter alia* complaints challenging the accession referendum results in the Estonian Supreme Court (case 3-4-1-11-03),[8] the Latvian Constitutional Court[9] and the Lisbon treaty judgment in the Latvian Constitutional Court. Moreover, this textual minimalism was an open invitation for the national judicial branch to interpret the role and meaning of the adopted constitutional amendments in relation to national constitutional orders. This invitation shortly materialized, even in 2003, but at the time was not welcome by national highest courts.[10] Neither the Estonian Supreme Court nor the Latvian Constitutional Court analysed submissions in substance but set aside the complaints on procedural grounds, clearly signalling inability or unwillingness to engage in creative judicial decision-making in 'hard' cases.

---

7 The speed of transformation, the novelty of the European integration process as well as socio-economic difficulties accompanying the reforms left little time or interest for national political elites to initiate full-scale public debate on the meaning of accession to the EU and particularly *vis-à-vis* national constitutional provisions on sovereignty. See for example, Pettai and Veebel (2005), who argue that the pre-accession process was expert-driven with low involvement of the public; the early stages of accession negotiations and pre-accession monitoring of public opinion indicate a large gap between the political elite's optimism and willingness to join the EU and public scepticism. For detailed discussion on various possible proposals, on national Constitutional amendments before accession to the EU, see for example, J Laffranque (2001, 2002, 2005), Albi (2002, 2005). Other new MSs, for example, Czechoslovakia and Hungary, have also had similar problems: see Kühn (2004, 2005, 2006), Sadurski (2005, 2006), Uitz (2007); for comparative analysis of the transfer of power provisions in the constitutions of Member States see for example, Claes (2005); For the comparative analysis of the relevant constitutional provisions in the new Member States, see Albi (2005).

8 Supreme Court of Estonia, case 3-4-1-11-03 of 24 September 2003.

9 Supreme Court of Latvia, decision of the 4th Chamber of 11 November 2003 to refuse to initiate proceedings in application registered Nr. 119–123.

10 A series of cases challenging the results of the accession referendum was brought in Estonia and Latvia. The applicants in the Estonian case (Estonian Supreme Court case nr. 3-4-1-11-03) argued that according to the text of the Constitution it is only possible to amend the existing articles of the Constitution and not supplement the Constitution. Thus, consequently the Constitutional Amendment Act that supplements the existing text of the Constitution violates the Constitutional provisions regulating the Constitutional amendment procedure. The argument of the applicants that is not fully developed in their submission goes to the root of the legal nature of the Constitutional Amendment Act. If the CAA amends the existing articles of the Constitution, specifically Article 1 on sovereignty, then the stringent constitutional procedure on amendment of fundamental provisions must be followed, otherwise adoption of amendments of the same nature but in another form, that is, in the form of the Constitutional Amendment Act, is unconstitutional.

Estonian Supreme Court

It was not until 2005 when the Estonian Supreme Court (ESC) substantively considered the meaning and nature of the Constitutional Amendment Act.[11] However, again, the ESC Constitutional Review Chamber in its *en banc* (!) decision provided no justification or reasoning as to what legal provisions or principles the supremacy of EU law in the national system is based on. Formally, the supremacy of EU law was acknowledged, 'European Union law indeed has supremacy over Estonian law'[12] but not discussed by the ESC.[13]

In a dissenting opinion, Justice Laffranque (joined by five other justices) harshly criticized this formalistic position of the court:

> It is regrettable that the highest court of the state that has the obligation to interpret the Constitution, did not explain the meaning and implications of the Constitution of the Republic Amendment Act, and did not give the foundations for interpreting the Constitution on the basis of the Act. Thereby the Supreme Court promotes legal vagueness.[14]

She argued for a more active and deliberative role of the Supreme Court and reasoned her position by (1) legal system coherency, (2) social and institutional dynamics of European integration considerations and (3) normative concerns related to interpretation of EU law.[15] As to the first point, Laffranque stated that the 'very laconic' formulation of the Amendment Act 'render[s] further interpretation of the Constitution by the Supreme Court indispensable.' Secondly, she emphasized that interpretation by the ESC would be especially welcome considering the debates and the upcoming decision of Estonia on the Treaty establishing a Constitution for Europe.[16] Finally, on the normative level, Laffranque stressed that the Constitutional Amendment Act 'does not constitute mere permission for Estonia to accede to the European Union' but rather a fundamental change on how the national Constitution must be interpreted.[17]

The impulse for a more open reason-based, normative communication of the Supreme Court on complex EU-related matters found reflection in the decision of

---

11 ESC Constitutional Review Chamber case 3-4-1-1-05 of 19 April 2005, *en banc* judgment.

12 Estonian Constitutional Review Chamber decision 3-4-1-1-05 para 49.

13 In this, the 'local elections case', the ESC adopted a rather EU law-friendly approach but failed to engage in deep analytical-normative discussion on the nature of EU law and the principle of supremacy.

14 Dissenting opinion of Justice Julia Laffranque to the judgment of the Supreme Court en banc in case 3-4-1-1-05, joined by Justices Tõnu Anton, Peeter Jerofejev, Hannes Kiris, Indrek Koolmeister and Harri Salmann, para. 6.

15 Case 3-4-1-1-05, para 6.

16 Ibid.

17 Ibid.

the Administrative Review Chamber a year later, in April 2006.[18] A three-member Chamber[19] engaged for the first time in considering the normative foundations of the application of EU law and the principle of supremacy.

The Administrative Chamber took two important steps forward. First, it acknowledged that the CAA is not only a competence transfer norm but importantly Article 2 CAA 'determines the relationship between Estonia and the European Union and conditions of EU membership – respect for the principles of the Constitution and supremacy as well as under certain conditions direct applicability of EU law.'[20] In other words, the CAA is not only of procedural importance for accession but also constitutes a fundamental change to the national constitutional system, so that the Estonian Constitution must be applied taking into consideration the rights and obligations flowing from the Accession Treaty.[21] Secondly, the Administrative Chamber connected and justified[22] the adopted position with reference to the results of the public accession referendum.[23]

The next step in development of Supreme Court reasoning on the normative basis for application of EU law and its supremacy came from the Constitutional Review Chamber judgment of 11 May 2006. In this decision the Constitutional Chamber, following the reasoning of the Administrative Chamber, stated regarding the nature of the adopted constitutional amendments:

> The Constitution was amended by a referendum of 14 September 2003, resorting to the model of constitutional amendment in which the amendments to the Constitution are enacted as separate constitutional acts and the provisions of the Constitution are not formally changed. At the same time the text of the Constitution must always be read with the amendments and only that part of the constitutional text shall be applied which is not in conflict with the amendments. Thus, the Constitution of the Republic of Estonia must be read together with the Constitution of the Republic of Estonia Amendment Act, applying only the part of the Constitution that is not amended by the CAA.[24]

In this quote, the Constitutional Chamber went considerably beyond the Administrative Chamber's position. Not only is the need to interpret the national

18 Judgment of the Administrative Chamber of the Supreme Court of Estonia 3-3-1-74-05 of 25 April 2006 and similarly following shortly after Administrative Chamber decision 3-3-1-66-05 of 10 May 2006, para 9.

19 Justice Laffranque and two other justices who joined the April 2005 dissenting opinion.

20 3-3-1-74-05, para 12.

21 Ibid.

22 Albeit only through a very short reference.

23 3-3-1-74-05, para 12.

24 Case 3-4-1-3-06 of 11 May 2006, Opinion of the Supreme Court of Estonia of 11 May 2006, RT III 2006, 19, 176, para 14.

Constitution in the light of the Amendment Act[25] stressed but also the supremacy of EU law over the national Constitution where only the part of the Constitution that is not amended by the CAA applies! This idea is further highlighted and developed by the Supreme Court, which stressed 'In the substantive sense this amounted to a material amendment of the entirety of the Constitution to the extent that it is not compatible with European Union law.'[26] Thus, in case of conflict between EU and national law, including national constitutional law, EU law applies! This position of the Estonian Supreme Court is outstanding in relation to other Supreme and Constitutional courts.

This enthusiastic and far-reaching position of the Constitutional Review Chamber was criticized in the dissenting opinion of Justice Kõve on three main accounts: first, the narrow reading of the CAA; secondly, over application of the principle of supremacy of the EU in the national constitutional order, and third, incoherence of the position of the Chamber with the earlier position of the Supreme Court *en banc*.

Kõve, relying on contextual-harmonization arguments, correctly stated that Article 2 of the CAA must be interpreted in conjunction with Article 1 of the same Act. Article 1 of the CAA refers to the fundamental principles of the Constitution as a condition under which Estonia may belong to the EU. Thus, analysis of Article 2 in the context of Article 1 of the CAA may provide a different reading of the overall implication of the CAA on the national constitutional order.[27] On this ground, Kõve argues that as a result of this narrow reading of Article 2 of the CAA 'For the time being, the relationship between §§ 1 and 2 of the CAA as well as e.g. the meaning of Chapter I [General Provisions] of the Constitution in its entirety, after accession to the European Union, remain unclear.'[28]

As a result of the narrow reading of Article 2 of the CAA, Kõve concludes, 'the Chamber "overestimated" the principle of supremacy of European Union law over the Estonian legal order.'[29] Kõve does not challenge *per se* the principle of supremacy of EU law, that as he agrees follows from Article 2, but rather the substantive scope of this principle that can be derived from the CAA:

> ...what is problematic for me is how this priority [of EU law over national law] is substantiated. ... the Chamber has, unfoundedly, concluded that the requirement – deriving from the case-law of the European Court of Justice – that upon application European Union law should have supremacy over a Member State law, amounts to amendment of the Constitution.[30]

---

25 3-4-1-3-06, para 15.

26 3-4-1-3-06, para 16.

27 Dissenting Opinion of Villu Kõve to the opinion of the Supreme Court of Estonia 3-4-1-3-06 of 11 May 2006, para 2.

28 3-4-1-3-06, Dissenting Opinion of Villu Kõve, para 2.

29 Ibid., para 3.

30 3-4-1-3-06, Dissenting Opinion of Villu Kõve, para 3.

Kõve rightly points out that the Constitutional Review Chamber's 'overestimated' reading of the principle of supremacy that a) provides for unconditional priority of EU law over national, including constitutional, law and b) results in material amendment of the entirety of the Constitution is substantively much broader than the reading of the general assembly of the Supreme Court.

Thus, if Justice Laffranque in her dissenting opinion to the decision of the general assembly of the Supreme Court[31] criticized the 'underestimation' of the meaning of the CAA, then later Justices Kõve and Kergandberg in their two separate dissenting opinions to Constitutional Review judgment 3-4-1-3-06 argued that the court derived overly broad implications as to the meaning of the CAA for the national constitutional order.[32] Regardless of the criticism voiced by some justices, the position of the Constitutional Review Chamber in the May 2006 decision, discussed above, at the moment remains the established legal doctrine that has been consistently followed in the three later decisions of the Supreme Court.[33]

For considerations of coherence, the Estonian case indicates that although national constitutional amendments only narrowly defined the relationship between national and European law, the Supreme Court took an active role in interpreting the constitutional amendments and through its jurisprudence placed EU law as the highest normative authority in the constitutional hierarchy, even above national constitutional norms. The debate between various Supreme Court justices through dissenting opinions in this context is not a threat but a health indicator of the maturity and independence of the national legal system that allows for a divergent position to be openly expressed and debated.

Latvian Constitutional Court

The normative position of the Constitutional Court is partly explained by a national doctrine of primacy of international law. Latvian constitutional doctrine and the jurisprudence of the Constitutional Court have repeatedly stressed the openness of the Latvian legal system and the primacy of international law:[34]

31 3-4-1-1-05.

32 Dissenting opinion of Eerik Kergandberg to the opinion of the Supreme Court of Estonia 3-4-1-3-06 of 11 May 2006 and dissenting Villu Kõve to the same opinion.

33 Administrative Chamber Decisions 3-3-1-87-07 of 07 April 2008 and 3-3-1-85-07 of 07 May 2008 directly quote paragraphs 15–16 of the Constitutional Review Chamber decision 3-4-1-3-06 of 11 May 2006; equally the Constitutional Review Chamber refers to para 16 of decision 3-4-1-3-06 in its judgment 3-4-1-5-08 of 26 June 2008.

34 For extensive discussion of international human rights law on the Latvian legal system, see for example, Mits (2010). The jurisprudence of the Estonian Supreme Court is also noted for its international law openness and long-standing direct application of international human rights treaties; for recent discussion see Lõhmus (2010); for early accounts of the role of international law in the Estonian legal system, see for example, Uibopuu (2005) and Vallikivi (1999b).

> … if there arises a discrepancy between international legal norms ratified by the Saeima and national legal norms of Latvia, international legal norms shall be applied. Besides, the international liabilities undertaken by Latvia on the basis of international agreements, confirmed by the Saeima, are also binding on the Saeima itself. It may not adopt legal acts which are at variance with the above liabilities.[35]

Constitutional protected adherence to international law has positively influenced Latvian legal thinking and played a significant role in re-establishing the national legal order after independence in 1991. The Constitutional Court has repeatedly pointed out that Article 89 of the Satversme imposes an obligation on the legislator to respect international legal norms binding on Latvia:

> The duty of the State to take into consideration the international liabilities in the field of human rights follow from Article 89 of the Satversme, which provides that the State shall recognize and protect fundamental human rights in accordance with the Constitution, laws and international agreements binding upon Latvia. This article clearly indicates that the objective of the constitutional legislator was to ensure harmony of the human rights norms with international human rights norms.[36]

The Constitutional Court further pointed out that the provisions of the Satversme must be understood considering the international liabilities of Latvia:

> When establishing the content of the norms included in the Satversme, it is necessary to take into consideration the international liabilities of Latvia in the field of human rights. International human right norms and the practice of their application serve as a means of interpretation on the level of constitutional law to determine the contents and scope of fundamental rights and the principle of the law-governed state, as far as it does not lead to decrease or limitation of fundamental rights included in the Satversme.[37]

Thus, application of international law norms, as well as reference to jurisprudence of courts of foreign jurisdictions and the European Court of Human Rights, became a 'common practice' of the Latvian Constitutional Court long before accession to the European Union. Against this background, application of liabilities following

---

35 Constitutional Court, 2004-01-06 of 7 July 2004.

36 Constitutional Court 2008-09-0106 of 16 December 2008, in case see also 2000-03-01 of 30 August 2000, para 5 of the Concluding Part; 2001-08-01 of 17 January 2002, para 3 of the Concluding Part and of 18 2007-03-01 of 18 October 2007, para 11; 2006-03-0106 of 23 November 2006.

37 2008-09-0106 of 16 December 2008; see also 2004-18-0106 of 13 May 2005, para 5 of the Concluding Part and 2007-03-01 of 18 October 2007, para 11.

from the European Union Accession Treaty, that is, application of EU law, was considered as a familiar practice to national Constitutional justices. Justice Aivars Endzinš (2004: 1–2), at the time chairman of the Constitutional Court of Latvia, after accession to the European Union stated:

> On the one hand, i.e. in the wider aspect, the entire activities of the Constitutional Court for the last almost eight years have been directed to approximating the Latvian legal system to that of the European State system. The idea of a democratic and law-based state is the basis for functioning of the state legal system within the European Union. As concerns the above, nothing has changed after May 1. Everyday activities are going on; so that, when reviewing particular cases, in every particular case Latvian legal norms shall be commensurable with the basic values of a democratic and law-based state. On the other hand, i.e. in the narrower aspect, the joining of Latvia to the European Union has advanced new and more complicated tasks for the Republic of Latvia Constitutional Court.

The jurisprudence of Latvian highest courts suggests that the doctrine of priority and friendliness of the Latvian constitutional system to international law that was primarily developed in the context of international human rights treaties is *de facto* applied to application of EU law.[38] Through ratification of international treaties (EU primary law), Latvia must respect obligations following from EU law. This 'international law' understanding of EU law explains why the Constitutional Court does not provide extensive judicial discussion on the consequences of accession to the European Union or the *sui generis* nature of EU law.

Albeit constitutionally justified, lack of an explicit position of Constitutional Court understanding on the normative position of EU law in the national legal system has resulted in a number of constitutional complaints challenging the constitutionality of Latvian accession to the European Union[39] and ratification of the Lisbon Treaty.[40] In the accession complaints,[41] applicants have challenged, *inter alia*, the constitutionality of the constitutional amendments adopted to join the EU (Articles 68 and 79) *vis-à-vis* the sovereignty provisions (Articles 1 and 2) of the Constitution.

---

38 See for example, Free Port Latvia decision of the Constitutional Court of Latvia case 2007-11-03 of 17 January 2008.

39 As referred to by Endzinš (2004), five applications on initiating a case in the Constitutional Court of Latvia, registration Nos 119-123, 2003 have been submitted to the Constitutional Court. Those applications claimed 1) parts of Articles 68 and 79 of the Republic of Latvia Satversme; 2) a referendum on the membership of Latvia in the European Union; 3) the Saeima decision on adoption (at first reading) of the draft Law 'On the Agreement between the Member States of the EU and the Candidate States on Accession to the EU' as unconformable with Articles 1, 2, 77, 89 and 40 of the Republic of Latvia Satversme. The 4th Panel of the Constitutional Court refused to initiate a case.

40 Constitutional Court of Latvia, case 2008-35-01 of 7 April 2009.

41 See n. 39.

The Constitutional Court has found that in principle the court has authority to review the constitutionality of the procedure selected by the legislator to adopt constitutional amendments. The Constitutional Court explained:

> … the aim of the legislator, when establishing the Constitutional Court was first of all to create an efficient mechanism for protection of the priority of Satversme norms … The Constitutional Court is authorized to review issues on the fact whether particular norms have become norms of the Satversme under the procedure established by law. Namely, whether the Saeima did not violate the procedure when passing the norms. At the same time one should take into consideration that the Satversme determines the procedure for amending it, while the Satversme does not envisage that the Constitutional Court will review compliance of one norm with other norms or the Satversme as a whole. If a norm has been incorporated in the Satversme, it is an integral part of it and has corresponding legal force.

However, the court further pointed out that this review must be based on a concrete constitutional complaint where the applicant must clearly define how a decision adopted by the legislator – that is, the choice of procedure for Constitutional amendments – violates fundamental rights provided in the Satversme. Because in the accession complaints the applicants failed to substantiate violation of fundamental rights, the Constitutional Court refused to initiate a case.

In the Lisbon Treaty case, the applicants specifically claimed that

> … the Contested Act [ratification of the Lisbon Treaty by Parliament] breached their fundamental rights guaranteed by Article 101 of the Satversme of the Republic of Latvia, namely, the right to participate in the conduct of State and municipal affairs and local government as provided by law.[42]

The Constitutional Court accepted the constitutional complaint on the Lisbon Treaty and discussed the case on the merits.

In discussing the constitutionality of the procedure of ratification of the Lisbon Treaty, the Latvian Constitutional Court followed its 'international law' approach to interpreting the provisions of the Satversme. The LCC pointed out that:

> Article 101 of the Satversme envisages a right which serves as a guarantee for democracy and is aimed at ensuring the legitimacy of the democratic State … The content of Article 101 must be interpreted in conjunction with Article 89 which determines that the State shall recognize and protect fundamental human rights in accordance with the Satversme, the laws and international agreements binding on Latvia. When interpreting the Satversme and the international obligations of Latvia, it is necessary to find a solution that ensures harmonious

42 2008-35-01 of 7 April 2009, para 3.

> interoperation of norms .... Therefore, international law and practice may serve as an instrument to establish the scope of the rules and principles established in the Satversme. (para 12–13)

In relation to understanding the European Union legal order,[43] the LCC stressed that the European legal order is a *lex specialis* of international law, derived from Member States which remain ultimately the 'masters of the Treaties'. Thus, the LCC understands the Lisbon Treaty as an amendment to international treaty obligations based on delegated authority and premised on national sovereign rights.

The issue of sovereignty as provided in Article 2 of the Satversme was addressed by the court in the Lisbon Treaty case exclusively in connection to amendments introduced by the Lisbon Treaty. The court went into considerable detail as to the meaning and concept of sovereignty:

> ... already prior to World War II in international law analysis of the legal consequences that arise when a state undertakes international obligations, sovereignty was treated as the exercise of sovereign rights rather than a restriction thereof. The Permanent Court of International Justice rejected the view that the conclusion of any such treaty according to which a State undertook to perform certain acts would mean that this state abandoned its sovereignty. At the same time, the right of entering into international engagements is an attribute of State sovereignty. The Permanent Court of International Justice noted [quote from Wimbledon decision CPJI Ser A 01 15, 1923, 25] when analysing international relations between States and international organizations, that it has been admitted that international organizations are institutions, in the frameworks of which States are merging their sovereignty and resources to solve common problems and find common solutions by acting in favour of national interests.[44]

Thus, relying on the modern understanding of sovereignty under public international law, the LCC argued that membership in the EU does not mean dilution of but rather exercise of sovereignty of the people. Consequently, the LCC concluded that the national principle of sovereignty is not infringed by the changes wrought by the Lisbon Treaty provisions.

Some arguments by the parties regarding the Lisbon Treaty, such as that political elites deliberately concealed information from society regarding the

43 When invited to discuss the meaning and scope of the constitutional amendments related to membership in the EU, the Latvian Constitutional Court took to the task with caution. First, the court explicitly stated that the arguments related to the procedure according to which Latvia joined the EU, as well as the lawfulness of the law ratifying the Constitutional Treaty, fall outside of the scope of the claim and would not be considered. Thus, the court limited itself to discussion of the nature of the Lisbon Treaty.

44 2008-35-01, para 17.

content and the consequences of the Treaty of Lisbon on the Constitutional provisions of sovereignty, may seem rather naïve than legal, but they point to fundamental discontent of the general public with issues of legitimacy related to the EU in general and EU law in particular.[45]

The international law-based normative position of the Constitutional Court *vis-à-vis* EU law *stricto sensu* is neither negative nor unfriendly to application of EU law. In fact, the Lisbon Treaty judgment has been rather positively appraised by legal commentators for its European integration friendliness (Reich 2009, Evas and Liebert 2010, 2012). However, from the perspective of the argumentative dimension of coherence, lack of explicit normative discussion by the highest court on the fundamental legal transformation of the legal system is regrettable. In this context, a more communicative approach by the Latvian Constitutional Court explaining normative considerations related to the impact of accession to the European Union for the national legal system would be welcome.

Comparative Conclusions

In conclusion, faced with the legal challenge of how to provide legitimate grounds for accession to the European Union against constitutionally protected provisions on 'sovereignty', Estonia and Latvia have selected different paths. Estonia, by means of a public referendum on accession, adopted the Constitutional Amendment Act. Latvia did not put constitutional amendments directly to a public referendum but instead adopted constitutional changes necessary for transfer of powers to supranational organizations like the European Union through the Saeima. Thus, at the time of accession, the political elites of neither Estonia nor Latvia were ready to engage with the public in debate on how accession to the European Union would impact the 'sovereignty' clause in the Constitution.

Following accession, the Estonian Supreme Court has actively engaged in discussion on the impact of EU law on the fundamental constitutional system. The Estonian Supreme Court, building on its long history of loyalty to international law, took an additional conceptual-theoretical step in developing the national legal system by elaborating the doctrine of the EU law-integrated constitutional interpretation. The Supreme Court has not only legitimized EU law in national constitutional doctrine through formal application of EU law, but also explicitly acknowledged that as a result of adopted constitutional amendments the entirety of the national constitutional order has changed to give full effect to the EU legal

45 2008-35-01 of 7 April 2009, para 18.10; Similar public detachment, disappointment and distrust were documented in analysis by printed press publications on the process of ratifying the Constitutional Treaty in Estonia and Latvia, Evas (2007) and in other European countries Liebert (2007a, 2008). For comparative analysis on the legitimacy and the democratic development of the EU during Constitutional and Lisbon Treaties debates in national contexts see Liebert (2005, 2006, 2007a).

order. Moreover, the Supreme Court has explicitly recognized the autonomous nature of the European Union legal order.

There is a remarkable difference in the approach by the Latvian Constitutional Court. Building on a well-established practice of directly applying provisions of international law and jurisprudence, the Latvian Constitutional Court did not intensively discuss the implications of EU membership for the national legal order. As analysis of jurisprudence indicates, the Latvian Constitutional Court has extended its international law-friendly approach to application of EU law. Neither in the Lisbon Treaty judgment nor in other cases did the Latvian court engage with theoretical conceptual considerations on the legitimacy of application of EU law in national constitutional space.[46] Rather, the court preferred to focus pragmatically on the formal legality of application of EU law following its international law-friendly approach. This position of the LCC may partly be explained by the procedure and wording of constitutional amendments adopted in Latvia,[47] and, in addition, partly as discussed above by understanding that openness of the national legal system to international law is sufficient to encompass and explain the position of EU law in national legal doctrine.

In a comparative perspective, developments in both jurisdictions may be classified in general as positive towards EU law. The Estonian Supreme Court may additionally be credited for initiating a legal debate on the implications of EU membership, while the Latvian Constitutional Court preferred not to explicitly discuss the nature of normative constitutional change in national legal doctrine following accession.

The position of the highest court on the constitutional validity of EU law in the national legal system is not *per se* an indicator of possible substantive incoherencies between EU and national law. Nevertheless, the position of the highest courts is important because they define the overarching parameters of national normative structures that guide resolution of potential EU law-related legal disputes, including clashes between substantive norms of EU and national law. The whole national legal system is then operated within those legal parameters. Consequently, I argue that a more clearly defined position of the national higher court on the normative validity of EU law facilitates more coherent application of EU law within the legal system. Against this background, the analysis in this section suggests that because the ESC more clearly defines and communicates its position on the validity of EU law, the Estonian legal system is less likely to generate substantive clashes between norms and therefore it has higher potential

46 For discussion of the contested constitutional meanings and the politics for a social Europe in the Lisbon process see Liebert (2007c), Closa (2009, 2012); for the analysis of the debates by major European intellectuals on the contentious issues of European democracy triggered by the Lisbon treaty see Liebert, U (2010).

47 The constitutional amendments are worded in the form of technical transfer of competences to the European Community. For discussion, see Albi (2005), Zukova (2009), Zigurds (2002).

for more substantive coherence. In contrast, the LCC is less clear and open and thus has lower coherence potential.

The Doctrine of Supremacy

The following section analyses whether and how the difference in the normative conception of EU law discussed in the previous section impacts reception of the doctrine of supremacy. The principle of supremacy is one of the defining aspects of substantive coherence as it provides conceptual guidance for national courts on the normative priority of legal rules in cases concerned with EU law. Similarly to the parameter of constitutional validity that comes from within the national legal system, the EU law principle of supremacy that is clearly defined, justified and consistently applied by national courts facilitates coherence of application of EU law within national legal systems.

Central issues and debates[48]

The doctrines of supremacy and direct effect in the words of ECJ Advocate General Trestenjak are fundamental structural principles[49] that regulate the relationship between national and EU law and the relationship between national and EU courts. In spite of the long-standing case law of the ECJ on supremacy (primacy)[50] and general acceptance of the doctrine by national courts, recent judgments of the ECJ and of national highest courts indicate that the issue remains in vogue and controversial.[51] In general, MSs can be clustered into three groups: those that have (1) fully accepted, (2) not accepted, or (3) conditionally accepted the doctrine of supremacy (Slaughter, Stone Sweet and Weiler 1998). Complete rejection of the doctrine of supremacy by MSs in the context of the EU is now history. Thus,

48 In this section (and in a similar section on other general principles of EU law), I do not attempt to provide an all-inclusive discussion of the principle, but rather to highlight recent EU law/case-law developments most relevant to development of the doctrine and its application in new MS.

49 C-445/06 Danske Slagterier v Bundesrepublik Deutschland [2009] ECR I-2119, Opinion of Advocate General Trstenjak delivered on 4 September 2008, para. 131.

50 Academic debate is ongoing on the definitions of supremacy and primacy. In the academic literature, supremacy is used most often to refer to the principle developed by the ECJ which holds that, in case of conflict, EU law prevails over national law. The same principle is referred to in judgments of the ECJ as 'primacy'. On the conceptual and linguistic difference, see for example, Mayer (2005). I will use both terms interchangeably, if not stated otherwise.

51 The relationship between European Union law and national law is one of the most debated issues of European constitutional law. The number of publications discussing the issue of supremacy primary is flourishing.

MSs either fully accept the doctrine of supremacy that according to the ECJ is necessary for the uniform and effective application of EU law and, at least in theory, provides the least conflicting and most receptive interaction between national and EU levels, or accept the doctrine of supremacy with conditions.

Full acceptance of the doctrine of supremacy means that all provisions of national law, including the Constitution, should be set aside by a judge and a provision of EU law applied.[52] In general, this condition is seen as unproblematic by national ordinary courts that according to national procedural rules do not have constitutional review competence. On the other hand, national highest courts that are obliged to safeguard national constitutions see the unconditional doctrine of supremacy as developed by the ECJ as problematic. The scope of the doctrine of supremacy, or rather acceptable limitations and derogations, are continuously contested by MSs (Craig 2003).

Thus, most recently in three requests for a preliminary reference submitted by the Polish Regional Administrative Court in *Filipiak* (Wojewódzki Sąd Administracyjny w Poznaniu), the German Administrative Court in *Winner Wetten* (Verwaltungsgericht Köln) and the French Cour de cassation in *Melki*, the courts have essentially asked the ECJ whether and if so on what conditions it is possible to derogate from the principle of primacy.[53] The *Melki* case concerned national interlocutory procedure for review of the constitutionality of national laws that are also allegedly in conflict with the provisions of EU law.

The ECJ stressed:

> … a national court which, in a case concerning EU law, considers that a provision of national law is not only contrary to EU law, but also unconstitutional, does not lose the right or escape the obligation under Article 267 TFEU to refer questions to the Court of Justice on the interpretation or validity of EU law by reason of the fact that the declaration, that a rule of national law is unconstitutional, is subject to a mandatory reference to the constitutional court. The effectiveness of EU law would be in jeopardy if the existence of an obligation to refer a matter to a constitutional court could prevent a national court hearing a case governed by EU law from exercising the right conferred on it by Article 267 TFEU to refer to the Court of Justice questions concerning the interpretation or validity of EU law in order to enable it to decide whether or not a provision of national law was compatible with that EU law.

52 European Court of Justice, case 106/77 Administrazione delle Finanze dello Stato v. Simmenthal SpA.

53 C-314/08 Krzysztof Filipiak v Dyrektor Izby Skarbowej w Poznaniu [2009] ECR I-11049; C-409/06 Winner Wetten GmbH v Bürgermeisterin der Stadt Bergheim [2010] ECR 0000; Joined cases C-188/10 and C-189/10 Aziz Melki (C-188/10) and Sélim Abdeli (C-189/10) [2010] ECR 0000.

The *Filipiak* and *Winner Wetten* cases concerned national provisions that were found by decision of the national higher courts to be contrary, *inter alia*, to the provisions of the EC Treaty.[54] However, based on national procedural considerations, higher courts have adopted temporal conditions when a contested national measure will remain valid in national jurisdiction.

The ordinary courts submitting references for a preliminary ruling to the ECJ have thus been confronted with the issue of either following the requirement of the doctrine of supremacy to apply the EC Treaty provision directly to the case in hand or to follow the guidance of the higher court and provisionally exclude the primacy of EU law. The European Commission in the Polish case argued that the principle of primacy of EU law and Articles 10 EC (now Article 10 TFEU) and 43 EC (now Article 49 TFEU) do not preclude application of a conflicting national provision:

> … the deferral by the Trybunał Konstytucyjny of the date on which the provisions at issue will lose their validity does not prevent the referring court from respecting the principle of the primacy of Community law and thus declining to apply those provisions … [T]he possibility, under … Polish Constitution, of deferring the date on which the provisions at issue will lose their validity, a possibility of which the Trybunał Konstytucyjny made use in its judgment of 7 November 2007, does not infringe either the principle of the primacy of Community law or Articles 10 EC and 43 EC, because it is not contrary to the obligation, imposed on national authorities and national courts, not to apply provisions of national law which are contrary to Article 43 EC.

The ECJ forcefully disagrees:

> … the primacy of law obliges the national court to apply law and to refuse to apply the conflicting provisions of national law, irrespective of the judgment of the national constitutional court which has deferred the date on which those provisions, held to be unconstitutional, are to lose their binding force.[55]

The ECJ recalled that according to settled case law starting from *Simmenthal*,[56] national courts are under a duty to give full effect to a provision of EU law, 'if necessary refusing of its own motion to apply any conflicting provision of national legislation, even if adopted subsequently, and it is not necessary for the court to

54 The Treaty Establishing the European Community (EC Treaty) is as of 1 December 2009 replaced by the Treaty of the Functioning of the European Union (TFEU). This book refers to the EC Treaty or TEC if at the time of the judgment the EC Treaty was still in force.

55 C-314/08 Krzysztof Filipiak v Dyrektor Izby Skarbowej w Poznaniu [2009] ECR I-11049, para 85.

56 European Court of Justice, case 106/77 Administrazione delle Finanze dello Stato v. Simmenthal SpA [1978] ECR 629.

request or await the prior setting aside of such provision by legislative or other constitutional means.'[57]

Conditional acceptance of the doctrine of supremacy by national highest courts is justified by three main considerations: structural constitutional provisions, 'essential' constitutional norms, and subject-matter limitations (*Kompetenz-Kompetenz*) (Craig 2003). All these limiting conditions arguments advanced by MSs essentially rooted in the claim to sovereignty are either procedural, that is, the power to decide on institutional competences and rights (structural constitutional and *Kompetenz-Kompetenz* arguments), or substantive, that is, the power to decide on substantive matters ('essential' constitutional norms limitations). Inevitably, this sovereignty-based conceptualization of the relationship between national and EU legal orders leads to direct conflicts that in principle cannot be fully resolved.

Theoretical debate addressing the issue of the *Kompetenz-Kompetenz* dilemma advanced by MacCormick essentially provides a viable normative construction that allows a conceptual relationship between national and European EU legal orders in non-conflicting terms (MacCormick 1999, Kumm 1999, Komárek 2005, Walker 2002). MacCormick and other scholars developing the idea of constitutional pluralism, most notably Maduro and Walker, argue that distinct but genuinely normative legal orders can coexist (Maduro 2000, 2003). Based on notions of legal pluralism and understanding of law as an institutional normative order, it is 'possible that each [normative order] acknowledges the legitimacy of every other within its own sphere, while none asserts or acknowledges constitutional superiority over another' (MacCormick 1999, also see Craig 2003), in other words, 'as a discourse among equals' (Maduro 2008: 11, see also Fossum and Menendez 2010a). This conception denies understanding of supremacy as a hierarchical subordination that inevitably leads to resistance and conflict, but rather advances communication between legal orders.

The idea of legal and constitutional pluralism as a form of reducing or managing potential conflict between legal orders requires three essential elements: *systemic compatibility*, *institutional awareness* and *a shared hermeneutic framework* (Maduro 2008: 12). The systemic compatibility requirement refers to the identity or the essential values that a legal system is based on. Institutional awareness refers to the understanding by the courts of their institutional role and jurisdictional limits *vis-à-vis* other institutions and acceptance that another legal order or institution may be better placed to resolve a particular legal issue. Finally, the hermeneutic framework relates to the conditions that shape interpretation of EU rules in the context of decentralized EU law implementation.

Beyond purely academic debate, an elegant analysis of the main limiting conditions to the supremacy advanced by MS and their conceptual fallacies was recently addressed by Advocate General Maduro in a reference for preliminary

57 C-314/08 Krzysztof Filipiak, judgment of 19 November 2009, para 81; Similarly see for example, Joined cases C-188/10 and C-189/10 Aziz Melki (C-188/10) and Sélim Abdeli (C-189/10) [2010] ECR 0000, paras 43–4.

ruling submitted by the *Conseil d'État* on the issue of conformity of EU law with the French Constitution.[58] Maduro begins his line of reasoning with full acknowledgement that the task faced by a national higher court that needs to reconcile its domestic obligation to protect the national Constitution with the EU obligation to respect the primacy of EU law may seem to the national court as 'an impossible task of having to reconcile the irreconcilable'. However, as Maduro convincingly argues, this conflicting approach to the requirement of primacy is not only unnecessary but also counterproductive to respect for fundamental rights.

Maduro builds the normative justification of his position through four main arguments:

1. Claims to legal sovereignty are the expressions of the legal pluralism that is integral and unique to the European integration process.
2. The constitutional foundations of the EU are based on constitutional principles common to the MS; moreover, through Article 6 TFEU the MSs are guaranteed that EU law will not threaten the fundamental values of their constitutions.
3. Thus, ultimately, it is a common (and not conflicting!) task of both national courts and the ECJ to protect fundamental values.
4. The 'structural congruence' that guarantees protection of fundamental values can only be fully and organically guaranteed through the mechanisms provided by the Treaty.

In this context the role of national constitutions and courts is not undermined but on the contrary becomes more essential, as through the process of ongoing dialog with the ECJ, which is confined at EU level to protection of fundamental values based on common constitutional traditions of the MS, national courts continuously contribute to development of the 'organic identity' of the Union.

Estonian Supreme Court

In the context of the EU integrated interpretation framework advanced by the Estonian Supreme Court, the doctrine of supremacy has been accepted by the court without major difficulties. Based on Article 2 of the Amendment Act, the Supreme Court has argued that:

> The effect of those provisions of the Constitution that are not compatible with European Union law and thus inapplicable is suspended. This means that within the spheres which are within the exclusive competence of the European Union or where there is a shared competence with the European Union, European Union

58 C-127/07, Société Arcelor Atlantique et Lorraine and Others v Premier ministre, Ministre de l'Écologie et du Développement durable and Ministre de l'Économie, des Finances et de l'Industrie, [2008] ECR I-09895.

> law applies in the case of a conflict between Estonian legislation, including the Constitution, with European Union law.[59]

The Supreme Court has accepted that only those provisions of the Estonian Constitution are applicable that are in conformity with EU law or that are not within the scope of EU competence. In the case of conflict between national legislation and EU law, conflicting national law is inapplicable and suspended so that EU law applies. This position was adopted initially by the Supreme Court in its opinion related to introduction of the Euro requested by the Parliament and not in the form of a judgment. In this context, as pointed out by the dissenting justices, the legal effect and significance of the opinion of the Supreme Court (that is procedurally very uncommon) is unclear. Justice Kõve argues that

> … it remains unclear whether an opinion of the Supreme Court has, for example, a meaning that is binding on the Supreme Court itself, analogously with its judgments, and whether such an 'opinion' excludes, for example, subsequent abstract or concrete norm control concerning the same matter.[60]

Justice Kergandberg shared this concern and continued that

> … bearing in mind the guiding nature of a Supreme Court opinion (one could not probably refer to a judges' opinion as a precedent) it would have been necessary to explain its legal meaning and to take a stand as to the possible binding effect of opinions of the kind both on the legislator and on subsequent constitutional review practice.[61]

However, the position of the Supreme Court on supremacy was repeated and confirmed by the Supreme Court in a later 2008 decision of the Administrative Chamber of the Supreme Court[62] that directly quoted the provisions of the 2006 opinion. This formula of legal construction accepting the supremacy of EU law over the national Constitution was applied by the Supreme Court in several cases: on the constitutional provision providing the exclusive right of the Bank of Estonia to issue banknotes;[63] on the constitutional provision that provides for competence of the Supreme Court to declare invalid any Act or legislation which is in conflict with the provisions or the spirit of the Constitution.[64]

---

59 3-4-1-3-06, para 16; see also 3-3-1-87-07, para 42.

60 Kõve dissenting opinion, Case 3-4-1-3-06, para 1.

61 Dissenting opinion of Justice Kergandberg, 3-4-1-3-06, para 3.

62 3-3-1-87-07, para 42.

63 3-4-1-3-06.

64 3-4-1-5-08 Ruling of the Constitutional Review Chamber of the Supreme Court of 26 June 2008.

In relation to the prospect of introduction of the Euro currency in Estonia, a conflict emerged between Article 111 of the Estonian Constitution[65] that guarantees the exclusive right of the Estonian Central Bank to issue Estonian currency and Article 106 of the EC Treaty (now Article 128 TFEU) providing for the exclusive right of the European Central Bank to authorize the issue of banknotes within the Community.[66] The Supreme Court opinion in this case states ' ... proceeding from § 2 of the Constitution of the Republic of Estonia Amendment Act, § 111 of the Constitution shall not be applied and Article 106 of the Treaty establishing the European Community shall be observed.'[67] Similarly in relation to the constitutional provision on the competence of the Supreme Court to declare invalid any legislation, the Supreme Court stated:

> If the Supreme Court exercised this competence [Art 152 (2) of the Constitution] in regard to the provisions of legislation of general application relating to EU law, this would create a conflict with European Union law. Proceeding from § 2 of the Constitution of the Republic of Estonia Amendment Act ... pursuant to which, as of Estonia's accession to the European Union, the Constitution of the Republic of Estonia applies taking account of the rights and obligations arising from the Accession Treaty.[68]

The Supreme Court of Estonia has unconditionally accepted the supremacy (primacy) of EU law. In its decisions discussing supremacy, the Supreme Court did not provide any limiting conditions coming from national constitutional law, including conditions related to the fundamental rights and principles protected in the Constitution.[69] In principle, as pointed out by dissenting justices Kõve and Kergandberg, interpretation of Article 2 of the Constitutional Amendment Act in the light of Article 1 of the same Act provides a convincing argument that Estonia may belong to the EU only in accordance with the fundamental principles of the Constitution of the Republic of Estonia. Thus, a strong normative argument may

---

65 § 111. The Bank of Estonia has the sole right to issue Estonian currency. The Bank of Estonia regulates currency circulation and upholds the stability of the national currency.

66 Article 106 EC Treaty (now Article 128 TFEU) '1.The ECB shall have the exclusive right to authorize the issue of banknotes within the Community. The ECB and the national central banks may issue such notes. The banknotes issued by the ECB and the national central banks shall be the only such notes to have the status of legal tender within the Community.'

67 3-4-1-3-06, para 18.

68 3-3-1-74-05, para 30.

69 See, however, the dissenting opinion of Laffranque: 'Within the framework of pertinent review the Supreme Court has the right and – on the basis of the Constitution of the Republic of Estonia Amendment Act – an obligation, upon interpreting the Constitution, to take into account the principles of law generally recognized in the European Union law, if these are not in conflict with the basic principles of Estonian Constitution' in Case 3-4-1-1-05 (Chancellor of Justice, election law, para 4).

be constructed to suggest that through systemic reading of the CAA the principle of supremacy is conditioned by fundamental rights protected by the Estonian Constitution. It remains to be seen in the future practice of the Supreme Court whether the Supreme Court will rely on the unconditional supremacy of EU law even against fundamental rights and principles protected in the Constitution or rather derive limiting conditions from Article 1 of the Constitutional Act.

Thus, the ESC has accepted the complete primacy of EU law, including primacy over the Estonian Constitution. The conceptual foundation for acceptance of supremacy as evidenced by the ESC opinion is Article 2 of the CAA and – although not implicitly mentioned by the ESC – general principles of EU law. The opinion of the ESC suggests that jurisdictional disputes similar to the earlier German *Solange* or Italian *Frontini, Granital* and *Fragd* cases are unlikely. The ESC's opinion did not provide any qualifications such as national constitutionally protected fundamental rights that would make acceptance of the primacy of EU law conditional.

A well-reasoned and elaborated application of the principle of supremacy by national lower courts may be found in two judgments of the Tallinn Administrative Court from 28 December 2005 and 14 June 2006, concerning a surplus stock fee calculated on the basis of national provisions applying European Commission Regulation 1972/2003/EC. Tallinn Administrative Court Judge Tiina Pappel went into substantial detail to explain the meaning of the supremacy of EU law and direct effect of the Commission Regulation in the national legal system.[70]

The applicants in both cases, each a private company due to pay a penalty fee for owning surplus stock of agricultural products, applied to the court, *inter alia*, to set aside EC Regulation 1972/2003/EC because of its alleged conflict with the Estonian Constitution. The applicants built part of their argument on Article 123 of the Estonian Constitution, which states that '(1) The Republic of Estonia shall not conclude foreign treaties which are in conflict with the Constitution. (2) If the Estonian laws or other acts are in conflict with foreign treaties ratified by the Parliament, the articles of the foreign treaty shall be applied.' Based on those provisions the applicants asserted that the Estonian Constitution, which is not 'a law or other act' ratified by the Parliament, enjoys supremacy over the EC Regulation.

The Tallinn Administrative Court disagreed with the applicants. First, the court stated that based on Article 2 of the CAA, adopted through public referendum and proclaimed by the President of the Estonian Republic, the provisions of European Union law are supreme in relation to national legal acts, including the Constitution. Thus, following accession, the specific relationship between national and EU law is regulated by CAA Article 2 and not Article 123 of the Constitution.

Secondly, the court continued by explaining that following accession to the EU it is no longer applicable to speak of Estonian legal space but rather European

70 The judge in both cases is Tiina Pappel. The reasoning of both judgments is very similar and in parts identical.

Union legal space. This means that in application of EU law it is necessary to take into consideration general principles of EU law. The two most important general principles of EU law are direct effect and supremacy. With direct citations from ECJ 26/62 *van Gend en Loos* and 6/64 *Costa* v *ENEL* judgments, the court concluded that based on the above reasons the request by the applicants to set aside application of EC Regulation 1972/2003/EC due to its unconstitutionality could not be upheld.

Supremacy puzzle under Latvian legislation

The amendments introduced to the Latvian constitutional text do not *per se* include a 'supremacy' provision similar to Article 2 of the Estonian CAA. Lack of a constitutional provision on 'supremacy' is remedied or more precisely attempted to be remedied in the text of Latvian legislative acts through provisions of procedural (administrative, civil and criminal) codes and interpretations by the Latvian Constitutional Court.[71]

The Administrative Procedure Act (LAPA) Article 1 (4) defines that legal norms are (a) regulatory enactments[72] and (b) general principles of law. Regulatory enactments are divided into internal and external. External enactments are the Constitution (*Satversme*), laws, government regulations and binding regulations of local government, as well as international agreements, and European Union (Communities) founding treaties and normative acts issued on the basis of the founding treaties.[73] Article 15 LAPA further regulates in detail the application of external regulatory enactments, general principles of law and legal norms of international law.[74] Specifically, Article 15 (1) provides that institutions and courts in administrative proceedings shall apply external normative acts, and international and European acts, and stipulates the hierarchy of external regulatory enactments as follows:

1. the Satversme;
2. acts and government regulations adopted on the basis of Article 81 Satversme;

71 One easy hypothetical illustrates that at least one of the problems of the Satversme as modified is just to join. A Latvian company after suffering adverse consequences from an EU regulation that provides norms contrary to Latvian law could argue in court that it is not subject to EU regulation because EU institutions constitutionally have no power over the company. Under Article 64 of the Satversme, the legislature is vested in the Saeima and the Latvian people. There is little doubt that a grammatical interpretation of the Satversme allows such a conclusion.

72 I will use 'external regulatory enactment' and 'external normative act' interchangeably.

73 Article 1(5) LAPA.

74 Article 15 LAPA, 'Application of External Regulatory Enactments, General Principles of Law and Legal Norms of International Law'.

3. government regulations, and
4. binding local government regulations.[75]

The hierarchical list of application of external normative acts includes neither international nor EU law. Formulation of the provisions regulating the relationship between national and international/EU law is somewhat ambiguous and circular.[76] Thus the first sentence of Article 15 (4) states that EU/EC legal norms shall be applied in accordance with their ranking in the external hierarchy of normative acts. A similar formulation is adopted in relation to the provisions of international law; regardless of the source of international legal norms, these norms are to be applied in accordance with their ranking in the external hierarchy of normative acts.[77]

Surprisingly, the LAPA is silent on a) how to determine the ranking of EU law in the national (!) hierarchy of norms, and b) on how to settle normative collision if a conflict occurs between a national legal norm and a EU legal norm of the same level of ranking.

According to the first sentence of Article 15 (4), in applying EU law, national judges must determine the ranking of EU law in the national hierarchy of normative acts. How exactly to determine the ranking of EU primary and secondary law is not stated under the LAPA. If in principle the hierarchical ranking of, for example, EU directives can arguably be determined on the basis of the Latvian implementing instrument, then how to determine the ranking of, for example, a directly applicable EU regulation? Therefore, national implementing provisions cannot be used as a yardstick measurement analogous to national provisions of the same hierarchical rank.[78] Relying on the ranking of national implementing measures is not only practically impossible but also normatively in direct conflict with the principle of EU law supremacy.

The normative puzzle of EU law supremacy is further complicated by the unclear relationship between national, international and EU law. Concerning

75 Article 15(3) LAPA.

76 Article 15 (3) 'The legal norms of international law regardless of their source shall be applied in accordance with their place in the hierarchy of legal force of external regulatory enactments. If a conflict between a legal norm of international law and a norm of Latvian law of the same legal force is determined, the legal norm of international law shall be applied.' Article 15 (4) 'The legal norms of the European Union (Community) shall be applied in accordance with their place in the hierarchy of legal force of external regulatory enactments. In applying the legal norms of the European Union (Community), institutions and courts shall take into account European Court of Justice case law.'

77 Article 15 (3) LAPA.

78 The question becomes somewhat trickier (and even less normatively convincing) if the ranking of such traditional EU instruments as regulations and directives must be compared with acts and government regulations. Thus if a regulation is adopted by the Council does it mean that it could be argued that its ranking is lower than an act because these are adopted by the legislature, but the regulation is adopted by a quasi-executive branch of power and thus is similar to the Latvian equivalent of a 'government regulation'?

international law, the second sentence of Article 15 (3) LAPA provides that 'If a collision is established between an international legal norm and a Latvian legal norm of the same legal force the international legal norm shall be applied.'[79] A similar provision as to EU law is lacking. However, the second sentence of Article 15 (4) LAPA provides that in applying EU law, institutions and courts shall take into consideration the case law of the European Court of Justice.[80] Thus, in addition to EU law, the case law of the ECJ is recognized by the LAPA as one of the sources of legal norms applicable in national jurisdiction. However, this provision fails to state clearly the priority rules.

Consequently, the LAPA acknowledges both international and EU law as sources of law in national jurisdiction while only in the case of international law providing guidance on settling collision of norms. This legislative lacuna (or inappropriate wording?) is questionable both from normative and practical considerations. Normatively, it is unclear why the LAPA does not address the methodology for settling the collision of norms between EU/EC and national law and ultimately does not provide for supremacy of EU law *vis-à-vis* national legislation while specifically acknowledging the primacy of international law.

One possible reading of the LAPA suggests that the supremacy of EU law in relation to national law is subsumed under the provision on primacy of international law. Although this construction may in functional terms lead to supremacy of EU law conceptually, it is, however, in conflict with a fundamental understanding of EU law as an autonomous legal order that is distinguishable in analytical terms from international law.[81] Another reading acknowledging the difference between international and EU law then suggests the *prima facie* preferential treatment of international law (and not EU law) in the national legal system. Notably, according to the legal commentary on Article 15 (4) LAPA, this provision was introduced to eliminate collisions between legal norms due to joining the EU. With due respect to the ambition of the legislator, it remains rather problematic to read directly from the provisions currently in force as to how possible collisions of norms are to be eliminated or settled.[82] Thus, in practical terms, a national judge faced with a legal dispute involving collision of EU and national norms is left without clear guidance and must rely on other methods than linguistic interpretation to give supremacy to EU law.

Unfortunately, systemic interpretations of LAPA provisions offer more questions than answers on the issue of supremacy of EU law. Provisions of LAPA regulating general collision of norms provide the conventional: '*lex superior*',[83]

79 Second sentence of Article 15 (3) LAPA.

80 Second sentence of Article 15 (4) LAPA.

81 C-6/64 Flaminio Costa v. ENEL [1964] ECR 585.

82 Legislative intent may be a helpful element utilized by the courts in constructing historical or teleological interpretive methods which are specifically recognized by LAPA Article 17 (1).

83 '*lex superior derogat legi inferiori*' Article 15 (6) LAPA.

'*lex specialis*'[84] and '*lex posterior*' principles.[85] According to the EU doctrine of supremacy as developed by the ECJ, these national principles must not be an obstacle to the application of EU law. Thus, according to EU law, a national judge cannot rely on the principle of '*lex posterior*' to set aside conflicting EU legislation and instead apply more recent national legislation. The grammatical reading of LAPA that provides no clear guidance on the status of EU law in national administrative proceedings does not in itself exclude application of the '*lex posterior*' rule, even against EU law. Note, however, that a similar effect will be excluded through the second sentence of Article 15 (3) in relation to international law.

The '*lex superior*' rule could be a solution to the 'supremacy problem' between national and EU law if the highest external normative enactment, the Constitution, clearly provided for a special role of EU law in the national legal system. However, as discussed in the previous section, this is not the case as the constitutional amendments adopted in Latvia deal primarily with transfer of competences provisions. Moreover, no clear national rules exist that would provide an answer to the question how conflict between the Latvian Constitution and EU law should be resolved.

Finally, a teleological interpretation of the legislative reference in the second sentence of Article 15 (4) LAPA to ECJ case law may provide an (in)direct (?) key to the supremacy issue in administrative proceedings. An EU law-conscious national judge who is willing to interpret the statement 'taking into consideration' broadly in principle may build an argument to set aside conflicting national legislation through reference to the autonomous nature of EU law and the well-known supremacy doctrine developed by the ECJ.[86] This 'hidden' way to supremacy of EU law in the LAPA may be an obstacle to judges inexperienced with EU law or hesitant to challenge the conventional national hierarchy of normative acts.

Other procedural codes – the Latvian Civil Procedure Act (LCCA) and the Latvian Criminal Procedure Act (the LCPA) – also address the relationship between national and EU law. According to the LCCA, the court decides civil cases in accordance with laws and other normative acts binding on Latvia, international agreements, and norms of European Union law. Similarly to the LAPA, the LCCA provides for primacy of international law and states that in case of conflict between national and international law treaties approved by the Parliament, international law provisions will apply.[87] In relation to EU law, the LCCA states that if the issue

84 '*lex specialis derogat generali*' Article 15 (7) LAPA.

85 '*lex posterior derogat legi priori*' Article 15 (8) and Article 15 (9) LAPA.

86 ECJ case law on the principle of supremacy, started in Costa (Case 6/64 Flaminio Costa v. ENEL) and further developed in Internationale Handeslgesellschaft (Case 11/70 Internationale Handelsgesellschaft GmbH v.Einfuhr- und Vorratsstelle fur Getreide un Futtermittel), Simmenthal (Case 106/77), Factoratame (C-213/89), Larsy (C-118/00), CIF (C-198/01) and Kapferer (C-234/04) indicate that constitutional law provisions or other national provisions cannot be invoked to challenge the supremacy of a directly applicable EU law.

87 Article 5 (2) LCCA.

at stake is regulated by EU law norms that are directly applicable in Latvia, Latvian laws apply so far as permitted by EU law.[88] This provision is welcome guidance for national institutions and courts on how to settle conflicts between national and EU law that is apparently missing from the LAPA. However, although the wording of the LCCA provision introduces the principle of supremacy of EU law (Latvian laws apply so far as permitted by EU law) at the same time it introduces a limiting condition (EU law that is directly applicable in Latvia).

According to Article 288 TFEU (ex 249 TEC), only regulations have general application and are directly applicable.[89] Thus, if to understand 'direct applicability' under Article 288 TFEU as meaning the way in which EU norms enter the national legal system, then it is not clear whether other EU instruments – directives, decisions, recommendations and opinions – fall within the scope of the 'supremacy' provision of Article 5 (3) of the LCCA. The broader reading of direct applicability that focuses on the substantive meaning of the concept rather than on the procedural avenue suggests that it should be understood as entailing a notion that individuals have rights from EU legislative instruments that they can enforce in national courts. However, this broader reading is now referred to as the principle of 'direct effect' rather than 'direct applicability'. True, the exact scope of the principles of 'direct applicability' and 'direct effect' was debated but it is now commonly understood in academic and judicial practice that direct applicability refers to methods of national incorporation while judicial enforceability is then understood as direct effect (Eleftheriadis 1996, Craig and de Burca 2008, Winter 1972). Considering this difference between direct effect and direct applicability, it is questionable why the Latvian legislator under the LCCA provided supremacy for EC regulations only. This approach runs clearly against the doctrine of supremacy as developed by the ECJ.

According to the Latvian Criminal Procedure Act (LCPA), the sources of criminal procedure are the Constitution, international law norms and the LCPA. The LCPA further states that in applying EC/EU legal norms the jurisprudence of the ECJ must be taken into consideration, while in applying the legal norms of the Latvian Republic interpretation of the norms given by the Constitutional Court must be considered. Thus, the LCPA similarly to the LAPA refers to ECJ case law as to the normative source but provides no 'clear' supremacy rule.

Bringing together discussion on provisions of Latvian procedural codes regulating the relationship and priority rules between national and EU law, it may be concluded that legislative regulation is complex, unclear and somewhat different in each procedural code. On the one hand, all procedural codes recognize EU law and ECJ case law as sources of law that must be taken into consideration in applying national rules. On the other hand, none of the codes clearly recognizes the primacy of EU law, while the Administrative and Civil Procedure codes do recognize primacy of international law. Problematically, the Civil Procedure

88 Article 5 (3) LCCA.

89 The meaning of 'direct applicability' is debated in the literature.

Code recognizes supremacy of directly applicable EU law and the Administrative Procedure Code provides for ranking of EU law in the external hierarchy of normative acts. Consequently, the supremacy of EU law is not excluded but equally, at least as far as the texts of the procedural codes provide, is not explicitly welcomed in relation to national law and even less so for the Constitution.

Latvian Constitutional Court

In this complex code-specific regulation of supremacy, interpretation provided by the Latvian Constitutional Court is crucial. The Constitutional Court has a duty under Article 16, item 6 of the Constitutional Court Law to review cases regarding compliance of national legal norms of Latvia with international agreements entered into by Latvia which are not contrary to the Constitution. According to the LAPA Article 17 (5), 'If the Constitutional Court has interpreted the relevant norm of law in a judgment, institutions and courts shall apply this interpretation.' Similarly, the LCPA provides that interpretation by the Constitutional Court must be taken into consideration. The LCCA refers more generally to case law as source of interpretation.[90]

In a case decided in July 2004 contesting imposition of a fine on a passenger ferry operator, the Constitutional Court was confronted with interpretation and application of conflicting provisions of national law, EU Directive 2001/51/EC and the International Convention on Facilitation of International Maritime Traffic. To establish the complex relationship and priority rules between conflicting public international, European Union, and national law provisions the Court stated:

> The Law 'The Procedure by which Laws and Other Acts, Adopted by the Saeima, State President and the Cabinet are Promulgated, Published, Take Effect and Being Valid' does not specifically stipulate the place of international agreements in the hierarchy of Latvian normative acts. However, one has to take into consideration that this Law was passed after the Law 'On the Republic of Latvia International Agreements' had taken effect. Article 13 of the Law 'On the Republic of Latvia International Agreements' determines that 'if an international agreement affirmed by the Saeima provides for other provisions than those in the Republic of Latvia legislative acts, the provisions of the international agreement shall be applied.'

Further, the court underlined its well-established position on priority of international law under Article 15 LAPA.

> The Administrative Procedure Law *inter alia* determines the application of external normative acts, general legal principles and international legal norms

90 Article 5 (6) LCCA 'In applying legal norms, the court shall take into account case law.'

> as well as the hierarchy of the legal force of the external normative acts in the administrative process. The third part of Section 15 of this Law establishes that 'the legal norms of international law regardless of their source shall be applied in accordance with their place in the hierarchy of legal force of external regulatory enactments'. The person applying legal norms, also the court, when establishing a discrepancy between an international legal norm and a national legal norm of Latvia, shall apply the international legal norm.

Specifically in relation to EU law, the Latvian Constitutional Court explained:

> After joining the European Union the Republic of Latvia has to honour the responsibilities following from the [Accession Treaty]. In accordance with the above act Council Directive 2001/51/EC is also binding on Latvia ... LAPA also envisages that the legal norms of the European Union (Community) shall be applied in accordance with their place in the hierarchy of legal force of normative acts. When applying the legal norms of the European Union (Community) the institution and the court shall take into consideration the judicature of the European Court of Justice. Taking into consideration the European Court of Justice Judgment in the case *Commission v. Italy (Case 10/61, [1962] ECR, p.11)* as concerns relations with other Member States, EU (Community) norms shall be applied, i.e., legal acts of the Community shall be applied.[91]

After examining national provisions regulating priority rules as well as substantive provisions of the relevant national, EU, and international law provisions on imposition of fines on maritime carriers, the court concluded that 'there is variance between the national legal norm (the challenged norm) and the norm of the Directive as well as the norm of the international agreement (Standard 3.15 of the Convention).'[92] In order to resolve conflict of rules between international and EU obligations, the Constitutional Court relied on Article 307 of the TEC (now Article 351 TFEU):

> European laws do not affect former agreements, but the Member States shall try to eliminate these unconformities. However, at the time when a Member State has not carried out any activities (denouncement, expression of pretexts) the international agreement shall be applied (*see the case C-158/91 Criminal proceedings against Jean-Claude Levy*).[93]

The court pointed out that EU law does not *expressis verbis* oblige MSs to disapply an international agreement; however, it obliges MSs to take measures to eliminate

91 Case 2004-01-06 of 7 July 2004, para 7.

92 Ibid.

93 Ibid.

inconsistencies between international law commitments and obligations following from EU law. At the same time, national law provides for supremacy of EU law:

> LAPA also envisages that the legal norms of the European Union (Community) shall be applied in accordance with their place in the hierarchy of legal force of normative acts ... Besides, if a Member State establishes unconformity of its international legal liabilities with the legal norms of the European Community, it shall undertake the necessary measures to eliminate the unconformity.[94]

After extensive discussion of the priority rules of international law in the national legal system, as well as the relationship between national, European Community and international law provisions, specifically as applied to the facts of the case, the Constitutional Court found that the provisions of the EC Directive must be applied to ships sailing under the flag of EU MSs while the provisions of the Convention must be applied to ships sailing under the flag of third countries. Consequently, the Constitutional Court confirmed that the international obligations of Latvia must take priority over national rules providing for a nuanced balancing between respect for public international law obligations and provisions of EU law.

This triangular balancing is, however, uncomfortable for the court and in conclusion the LCC stresses that the Latvian authorities must take steps to eliminate inconsistencies between relevant national, European Community and international law commitments:

> ... taking into consideration the provisions of Article 307 of the Foundation Agreement of the Consolidated European Community, which establishes the duty of the State to attain conformity of formerly concluded international agreements with European Law, Latvia shall undertake the relevant and necessary measures.

Further, the principle of supremacy was discussed by the LCC in a dispute between an environmental association and Riga City Council.[95] The association challenged the constitutionality of provisions of the Riga Land Use Plan covering the territory of Freeport Riga. The applicant argued that by failing to conduct an environmental assessment before adoption of the Riga Land Use Plan, *inter alia*, Riga City Council violated Article 175 of the EC Treaty (now 192 TFEU), Directive 2001/42/EC,[96] Directive 79/409/EEC[97] and Directive 92/43/EEC.[98]

---

94 Ibid.

95 2007-11-03 of 17 January 2008.

96 Directive 2001/42/EC of the European Parliament and of the Council of 27 June 2001 on the assessment of the effects of certain plans and programmes on the environment.

97 Council Directive 79/409/EEC of 2 April 1979 on the conservation of wild birds.

98 Council Directive 92/43/EEC of 21 May 1992 on the conservation of natural habitats and of wild fauna and flora.

The Constitutional Court, following discussion on the constitutionally protected right to a benevolent environment and the standing of a public interest association to challenge the constitutionality of the Riga City Council Land Use Plan, underlined the relevance of EU law and ECJ jurisprudence:

> Moreover, simultaneously with ratification of the Treaty on Accession of Latvia to the European Union, European Union law has become an integral part of the Latvian legal system. Therefore, legal acts of the European Union and interpretation provided in the jurisprudence of the European Court of Justice is to be taken into account when applying national regulatory enactments.[99]

Specifically as relates to the balancing between economic interests of port area development and environmental rights and obligations flowing from EU law, the Constitutional Court remarked:

> Taking into account the fact that *Natura 2000* is the designation of a site established by European Union law and taken over in Latvia, Latvian law must be interpreted so as to avoid any conflicts with the obligations of Latvia towards the European Union, unless the fundamental principles incorporated in the Satversme are affected. Thus also regarding the *Natura 2000* territories the requirements of directives transposed by Latvia and interpretation of directives established in the case law of the European Court of Justice should be observed.[100]

Undertaking analysis of applicable EU law and ECJ jurisprudence, the Constitutional Court found:

> According to European Union law, the obligations of Latvia regarding conservation of the environment are a part of the common responsibility of the Member States, because the nature in Latvia is a part of the common heritage of the entire European Community. Latvia has no legal basis to make alterations to these territories, because this would hinder reaching the objectives established in directives of the European Union [ECJ cases cited]. Moreover, the Court of Justice of the European Communities, when interpreting Article 6 of the Directive 92/43/EEC, has stated in its case law that land use plans before adoption should be subject to appropriate assessment of possible implications for the environment of the respective site in order to reduce any potential damage [ECJ case law]. This assessment is to be performed for plans that affect *Natura 2000* territories, as well as to land use plans that are adjacent to *Natura 2000* territories that are located in a protected site or in its vicinity.

99 2007-11-03 of 17 January 2008.

100 2007-11-03 of 17 January 2008, para 25.4.

Following analysis of the procedure for adoption of the Land Use Plan against the constitutionally protected rights and provisions of European EU norms, the Constitutional Court concluded that 'Riga City Council has exceeded the limits of its discretion because, when adopting the Contested Plan, it did not assess its effects on *Natura 2000* territories.'[101]

In both the 'Ferry Fine' and 'Freeport Riga' cases discussed above, the Constitutional Court intensively analysed EU law and ECJ jurisprudence and applied the principle of supremacy of EU law. The principle of supremacy of EU law is a guiding principle of Latvian Constitutional Court adjudication and settlement of conflicts between national, supranational and international legal norms. Therefore, in spite of confusing legislative regulation of conflict of norms in national procedural law, the principle of supremacy is applied in national court practice.

The limits of acceptance of the principle of supremacy were discussed by the Constitutional Court in its recent 2009 Lisbon Treaty judgment.[102] The court clearly indicated that the principle of supremacy of EU law is conditioned by constitutional principles of a democratic state and sovereignty:

> ... the integration of the legal acts of the European Community into our legal system places certain restrictions that can be acceptable only if EU law is compatible with the principles of a democratic State and the sovereignty of people that are derived from Articles 1 and 2 of the Satversme.[103]

In the same Lisbon judgment, the court stressed that 'The Constitutional Court has the duty to ensure the supremacy of the Satversme.'[104] Thus, the formulation of the court suggests that the supremacy of the national Constitution should be the lens through which the relationship (and possible conflict) with EU law should be assessed. The Constitutional Court in analysing the provisions of the Lisbon Treaty concluded that:

> Neither the effective Treaties nor the objectives set in Article 3 of the Consolidated Treaty of the European Union ... are contrary to the values and interests established in the Satversme. At the same time, as EU integration proceeds, it is necessary to take into account that Article 2 of the Satversme does not allow an unlimited transfer of competences which would preclude Latvia from being regarded as a sovereign State.[105]

Thus, according to the interpretation of the Latvian Constitutional Court, national legal doctrine places limits on its acceptance of EU law supremacy from its own

101 Ibid.

102 2008-35-01 of 7 April 2009.

103 Ibid.

104 Ibid., para 11.1.

105 Ibid., para 18.3.

national constitutional provisions on sovereignty and democracy. In contrast, the Estonian Supreme Court regards the supremacy of EU law as trumping all national law, including the Constitution. Thus, the Estonian Supreme Court conceptually derives the supremacy of EU law from the national Constitution, although accepting that the Constitution itself is not a limiting condition to the supremacy of EU law. On the other hand, the Latvian Constitutional Court derives the supremacy of EU law from international obligations of the state as further provided under national procedural law and ECJ jurisprudence.

Practice of higher courts in both jurisdictions suggests that the principle of supremacy is well understood and applied by national courts. The Estonian Supreme Court has clearly defined and explained the parameters on conflict-settlin rules between EU and national law and ruled that the principle of supremacy should be applied unconditionally in national law. The Latvian legal system provides differentiated, code-specific regulation of the principle of supremacy. Incoherent legislative provisions are interpreted by the national Constitutional Court to give full effect to the principle of supremacy of EU law. Fundamental constitutional principles of sovereignty and democracy are considered by the Constitutional Court as conditions that could potentially limit the principle of supremacy.

The Doctrine of Direct Effect

Following the analysis of supremacy, this section examines another fundamental EU law principle, the doctrine of direct effect, which is crucial for judicial enforcement of EU law by individuals (Reich 2005: 13–35).

Central Points

ECJ doctrine on the direct effect of Treaty provisions and regulations is straightforward. National courts must enforce the provisions of EU primary and secondary law if provisions of EU law are sufficiently clear, precise, unconditional, and if they confer specific rights on citizens.[106] In the context of recent enlargements, the ECJ *Skoma-Lux* judgment discussed whether the unavailability of regulation in the national language may preclude direct effect of a regulation against individuals. In other words, the central question was whether a MS must enforce sanctions against individuals that follow from a regulation if this specific regulation has not been published in the official EU publication in the national language. The ECJ held that a EU regulation which is not published in the language of a Member State is unenforceable against individuals in that State.[107]

---

106 This generally applies to EU primary law provisions and regulations, for discussion on direct effect of directives see S Prechal (2005).

107 Case C-161/06, Skoma-Lux sro v Celní ředitelství Olomouc, paras 57–61.

The debated field relates to the horizontal direct effect of directives (Prechal 2005). It has long been contested whether in the case of incorrect or delayed implementation of a directive by a MS, it is nevertheless possible to enforce rights flowing from the directive in the national court in a person vs. person dispute. Generally, the ECJ has denied the horizontal direct effect of directives. However, a new wave of debate has recently been triggered by the ECJ *Kücükdeveci* judgment of January 2010.[108] The court, interpreting the age discrimination directive, concluded that although directives do not have horizontal direct effect, the general principles of EU law that a directive promotes (in the given case, non-discrimination based on age) and which are included in EU primary law nevertheless have 'negative' horizontal direct effect.[109] Estonian and Latvian courts have not yet been directly confronted with issues related to horizontal direct effect of directives. The direct effect of EU primary law and regulations is well understood and taken up by national courts.

In cases of insufficient or incorrect implementation of directives that create individual rights but do not have horizontal direct effect, the principle of EU-conforming interpretation of national law is central. The principle of conforming (harmonious) interpretation requires interpretation of national law in the light of the wording and the purpose of EU law.[110] This principle has various dimensions that have been gradually developed and sharpened through ECJ case law (Craig and de Burca 2008: 287–96). The central elements include the following: the principle applies not only to national courts but also to all competent authorities;[111] the principle is inherent in the Treaty system and follows from Article 10 TFEU (ex 10 TEC);[112] the principle applies to all national law, not only to legislation implementing a directive;[113] the principle applies to 'horizontal' cases between private parties,[114] and the obligation of harmonious interpretation does not require a *contra legem* interpretation of national law.[115]

The up-to-date doctrine of harmonious interpretation doctrine is well summarized by the ECJ in the recent *Kücükdeveci* case:

> It follows that, in applying national law, the national court called on to interpret it is required to do so, as far as possible, in the light of the wording and the purpose of the directive in question, in order to achieve the result pursued by the

108 Case C-555/07, Seda Kücükdeveci v Swedex GmbH & Co. KG.

109 Similarly, the court also supported the theory of 'negative direct effect' in case C-144/04 *Werner Mangold v Rüdiger Helm* [2005] ECR I-9981.

110 Case 14/83 Von Colson and Kamann v. Land Nordrhein-Westfalen.

111 Case C-218/01 Henkel KGaA [2004] ECR I-1725, para.60; Case C-555/07 Kücükdeveci, para 47.

112 Case C-397-403/01 Pfeiffer.

113 Ibid.

114 Case C-106/89 Marleasing, para 7–8.

115 Case C-555/07 Kücükdeveci, paras 47–8.

> directive and thereby comply with the third paragraph of Article 288 TFEU … The requirement for national law to be interpreted in conformity with European Union law is inherent in the system of the Treaty, since it permits the national court, within the limits of its jurisdiction, to ensure the full effectiveness of European Union law when it determines the dispute before it … .[116]

The ECJ continued by expressly acknowledging that, in considering a clear and precise provision of national law, harmonious interpretation in conformity with an EU directive may be not possible.[117]

Estonian Courts

Concerning the direct effect of EU primary law, in a 2006 case related to the Surplus Stock Act, the Estonian Supreme Court stated that if necessary national courts must directly rely on the provisions of the EC (now TFEU) Treaty.[118] In the absence of a national procedure for stay of proceedings to submit a preliminary reference to the ECJ, the national court must directly rely on Article 234 EC (now 267 TFEU).[119] Thus, the court straightforwardly suggested that lack of national procedural rules[120] must not be an obstacle to effective application of EU law in a national jurisdiction. Consequently, the court argued that a legislative lacuna can and should be resolved by national courts by direct reliance on EU primary law.

The Estonian Supreme Court in several cases has also discussed the legal nature and the direct applicability of EC regulations.[121] The court has expressly and neatly repeated EU law and ECJ jurisprudence on the legal nature of a regulation and explained that 'As a rule, according to Article 249 para 2 of the EU Accession Treaty an EC Regulation is in its legal nature generally applicable in all MS (including Estonia) binding in its entirety and directly applicable.'[122] The court then discussed that, as a general rule, regulations do not require national implementing measures and in fact rewriting provisions of a regulation into national law is contrary to ECJ jurisprudence.[123] However, in some cases, national implementing measures are nevertheless necessary, for example, in order to define national institutions and

116 Ibid., paras 47–8.

117 Ibid., para 49.

118 3-3-1-74-05.

119 Ibid., para 23.

120 Following amendments to the Civil Procedure Act, from 2006 a provision allows for stay of proceedings (Article 356 Civil Procedure Act).

121 See for example, cases 3-3-1-33-06; 3-3-1-74-05; 3-3-1-87-08; 3-3-1-11-09.

122 No 3-3-1-74-05 of 25 April 2006, para 12 ; 3-3-1-79-08, para 14.

123 3-3-1-33-06, para 15. To support its argument, the court cites ECJ case law: Case 39/72 Commission v. Italy and Case 50/76: Amsterdam Bulb BV v. Produktschap voor Siergewassen; see also 3-3-1-79-08, para 14.

to determine sanctions for breach of EU law.[124] A national implementing measure must not be contrary to EU law and the substance of national law must be in accordance with the scope of the delegated norm provided by EC regulation.[125] Estonian national law must be applied if the national implementing measure is in accordance with the EC regulation. However, if the court determines that a national implementing measure is contrary to the regulation, then the court must determine if the regulation can be directly effective regardless of national law.[126]

In distinguishing direct applicability from direct effect of the specific provisions of a regulation, the Supreme Court has explained:

> As a rule, a regulation imposes public-law obligations on individuals and simultaneously provides them rights in relation to a state. The direct applicability of a regulation in itself does not mean that all provisions of a regulation have direct effect. Norms of a regulation have direct effect only if they are formulated clearly and do not leave discretion to Member States.[127]

Applying those principles, for example, in cases related to structural funds, the Supreme Court has found that although EC Regulation 817/2004/EC is directly applicable, specifically Article 73 of this regulation is not directly effective:[128]

> As a follow up to the ECJ *Skoma-Lux* judgment, the Supreme Court has discussed whether the direct effect of a regulation may be unenforceable against individuals. The Court has stated that based on EC law, determination of penalties following from a regulation is connected to the proper publication of the regulation in the Estonian language.[129] Thus, applying the criteria developed by the ECJ in *Skoma-Lux* the Supreme Court found that because the contested regulation had not been properly published in the Estonian language at the time of submission of the declarations serving as the basis of tax liability, the regulation could not have obligated the company to pay *erga omnes* customs duty.[130]

The principle of conforming interpretation as developed by the ECJ is well taken into the jurisprudence of the Estonian Supreme Court. Inspired by the *Von Colson/*

124 3-3-1-33-06, para 15; 3-3-1-79-08, para 14.

125 3-3-1-33-06, para 15.

126 3-3-1-74-05 of 25 April 2006, para 12. In this case, the Supreme Court relying directly on the provisions of the regulations set aside a conflicting national provision.; 3-3-1-79-08, para 14.

127 Case 3-3-1-79-08, the court refers to the ECJ decision in case C-403/98 Azienda Agricola Monte Arcosu.

128 3-3-1-79-08, para 14; 3-3-1-80-08, para 10.

129 3-3-1-87-08, para 41.

130 3-3-1-36-08 of 13 October 2008.

Marleasing ECJ jurisprudence, the Supreme Court arguing *a contrario* stated in a 2008 case:

> If the court adjudicating a legal dispute had no obligation to review the conformity of Estonian law with EU law or if the court did not fulfil this obligation, it would be impossible to ascertain possible conflicts with EU law. This would undermine performance of the duty of the Estonian courts under Article 10 EC to ensure fulfilment of the obligations arising out of the EC Treaty or resulting from action taken by the institutions of the Community, and to facilitate achievement of the Community's tasks.[131]

Consequently, the Supreme Court adopts an understanding of the principle of conforming interpretation as closely resembling ECJ doctrine. The Supreme Court further explained that without accepting the obligation of conforming interpretation the national courts could not fulfil their EU law mandate and guarantee full legal effect of EU law provisions.[132] If various interpretations of legal provisions are possible, courts should if possible prefer an EU law conforming interpretation.[133] Moreover, the court stressed that if a conflict between Estonian and EU law cannot be resolved through EU law conforming interpretation, then the court must refuse to apply the provision of national law and directly apply the effective provision of EU law instead.[134]

Most recently, the issue of direct effect in the context of insufficient implementation of the directive was addressed by the Estonian Supreme Court in a complex case concerning VAT.[135] OÜ Esoni, a real estate development company, disputed a decision of the national tax authorities to tax two transactions. In the first disputed transaction, the applicant gave a legal right of use over a real estate property for the construction of water and sewerage pipelines to another unrelated undertaking. The Estonian Tax Board (ETB) taxed the supply of establishing the right of use over property. In the second disputed transaction, the applicant handed over communication cables and communication underground workings to another unrelated undertaking. In determining the taxable amount, the ETB adjusted the sale price between the applicant and the unrelated undertaking up to the open market value. The applicant disputed the VAT obligation on the right of use over

131 3-4-1-5-08 of 26 June 2008, para 31.

132 'If the courts had no obligation to review the conformity of the Estonian law to the EU law, the courts could not fulfil its duty to interpret the Estonian law in the EU-law conforming manner, i.e. the duty to interpret the Estonian law, as far as possible, taking account of the wording and objectives of the European Union law' (see in this regard C-106/89 Marleasing, [1990] ECR I-04135, paragraph 8, and C-268/06, Impact [2008], para 98–101.)." Case 3-4-1-5-08, judgment of 26 June 2008, para 31.

133 3-3-1-85-07 of 7 May 2008, para 38.

134 Case 3-4-1-5-08 of 26 June 2008, para 32.

135 Supreme Court of Estonia case 3-3-1-36-10 of 16 June 2010.

property and adjustment of consideration up to the open market value among unrelated undertakings.

In relation to the second transaction, the applicant *inter alia* argued that national law (Article 12 para 4 of the VAT Act),[136] that also allows adjustment of consideration up to the open market value among unrelated undertakings, is contrary to the provisions of EU Directive 2006/69/EC that allows such an adjustment only on transactions between related undertakings. The national lower courts, based on the evidence related to the factual circumstances of the case, refused to apply the directives to the facts of the case. However, the Administrative Chamber of the Supreme Court analysed the issue of application of EU directives in detail.

The court first pointed out that the disputed transaction took place after the implementation date of Directive 2006/69/EC had passed but before relevant national amendments came into force. Thus, application of the national law provision that at the time when the transaction took place was contrary to the EC was not legitimate:[137]

> The Supreme Court has emphasized (see e.g. case nr. 3-3-1-85-07 of 7 May 2008 and case nr. 3-4-1-5-08 of 26 June 2008) the obligation of national courts to interpret Estonian law in conformity with EU law namely the obligation to interpret Estonian law as far as possible in the light of the wording and the purpose of EU law (see e.g. ECJ decision *Marleasing* and *Impact*). In case of a conflict between national and EU law, Estonian law should be interpreted in conformity with EU law. In case of a conflict between Estonian and EU law the conflicting Estonian law must not be applied. If conforming interpretation is not possible then the direct effect of the directive should be considered.[138]

In this case, the Supreme Court clearly established analytical steps that national courts must take in cases involving disputes between national and EU law: first, EU law-conforming interpretation of national law; secondly, if conforming interpretation is not possible, then national law is to be set aside and direct effect of the specific provision of EU law is to be considered. Concerning the conditions for direct effect of the provision of the EU directive, the Supreme Court repeated the well-known test of 'clear, precise and unconditional'.[139]

Specifically as applies to the facts of the *Esoni* case, the Supreme Court stated that it is not possible to interpret national law in conformity with EU law. Consequently, the court set aside application of the national law contrary to the

136 Article 12 para 4 of the Value Added Tax Act in the version contested in the case 3-3-1-36-10 was in force until 1 January 2009 and was repealed by the legislator prior to the decision of the Supreme Court as inconsistent with the provisions of Directive 2006/112/EC.

137 3-3-1-36-10, para 19.

138 Ibid., paras 19–20.

139 Ibid., para 21.

EU directive and annulled the decision of the lower courts.[140] The Court concluded that the applicant had a right to directly rely on the provision of the EU directive while the national ETB had no legitimate right to tax a transaction on the basis of national law that was in conflict with EU law provisions.

Analysis of the jurisprudence of ordinary courts indicates that national courts in general follow the guidance of the Supreme Court and there are no major difficulties or inconsistencies in application of the principle of direct effect in the jurisprudence of lower courts.[141]

Latvian Courts

Latvian courts in several cases have addressed the principle of direct effect and direct applicability of EU law.[142] However, scholarly articles and the jurisprudence of Latvian national courts are not always terminologically consistent about translation into the Latvian language of the terms 'direct effect' and 'direct applicability'. This is especially relevant in cases related to the direct effect of directives. Therefore, before conducting a closer substantive analysis of the national jurisprudence on direct effect, a short terminological note is necessary.[143]

A review of scholarly articles in the publication *Jurista Vārds* suggests that although various authors substantively correctly (!) distinguish between the notion of direct applicability and the principle of direct effect, they diverge in translating this principle into the Latvian language. Thus, for example Parfjonova (2002: 247) discussing the European Association Agreement uses the term '*tiešā spēkā esamība*' to refer to direct applicability and '*tiesību tiešā piemērojamība*' to denote the principle of direct effect.[144] Škutāns (2006: 437), in an article discussing

---

140 Ibid., paras 23, 31.

141 For application by lower courts see for example, judgments 3-04-406; 3-05-272; 3-05-617; 3-04-415; as well as analysis by Kanger (2007: 31–2). For application by Supreme Court, see for example, cases 3-2-1-4-06, 3-3-1-33-06, 3-3-1-90-06, 3-3-1-33-07, 3-3-1-79-08, 3-3-1-57-09, 3-3-1-36-10.

142 See for example, Supreme Court cases SKA-46 judgment of 8 March 2005 on application of Directive 2003/109/EC; SPC-37/2008 judgment of 14 May 2008 on application of Directives 93/13/EEC and 98/27/EC.

143 The 'terminological background' is key to the understanding of jurisprudence of national ordinary courts as in some cases it is linguistically not clear whether the court refers to direct applicability or direct effect.

144 'Ir svarīgi atcerēties, ka pastāv atšķirība starp Kopienas tiesību tiešo spēkā esamību un Kopienas tiesību tiešo piemērojamību. Kopienas tiesību tiešā spēkā esamība (angl.: *direct applicability;* franc.: *applicabilié*) nozīmē to, ka Kopienas tiesības ir spēkā dalībvalstīs kā daļas no valsts iekšējās jurisdikcijas un to realizāciju nav nepieciešams ieviest ar īpašu nacionālo tiesību aktu. Kopienas tiesības darbojas dalībvalstīs, sākot ar to spēkā stāšanās brīdi. Kopienas tiesību tiešā piemērojamība (angliski: *direct effect;* franciski: *effet direct*) nozīmē konkrētu un faktisku fizisku un juridisku personu tiesību pamatojumu dalībvalstīs ar kādas Kopienas tiesību normas starpniecību. Kādas Kopienas tiesību normas

national and EU regulations of public-private partnerships in procurement, also refers to '*tiešās piemērojamības doktrīnu*' as to the doctrine of direct effect. In contrast, Čakste (2000: 188) refers to direct applicability as '*tiešā piemērošana*' and to direct effect as '*tiešais juridiskais spēks*'.[145] Other scholars – for example, Škoba (2003: 300) in an article discussing the direct effect of directives – refer to the principle of direct effect as '*tiešā iedarbība*'. Similarly, direct effect as '*tiešā iedarbība*' is most recently referred to by Borkoveca (2010: 608)[146] and Pelša (2009: 564).[147]

The EU's multilingual terminology database IATE suggests that direct effect should be translated into Latvian as '*tiešā iedarbība*' and directly applicable as '*tieši piemērojams*'.[148] This practice is followed by EU translation services in the translation of ECJ jurisprudence into the Latvian language.[149]

The first case where the legal nature of an EU directive and its application at the national level were substantively analysed by national courts is the *OCMA* case. In this case, related to the term of validity of a travel document, the applicant attempted to rely on the principle of direct effect of an EU directive provision against conflicting national law.[150] The applicant argued that the Office of Citizenship and Migration Affairs (OCMA), the national administrative agency, acted contrary to the provisions of EU directives on free movement of persons,[151]

---

piemērojamības gadījumā kāda atsevišķa persona nacionālajās tiesās un iestādēs var tieši atsaukties uz šo normu.'

145 'Tiešā piemērošana (*directly applicable*) attiecas uz visiem ES tiesību aktiem, kas ir saistoši Dalībvalstīm un kam ir obligāts raksturs, un kas neprasa to tālāku implementēšanu Dalībvalsts tiesībās. Tiešais juridiskais spēks (*directly effective*) nozīmē šo tiesību normu attiecināšanu uz Dalībvalstu privātpersonām, respektīvi, Dalībvalstu privātpersonu tiesības griezties Dalībvalstu tiesās sakarā ar Eiropas Savienības tiesību normu pārkāpumiem un tieši atsaukties uz ES tiesību normām.'

146 'Tiešā iedarbība, ar to saprotot indivīda tiesības (iespēju) atsaukties uz ES akta noteikumu dalībvalsts tiesā, attiecībā uz dibināšanas līgumu, regulu un lēmumu normām atzīta Tiesas judikatūrā jau vairāk nekā pirms 30 gadiem.'

147 'Nenoliedzami, tā palīdz arī dažādu ārējo normatīvo aktu "robu" aizpildīšanai, jo Eiropas Kopienu tiesībām piemīt tiešā iedarbība (*direct effect*) un pārākums pār nacionālajām tiesībām (*supremacy*).'

148 InterActive Terminology for Europe: http://iate.europa.eu/.

149 See for example, translation into Latvian, Joined cases C-471/07 and C-472/07 Association générale de l'industrie du médicament (AGIM) ASBL and Others (C-471/07 and C-472/07), Janssen Cilag SA (C-471/07) and Sanofi-Aventis Belgium SA (C-472/07) v Belgian State [2010] ECR I-0000.

150 A42347606, Judgment of Regional Administrative Court AA43-111-08/13 of 30 October 2008; Judgment SKA-175/2009 of Supreme Court of 5 March 2009; judgment of Regional Administrative Court AA43-2025-09/11 of 29 May 2009.

151 Council Directive 68/360/EEC of 15 October 1968 on the abolition of restrictions on movement and residence within the Community for workers of Member States and their families [Official Journal L 257 of 19.10.1968].

or alternatively on freedom to provide services.[152] By issuing an identity document for a period of one year instead of five years, the OCMA had violated the rights of the applicant as provided under EU directives.

Confronted with the cases, the administrative court of first level correctly identified the nature of the legal problems: 'Whether provision 10.2.1. of the Cabinet of Ministers Regulation 378 is contrary to EU law and whether the national agency was required without the applicant's specific request to issue passports for the applicant's children with a validity period of five years.'[153] In reply to those questions the administrative court of first instance explained

> Article 249 EC Treaty (ex Article 189) in the third paragraph provides that a directive shall be binding, as to the result to be achieved, upon each MS to which it is addressed, but shall leave to the national authorities the choice of form and methods. Therefore, Directives 68/360 and 73/148 are not *directly applicable* [*tieši piemērojamas*] [[154]] in MSs including Latvia.[155]

The court then continued by stating that the applicant does not fall under the material scope of the directive on free movement of workers because her intention in travelling was not connected to any work-related activities. Consequently, the decision of the OCMA did not constitute a violation of the legitimate interests of the applicant and her children as provided under the directives.[156] Moreover, the court underlined that national regulation and practice of the OCMA to issue

---

152 Council Directive 73/148/EEC of 21 May 1973 on the abolition of restrictions on movement and residence within the Community for nationals of Member States with regard to establishment and the provision of services. Directive 2004/38/EC of the European Parliament and of the Council of 29 April 2004 on the right of citizens of the Union and their family members to move and reside freely within the territory of the Member States.

153 AA43-1111-08 para 4.2.

154 In the quotes from the national courts judgments, I will translate terms as most closely connected to the meaning and indicate original Latvian language terminology in parentheses.

155 AA43-1111-08 para 4.3.1.

156 'The above mentioned directives consolidated the rules on free movement of workers within the Community, determining what measures should be taken to remove still existing restrictions on movement and residence within the European Community. Thus, with the purpose of ensuring the free movement of labour, the Member States were obliged to provide Community citizens, their spouse, their children and their spouses' relatives in ascending and descending lines, which are dependent on them, with passports valid for a period of not less than five years … The Court finds that decision of the CMB did not limit the opportunities of the applicant to reside and move freely within the European Community. Since the applicant [did not have an aim to travel for work related purposes] the decision of the CMB did not violate legitimate interest of the applicant and her children as provided in the Directives 68/360 and 73/148' AA43-1111-08 para 4.3.2.

passports for children under the age of five for a term of validity of one year is considered to be reasonable and justified.[157]

The applicant, relying on fundamental principles of EU law and jurisprudence of the ECJ on supremacy (*Costa v ENEL*;[158] *Simmenthal*[159]), direct effect (*Van Duyn*,[160] *Ratti*[161]), pointing to the principle of state liability as established in *Francovich*[162] and the underlying principle of harmonious interpretation (*von Colson*,[163] *Marleasing*[164]) appealed to the Regional Administrative Court.

Specifically in relation to the principle of direct effect the applicant pointed out that according to the cases of *van Duyn* and *Ratti*, the European Court of Justice has recognized the principle of direct effect (*tiešās iedarbības*) of directives.[165] In reply, the Regional Administrative Court explained first that as a rule the provisions of the directive are not directly applicable:

> The EC norms pre-empt national norms only if national norms are contrary to the EC norms or narrow them. Article 249 of the EC Treaty allows the member states to choose methods and form for reaching the goals set in the Directive. Thus, directives are not directly in force [*tiešā spēkā esamība*] and not directly applicable [*tieši piemērojamas*].[166]

---

157 'The appearance of the child, not only in its first months of life, but also during the first years of life is changing very rapidly. Consequently, by issuing a passport for longer than one year there is a possibility that the child's photo in the passport is no longer recognizable. Provision determining the issue of the passport for a period of one year for children less than five years of age provides a national protection of a child. At the same time regulation leaves the children's parents or legal representatives to decide if there is a need to obtain a passport for a longer period than one year. The Court considered that restriction provided in the Article 10.2.1 of the Regulation 378 pursues a reasonable goal' AA43-1111-08 para 4.6.

158 C-6/64 Flaminio Costa *v.* ENEL [1964] *ECR* 585 (establishing principle of supremacy).

159 Case 106/77 Amministrazione delle Finanze dello Stato v Simmenthal [1978] ECR 629. (Duty to set aside provisions of national law which are incompatible with EU law).

160 Case 41/74 Van Duyn v Home Office [1974] *ECR* 1337 (direct effect).

161 Case 148/78 Pubblico Ministero v Tullio Ratti [1979] ECR 1629 (direct effect).

162 Joined Cases C-6/90 and C-9/90 Francovich and Others v Italian Republic [1991] ECR I-5357.

163 Case 14/83 Von Colson und Kamann V. Land Nordrhein-Westfalen [1984] ECR 1891 (conforming interpretation).

164 Case C-106/89 Marleasing SA v La Comercial Internacional de Alimentacion SA [1991] 1 ECR 4135 (a duty to interpret national legislation in light of unimplemented directive).

165 AA43-1111-08 para 12.

166 Ibid. Note however, that last sentence could be also translated as 'Directives are not directly applicable and do not have direct effect.'

However, ECJ case law recognizes that under certain circumstances, a directive may be important to an individual and it may contain rights granted to an individual. However, this is only when a Member State does not implement a directive or implements it incorrectly and this places an individual at a disadvantage. Thus, some provisions of a directive, if they fulfil certain preconditions, may be applied directly (*piemēroti tieši*).

The court then stated with reference to the ECJ judgment in case 8/81 *Becker*[167] and a national legal publication[168] the conditions under which the provisions of the directive may be applied directly (*piemēroti tieši*):[169]

> The directive is directly applicable [*tieši piemērojama*] only if the following conditions are met that is, if (1) the implementation date of the directive has passed; (2) a Member State has not implemented the directive or has implemented it incorrectly; (3) the norm of a directive is sufficiently clear. (4) the norm of a directive is not conditional upon coming into force of another norm.[170]

In this quote, in substance the court seems to discuss not 'direct applicability' but conditions for the principle of direct effect. It is not clear why, if the court attempted in fact to discuss the principle of direct effect, it did not use the same terminology as referred to by the applicant, who claimed direct effect (*tiešās iedarbības*) of the directive. The court equally does not refer to any cases of the ECJ establishing direct effect of the directives mentioned by the applicant.

Following discussion of the four conditions established in *Becker*, the Regional Administrative Court concluded that the applicant could not rely on those directives to protect individual rights:

> The Regional Administrative Court finds that in the particular case not all four conditions are fulfilled in order for a person to rely on direct applicability/direct effect[171] [*tiešu piemērošanu*], that is, national law provides for individual rights similar to those confirmed by Directive 68/360 and 73/148. The court concludes that national law does not restrict rights of an individual provided

---

167 Case 8/81 Ursula Becker v Finanzamt Münster-Innenstadt [1982] ECR 53.

168 The court refers to S Gatawis, E Broks and Z Bule, *Eiropas Tiesības* (Rīga, EuroFaculty, 2002).

169 The court refers to direct applicability of the directive 'Direktīva ir *tieši piemērojama* tikai pie šādiem priekšnosacījumiem' (emphasis added); however, in fact the court discussed the conditions for the 'direct effect' in Latvian 'tieša iedarbība" of the directive. Confusingly, the court also discussed direct effect of the directive in total and not in relation to any specific provision of the directive.

170 AA43-111-08/13 of 30 October 2008, para 12.

171 Here linguistically it is more correct to translate as 'direct applicability' but substantively as 'direct effect'.

> under directives. Thus, Latvia has implemented the Directives properly and the applicant has no basis to rely on the Directives as a source of individual rights.

It remains puzzling how after comparing the provisions of national law stipulating that 'children ... shall be issued a passport for one year or [under specific conditions] for a longer period than one year'[172] and Article 2 (3) of the Directive 73/148/EEC 'its [passport] period of validity shall be not less than five years',[173] the court concludes that 'Latvia has implemented the Directive properly' and thus the applicant has no need to rely on the directive as a source of individual rights. Clearly, the mere possibility to have a passport valid for over one year (which the applicant could have requested) is not the same as a default rule to have a passport valid for five years as provided under the directive. However, the court seems to consider that existence of the possibility to acquire a passport valid for five years is sufficient to conclude that the directive is implemented correctly. Fuzziness of the lower courts on the principle of direct effect in contrast to the notion of direct applicability could also partly explain the court's conclusion denying that an individual can rely directly on the provisions of the directive against a conflicting provision of national law.[174]

It is well-established and consistent practice of the ECJ that 'where a directive is intended to create rights for individuals, the persons concerned must be able to ascertain the full extent of their rights and, where appropriate, rely on them before the national courts.'[175] The fact that national law has transposed the directive *per se* could not be a reason to deny the possibility for an individual to rely directly on the provisions of the directive for protection of individual rights. As the Advocate General pointed out in relation to the rights conferred by Directives 68/360 and 73/148:

> Free movement of citizens of the Union, i.e. persons possessing the nationality of a Member State, within the territory of the Member States is guaranteed at Treaty level by the combined effect of Articles 18, 39, 43 and 49 EC, all of which have direct effect, in conjunction with the secondary Community legislation adopted in order to give effect to these provisions, in particular Regulation No 1612/68, Directive 68/360, Directive 73/148 and Directives 90/364, 90/365 and 93/96.[176]

172 Cabinet of Ministers Regulations No. 378 of 22 April 2004.

173 A similar provision is also included in Article 2(3) of EC Directive 68/360/EEC.

174 If the court was not sure about direct effect of relevant provisions of most fundamental EC directives on free movement of workers and freedom to provide services it should have turned to the ECJ with a request for a preliminary reference instead of concluding that individuals cannot rely on the provisions of directives.

175 See for example, Case C-9/92 Commission of the European Communities v Hellenic Republic para 20.

176 Case C-1/05 Yunying Jia v Migrationsverket, Opinion of Advocate General Geelhoed [2007] ECR I-1, para 31.

The applicant, dissatisfied with the outcome and reasoning of the lower courts, again relying on the fundamental principles of EU law and ECJ jurisprudence, including the principles of direct effect and supremacy, appealed the case to the Supreme Court. *Inter alia*, the applicant requested the Supreme Court to submit a request for a preliminary reference with two questions: first, whether national law complies with Article 4 of EU Directive 2004/38,[177] and secondly, whether the directive allows derogations.

The Senate of the Supreme Court (Department of Administrative Cases) found that national law is contrary to the provisions of EU Directive 73/48/EEC and overruled the decision of the Regional Administrative Court.[178] The court, based on extensive reference to the jurisprudence of the ECJ, established that Directive 68/360 was not applicable to the applicant and her family because she did not qualify as a worker. However, Directive 73/148 did apply to the applicant because she requested identity documents for her children with the intention of going on a tourist trip so that they can be considered as recipients of services:

> In the Senate's view such national legislation comes into conflict with Article 2.3 of EC Directive 73/148/EEC (Article 2.3. of EC Directive 68/360/EEC and Article 4.4. of EC Directive 2004/38/EC, as the provision of the Directive requires a passport with validity of at least five years. The Directive does not allow MS to make additional reservations or conditions, such as establishing the necessity to travel or the length of travel, as a prerequisite. The Senate therefore concludes that the State had not properly implemented into national law Article 2.3 of EC Directive 73/148/EC. Considering that the applicant has requested a child's passport after the date for implementation of the Directive had expired, the State was required to directly apply [*tieši piemērot*] Article 2.3 of EC Directive 73/148 to issue passports to children for five years.[179]

Therefore, finally, the Supreme Court enforced the doctrine of direct effect, suggesting that national law should be set aside and the provisions of the directive applied instead. As a result, the Supreme Court overturned the decision and sent the case back for consideration on the merits to the Regional Administrative Court. The Regional Administrative Court, following the reasoning of the Supreme

177 Directive 2004/38 amends directives 73/148/EEC and 68/360/EEC.

178 The court denied a plea by the applicant to submit a request for a preliminary reference to the ECJ on the basis of the *acte claire* doctrine. The court refers to ECJ case 283/81 Srl CILFIT and Lanificio di Gavardo SpA v. Ministry of Health.

179 The court then continued to explain that it was not relevant that the applicant requested the passports for a one-year validity period. Derogations under directives are allowed only on grounds of public policy, public security, or public health and in the present case that did not seem to be the case as a passport is only a travel document and may not be used by children otherwise than for these purposes. Therefore, national regulation did violate the norms of Directive 68/360, Directive 73/148 and Directive 2004/38/EC.

Court, first restated the four conditions on direct effect of the directive and then pointed out that under Directive 73/148/EEC, the date of implementation of which had passed, the validity of the travel document was five years and derogations did not apply. Finally, the court as moral compensation for incorrect application of the directive, ordered a letter of apology from the administrative agency.[180]

After a lengthy procedure through all three levels of the judicial system, finally the Supreme Court, relying on the principle of direct effect and supremacy, correctly applied the provisions of the EU directives and guided the appeal court to reconsider the decision.[181] The *OCMA* case indicates that application of fundamental EU law principles such as direct effect by national lower courts is not always uncomplicated. Nevertheless, on a positive note, albeit with a detour through the Supreme Court's extensive analysis and guidance to the appeal court, the applicant was nevertheless able to rely on the provisions of the directive.

More recent jurisprudence of national courts, especially jurisprudence of the Senate of the Supreme Court, indicates that gradually national courts are increasingly becoming accustomed to application of the doctrine of direct effect and more clearly distinguishing both substantively and terminologically between the notion of direct applicability and direct effect:

> … after the implementation date [of a directive] the state authorities and national courts are obligated to directly apply [*tieši piemērot*] a directive. The European Court of Justice recognized that under certain circumstances a directive may have direct effect [*tieša iedarbība*], concluding that market participants have the opportunity in relationship with a state to directly refer to the provisions of the directive if the state has not yet transposed the directive (European Court of 5 April 1979 in Case 148/78, Criminal proceedings against Tullio Ratti).[182]

More nuanced questions related to the horizontal direct effect of directives were discussed by national courts in a case related to the dismissal of a pregnant member

180 AA43-111-08 of 29 April 2009.

181 For the applicant it took over three years in order to enforce her rights under the EC directive. The OCMA rendered its administrative decision on 20 January 2006. The final judgment of the Regional Administrative Court was issued on 29 May 2009.

182 Case A8080309/2 judgment SKA – 293/2010 of 24 March 2010 para 17. This is the first case where the Supreme Court uses terminology consistent with the IATE database and practice of the ECJ lawyer-linguists translating ECJ jurisprudence into the Latvian language. Compare, however, that in another judgment of the Senate of the Supreme Court (Case A42270505, judgment SKA-146/2009 of 11 June 2009) concerning Article 17 of the VAT Directive 'The Senate considers as an *obiter dictum* to point out that after accession of the Latvian Republic to the European Union, the first part of Article 17 of the above mentioned directive is directly applicable/directly effective [?] (*tieši piemērojama*), since its content is sufficiently precise and unconditional and it requires MS to follow a certain course of action' para 11.

of a board of directors.[183] In the *Pregnancy Dismissal* case, the parties argued whether the applicant is considered to be a 'worker' under EU law and therefore falls under the protection of an EU directive prohibiting dismissal of pregnant women and whether a provision of the directive can be horizontally relied on by the applicant against a private company. The applicant, directly relying on Article 10 of Directive 92/85/EEC, argued that her dismissal by a private company was contrary to EU law. In reply, the respondent, *inter alia*, stated that EU directives do not enjoy horizontal direct effect and therefore cannot be directly relied on in a dispute between two private parties:

> Directive 92/85/EEC cannot be directly applied in the particular dispute between applicant and respondent. The ECJ under Article 249 EC Treaty has consistently rejected the possibility that a directive may impose obligations on individuals and therefore it cannot be applied in private law disputes (Case C-91/92 para 20 judgment of 14 July 1994; case C-201/02 para 56 judgment of 7 January 2004). The ECJ has further stated that even '(…) a clear, precise and unconditional provision of a directive seeking to confer rights or impose obligations on individuals cannot of itself apply in proceedings exclusively between private parties.' (see Joined cases C-397/01 and C-403/01 para 109, judgment of 5 October 2004). Thus, … if the applicant is not satisfied with the way in which the Latvian legislator introduced Directive 92/85/EEC into national law, the applicant must address the Latvian state, rather than reference to the Directive should be used in a dispute between private parties.[184]

The Supreme Court, confronted with issues related to interpretation of EU law, submitted a reference for a preliminary ruling.[185] Advocate General Bot in his opinion in this case relying on *Kücükdeveci* argued that the principle of equal treatment between men and woman must be given fullest protection including in disputes between private individuals:

> Admittedly, as LKB pointed out, Article 10 of Directive 92/85 cannot be applied directly in a dispute between individuals although it could in a dispute with a public-sector employer. (37) However, it is important to remember that the national court must interpret its domestic law so far as is possible in conformity with EU law so as to achieve the result envisaged by the latter and, if such an interpretation is not possible, it must disapply the provision of national law that is contrary to EU law if it has the power to do so under its procedural rules. (38) It is also important to add that, in accordance with Kücükdeveci, (39) in so far

183 SKC-88/2009, C-232/09 Dita Danosa v LKB Līzings SIA [2010] ECR I – 0000.

184 Supreme Court of Latvia case SKC-88/2009 of 13 May 2009, paras 4.2.7 and 4.2.8.

185 C-232/09 for discussion see the section 'Latvia: Preliminary Reference Procedure'.

> as Article 10 of Directive 92/85 merely implements the fundamental principle of equal treatment between men and women by prohibiting the dismissal of a pregnant woman on grounds of pregnancy, a national court which cannot find in national procedural law a sufficient basis for disapplying the provision of national law justifying such dismissal, derives that power from the primacy of the fundamental principle. (40)[186]

National case law related to the direct effect of regulations is more consistent and straightforward.[187]

In conclusion, both the Estonian and the Latvian courts have had an opportunity to discuss the principle of direct effect. The Estonian Supreme Court as well as the ordinary courts have, with detailed references to ECJ jurisprudence, discussed differences between the notions of direct applicability and direct effect and applied the doctrine accordingly. Latvian jurisprudence suggests that there is at least a terminological inconsistency between the notion of direct applicability and the doctrine of direct effect. Ordinary courts, as the *OCMA* case indicates, initially have not been comfortable to rely on the principle of direct effect of a directive. However, more recent cases denote a tendency towards a more consistent terminological and substantive application of the doctrine of direct effect of EU legislation.

The principle of harmonious interpretation, developed in national jurisprudence through cases related to the application of norms of international law, is generally also applicable in EU law-related cases.

---

186 C-232/09 Opinion of AG Bot [2010], paras 110–11.

187 See for example, cases of the administrative district *court of first level*: case Nr. A42723808, judgment Nr. A2206-10/12 of 19 February 2010 of the (consumer protection); case Nr. A42546208 judgment A01389-10/18 of 26 January 2010; case Nr. A42428007 judgment A2039-08/6 of 1 April 2008; case Nr. A 42603908 judgment A 01631-10/21 of 29 January 2010; case Nr. A42423007 judgment A373-09/5 of 10 March 2009 (VAT case); case Nr. A42588507 judgment A 1178-09/23 of 31 March 2009; case Nr. A42388607 judgment A261-09/7; Regional Administrative Court (*second level*) case Nr. A42428007 judgment AA43-0063-10/19 of 11 January 2010 of in case related to consumer protection rights; case Nr. A42389006 judgment AA43 – 0303 – 09/8 of 3 July 2009; Senate of the Supreme Court (*third level*) case Nr. A42207705 judgment SKA – 153/2008 of 8 May 2008.

Chapter 3
Institutional Coherence: Interests and Interactions

The previous chapter covered analysis of EU law principles that structure the relationship between EU and national law. This section focuses on the institutional dimension of coherence and aims to analyse institutional and procedural arrangements that guide interactions between national courts and political actors and national and European courts in EU law-related matters. Litigants, national courts and the ECJ are centre staged. I assume that more clearly defined institutional competences and procedural rules that guide resolution of EU law-related cases and more open access to courts, including access to jurisprudence, contribute to a more coherent resolution of EU law-related disputes. Put differently, a national institutional structure has a higher degree of coherence when litigants (a) are well informed of their legal rights and (b) have access to jurisprudence and legal process is understandable and affordable; when national courts have (c) clear, uncontested rules on which institution has what competence to resolve a particular EU law-related case and (d) have clear guidance under what conditions and how a preliminary reference should be requested from the ECJ. Acknowledging the importance of both litigants and courts in the institutional structure, the role they play *vis-à-vis* institutional coherence is different. Malfunctioning of courts could be a substantial disturbance while low activity of litigants may be unwelcome but not detrimental to the application of EU law in the national legal system.

Considering the different roles of litigants and courts, Chapter 3 does not have the same normative yardstick for examining the impact of those actors on institutional coherence. In relation to litigants, I argue that although they are an integral part of the institutional system their role is primarily limited to initiation and quality[1] of the litigation process and not in sustainability of institutional coherence. Active citizens that engage in the litigation process are not a threat to coherence but a litmus test as to the ability of the legal system to resolve EU law-related conflicts. On the other hand, courts are institutions that are vital to the sustainability of institutional coherence. A competent and independent judiciary and a well-organized judicial system are necessary elements of the coherent application of EU law. Even where substantive EU norms are implemented into national law, if the judicial institutions fail then effective application of EU law in the national context may be jeopardized.

1 Here by quality I mean a well-structured and argued legal submission and representations in court.

Litigants

Litigants are the main actors that bring to the fore substantive incoherencies between norms. Thus they are an integral part of the institutional structure of application of EU law. Taking into account the coherence argument, I focus in this section on the conditions that facilitate or impede access to courts and the quality of the litigation process. However, I start the discussion of litigants with arguments related to the role of litigation in a deliberative democracy, because I consider active participation of citizens in the legal process as important, especially in the context of post-Communism transformation.

Normative preferences, institutional constraints and established practices at the national level may be slow to accept change even after formal adoption of EU legal rules and national implementing measures. To challenge the existing boundaries of national legislation, or established administrative or legal practice that may be not in line with EU law provisions, requires an affected active citizen (resident) with legal standing in a given jurisdiction. Through national citizenship or residence status, an individual has access to various rights that in turn allow participation in a given political community.

Participation in a political community is conventionally exercised through participation in elections, active citizenship practices such as petitioning or demonstrations, and membership and participation in civic or social movements and NGOs.[2] However, what is less evident is that participation in a given political community may also be exercised through litigation. Participation through litigation requires (a) full and transparent access to information, including for example access to national and European legislation and case law; (b) access to courts (both in terms of procedures and resources); (c) active, educated citizens, and (d) a professional and independent court system (discussed below in section 2 of this chapter).[3]

Access to information

Access to information contributes to the democratic formation of opinion where individuals, as a result, can arguably make reasoned decisions and participate in the political process. However, access to and availability of information may result not only in increased awareness of the applicable formal rules but may also

2 For discussion on the role of civil society as a mechanism for reconstitution democracy in Europe see Liebert (2009).

3 For detailed discussion on the notion of litigation through European Courts as democratic participatory practice see Evas (2011), Evas, Liebert, Lord (2012) and Evas and Liebert (2013). On the litigation in the European courts see also for example Cichowski and Stone Sweet (2003), Alter (2006), Börzel (2006), Conant (2006), Schiek (2010, 2012). For theoretical discussion on public interest litigation at EU level see for example Micklitz and Reich (1997).

contribute to increased contestation of those rules and procedures. Therefore, the right to information not only implies the 'right to know' but also to the 'right to contest'. The right to contest, that is, the right to judicial recourse to challenge in a court of law existing formal rules that mediate an individual's relation to the state or other individuals, creates a public 'deliberative space'. Consequently, I consider litigation as an instrument for contesting substantive incoherencies among legal norms where legislative boundaries are challenged with the aim of either extending or limiting existing legislative regulation.[4]

Although Estonia and Latvia are countries with a civil law tradition where court cases do not have the force of legal precedent, nevertheless access to court cases can help clarify otherwise ambivalent legal obligations and ensure coherent application of norms.

In Estonia, through state commitment to e-technologies, access to legislative and judicial information is relatively easy, comprehensive and inexpensive. By contrast, in Latvia until very recently, access to legal information was partial, difficult and expensive. Even now, after substantial improvements from 2009, full public access to court cases in Latvia remains problematic. Table 3.1 below summarizes the public availability of the main electronic databases of legal materials.

Access to courts

Both Estonian and Latvian legislation guarantee access to justice. However, a number of important obstacles have recently been discussed: (1) limited access to legal aid, (2) high state fees and (3) costs of legal proceedings.

Access to legal aid provisions remains contested.[5] Justice Rask (2010) (the head of the Estonian Supreme Court) recently pointed out that in Estonia state aid for court proceedings in substance is more a loan than legal aid. Even when legal aid is provided, the low fees paid to appointed bar association lawyers raise concerns in the professional community regarding the quality of representation. There are also concerns regarding accessibility of legal aid to the ethnic minority (Evas 2006).

Recently, the Constitutional Review Chamber of the Supreme Court addressed the issue of extra-high state fees to initiate court proceedings. The court found that a state fee of 75,000 EEK (approx. €4820) is disproportionate. The court pointed out that the state fee in a case involving annulment of a decision of a building association that equals about six times the average monthly Estonian salary or 17 times the Estonian minimum wage violates the principle of proportionality and

4 In other words, court cases deal with issues where at a given time given boundaries (in substantive or procedural terms) of a given policy or regulation are at stake. They may (but need not) trigger political processes leading to formal legislative codification (regulation) or changes.

5 On access to justice reform in Estonia see Evas (2005). For a comparative report, please see Roger (2007: 261–80).

Table 3.1 Legal databases

	Estonia	Latvia
Database of national legislation	Riigiteataja http://www.riigiteataja.ee Fully searchable official free-of-charge electronic database that includes all legislation currently in force (and an archive of older legislation). Electronic version has equal legal force as the paper version of the official journal.[a]	Latvijas Vēstnesis http://www.vestnesis.lv/ www.likumi.lv Fully searchable free-of-charge electronic database that includes all legislation currently in force (and an archive of older legislation). Electronic version does not have official publication status.[b]
Database of national case law (first and second instances)	KOLA database (public) http://kola.just.ee/ Searchable database of all public judgments entered into force before 31 December 2005; free of charge. KIS database (public) http://www.kohus.ee/kohtulahendid/index.aspx Searchable database of all public judgments from 1 January 2006 up to date; free of charge.	LURSOFT (commercial) http://www.lursoft.lv/lapsaext?act=NISMAIN From 2009, the database is searchable free of charge (previously fee-charging), but the full text of the judgment available only by subscription and a fee charge.[c] www.tiesas.lv Started to operate from 2008; at the beginning not searchable from 2009; search functions have been considerably improved but database still very limited and partial.[d]

[a] https://www.riigiteataja.ee/ert/ert.jsp?link=introduction.

[b] http://www.vestnesis.lv/?menu=parmums.

[c] http://www.lursoft.lv/Latlex_abonements.html; the price of one judgment is between 0.99 LVL (1.41 EUR) to 1.18 LVL (1.68 EUR) depending on the court.

[d] As of 27 April 2010, the database includes 217 civil law cases; 258 criminal law cases and 332 administrative law cases. Just as an example, by entering the search term 'European' into the commercial database Lursoft returns 1,158 court cases; while a search with the same key word in www.tiesas.lv database returns only 139 cases.

may restrict individuals' rights of access to the court.[6] The issue of high state fees was also addressed by the head of the Estonian Supreme Court in the annual speech before the Parliament, urging the legislator to revise regulations on state fees.

Active citizenship

Private litigation, especially by private individuals against the state – for example, in human rights cases – in post-Communist MSs is a relatively new phenomenon,

6 3-4-1-25-09 of 15 December 2009, RT III, 28.12.2009, 60, 440.

and is one of the aspects of a broader process of fundamental legal-political transformation in the region.

The recent ECJ *Metock* case is an example of a 'collective action'[7] by ten individuals,[8] first at the national level and then through a preliminary reference at EU level, which resulted not only in changing a national expulsion decision but also contributed to development of EU law doctrine on European citizenship.[9]

National Courts

Following the discussion on litigants, I now turn to analysis of national courts. The EU legal system is uniquely and intimately concerned with the performance and cooperation of national courts. Individuals, for enforcement of their EU law-related rights, first turn to the ordinary national courts, which consider the matter on its merits. At the same time, lack of judicial independence and judicial review mechanism were central negative drawbacks of the Soviet legal system and the starting position of the post-Communist transformation. Against this background, the organization of the national judicial system, its independence and professionalism, and the relationship between national and European courts are central factors that contribute to assessment of the institutional dimension of coherent application of EU law.

National court systems

In general, both Estonian and Latvian courts are structured as a three-tier system where, as a common rule, single-judge courts of first instance hear all cases; three-judge courts of second instance hear cases on appeal, and finally the Supreme Court hears cassation cases. However, the court system in Latvia differs from the Estonian system in two important aspects.[10] First, the Estonian Supreme Court hears only cases on cassation while the Latvian Supreme Court also in certain cases exercises jurisdiction as an appeal court. The appellate instance of the Latvian Supreme Court has two court chambers (Civil and Criminal) and the cassation

7 Formally, the 'class action', similar to the US or some national EU jurisdictions that allow cases for the 'public good', is not allowed in the ECJ, except indirectly through reference proceedings submitted by national courts.

8 In Case C-127/08 Metock et al. v Minister for Justice [2008] ECR I-6241, a group of third-country nationals and their Union citizen spouses brought a legal action in national courts against refusal by the Minister for Justice, Equality and Law Reform to grant a residence card. To avoid expulsion from Ireland, they relied on a provision of the Citizenship Directive to challenge national norms. The High Court submitted to the ECJ a reference for a preliminary ruling concerning interpretation of the Citizenship Directive.

9 For analysis of ECJ EU citizenship case law developments, see Evas and Liebert (2009, 2013), Liebert (2007b).

10 Generally on the court system and court reforms in Latvia see Aigars (2001).

has three Senate departments (Criminal, Civil and Administrative). Secondly, the Estonian judicial system does not have a separate Constitutional Court but rather a constitutional review chamber is institutionally integrated into the Estonian Supreme Court. This exercises constitutional review jurisdiction while Latvia has an institutionally separate Constitutional Court.

Table 3.2 Estonian and Latvian court systems

Estonia		
First instance	*Second instance*	*Third instance*
Four county courts Harju, Tartu, Parnu, Viru	Two circuit courts Tartu, Tallinn	Supreme Court Tartu
(all cases)	Cases on appeal	Cassation cases/discretion of the SC
One judge	Three judges	Three judges (chamber) Five judges (special panel) Nineteen judges (*en banc*)
Latvia		
First instance	*Second instance*	*Third instance*
Thirty-four city/ district courts	Five regional courts	Supreme Court
(all cases)	Cases on appeal (also may be the court of first instance in cases on • property right to immovable property • rights in regard to obligations over 150,000 LVL (~ €214,285) • patent and trademark rights • insolvency and liquidation of credit institutions)	Appeal Cases (Chamber) Cassation cases (Senate)
One judge	Three judges	Three judges (chamber) Five judges (special panel) Nineteen judges (*en banc*)

Reform of the court system, independence of the judges and administration of courts were central themes in the transitional period (Bobek 2010: 251). The European Commission's regular pre-accession reports (2003) included independence of the judiciary as one of the assessment criteria. The last comprehensive report on

Latvia's preparations for membership concluded that although the judicial system is in place further efforts are necessary to ensure full implementation of the *acquis*:

> As regards overall administrative and judicial capacity, sufficient conditions are in place for the implementation of the *acquis* by the Latvian public administration and judiciary, but there is room for further improvements … Particular attention needs to be paid to the reform of the judiciary, and in particular the completion of the legislative framework, especially the urgent need to adopt the new Law on Judicial Power, as well as the Law on Criminal Procedure, and to the implementation of legislation on Court administration. The fight against corruption should continue to receive high priority. (European Commission 2003b: 56)

However, transformation of the court systems was not without difficulties. Not to mention the first years of transition, most recently the Latvian judicial system has faced two large scandals related to corruption (Sikk 2009) and the independence of judges, as well as a series of constitutional cases on remuneration of judges.[11] In 2007, journalist Lato Lapsa (Jānis Brūklenis), published a book *Litigation Kitchen* (Tiesāšanās kā ķēķis), which included secretly tapped, allegedly authentic, telephone conversations of one of Latvia's largest law firms. Leading advocate Grutaps was recorded as contacting leading judges, the prosecutor's office and politicians to discuss cases on behalf of his clients. The book has shaken the legal community and a special parliamentary commission was formed in 2008 to investigate allegations of judicial corruption. Immediately following publication of the book, Judge Levits (the Latvian judge at the ECJ) stated that 'the disclosure of the telephone conversations could become the biggest judicial scandal in Latvian history.'[12] In his turn, President Zatlers predicted that 'the book could become a bestseller.'[13] As a result of this indeed extremely popular and widely discussed 'bestseller', no public officials were formally charged with crimes, but three judges resigned as a result of the allegations.[14]

The second corruption controversy unfolded more recently. This time, tension developed between the Supreme Court and Parliament when, in a secret ballot, Parliament without specifying reasons, refused to appoint Administrative Court Judge Māris Vīgants to the Supreme Court. The nomination of Judge Vīgants was formally supported by the Latvian Judicial College (the self-governing professional body of judges) and even the judicial committee of the Parliament. However, for

11 Constitutional Court of Latvia, Case 2009-11-01 of 18 January 2010, Case 2009-111-01 of 22 June 2010.

12 http://easyget.lv/kultura/read/2251/ (last accessed on 1 December 2010).

13 Ibid.

14 See also the 2009 US Human Rights Report that also covers and refers to publication of this book.

allegedly political reasons[15] unrelated to his professional competence, Vīgants was nevertheless not nominated. The failed nomination triggered considerable public criticism including by high-level politicians such as former Latvian president Viķe-Freiberga. However, the dispute between the Supreme Court and Parliament did not end following the failed nomination. In spite of a negative vote in the Parliament, in January 2010 the Chief Justice of the Supreme Court appointed Judge Vīgants as a justice to the Civil Cases Chamber of the Supreme Court, an appointment based on Article 79 of the Law on Judicial Power, providing for a special procedure on temporary replacement of the vacancy of judge.

In April 2010 on nomination of the Chief Justice of the Supreme Court (and with the public support of President Zatlers and Prime Minister Dombrovskis), Parliament voted against candidate Janis Maizitis for the position of prosecutor general. Maizitis had already served as prosecutor general for two terms and re-election would have continued his mandate for another five years. Similarly to the Vīgants nomination, the scandal was connected to powerful politician-businessmen, including Lembergs, against whom criminal cases had been initiated during the term of office of Janis Maizitis. As one German news source put it 'Latvia's prosecutor-general, a prominent anti-corruption fighter, has failed to gain re-election. It's thought that Latvia's oligarchs, many of whom had cases brought against them, were behind the parliamentary vote.' Two failed nominations triggered public discontent and resulted in a petition signed by more than 2,000 individuals, including two former presidents and various heads of international and human rights NGOs.[16] The petition among other things called for more transparency and responsibility of the parliamentary approval procedure:

> Taking into consideration that the Saeima has twice, without giving any reasons, voted down two of Supreme Court Chief Justice Ivars Bickovskis' candidates for top jobs in the judicial system – Maris Vigants and Janis Maizitis ... that part of Saeima members openly demonstrated their hypocrisy by publicly promising their support for Maizitis' candidacy but then voting against him in a secret ballot, we call on Saeima members to decide the matter by open vote.[17]

---

15 Vīgants was one of the judges who sent the controversial politician, long-term mayor of Venspils (an important Latvian port) and oligarch Aivars Lembergs, to prison in 2007. Lembergs is also believed to be an 'owner' of a political party in the Parliament that allegedly voted against Vīgants (voting was by secret ballot). On criticism of Lemberg, see for example, a legal dispute between newspaper *FAZ* and Lemberg adjudicated by Landgericht Hamburg, judgment (324 O 507/06) of 30 March 2007.

16 Sarmite Elerte, founder of the Meierovics Society for Progressive Reform and former editor-in-chief of the newspaper *Diena*, representatives from Transparency International – Latvia and others also signed the petition.

17 http://www.ipetitions.com/petition/partiesiskuvalsti/ (last accessed on 1 December 2010).

Finally, in 2010, the Constitutional Court was confronted with a complex, politically and socially sensitive dispute between the legislative and judicial branches. In a series of constitutional complaints, a group of judges challenged the constitutionality of legislative amendments concerning remuneration of judges.[18] The legislator was unable to keep to commitments on reform of the system of remuneration of judges initially envisaged in 2003.[19] Faced with a deep economic recession and significant shrinking of the state budget, the Saiema introduced a number of legislative amendments; first, freezing the amount of judges' remuneration and then introducing further reductions.[20] Therefore, in sum, if the reforms of judges' remuneration were implemented as initially planned in

---

18 The system of remuneration as an important element of judges' independence was a matter of concern pointed out by the European Commission in pre-accession monitoring reports, see for example, 2002 report. In the 2003 report, the European Commission welcomed reforms of the system of remuneration of judges introduced in 2003 but pointed out that 'In order to address the independence of the judicial system, amendments to the previous Law on Judicial Power, adopted in June 2003, introduced a timetable for gradually raising judges' remuneration, starting from July 2003 (until 2006), when they will be several times higher than before the reform, e.g. LVL 720 (€ 1 137) for a newly appointed judge, compared to LVL 269 (€ 425) today. It will be important now to keep up the work and duly implement commitments undertaken in order to increase the standing of the profession and the judicial system as a whole' European Commission 2003 pre-accession monitoring report on Latvia, p. 13.

19 This 2003 national reform of the judicial system was positively supported by the European Commission in the 2003 comprehensive monitoring report and was a ground for more positive evaluation of the Latvian judicial system as compared to 2002. See European Commission Report (2003: 12–13).

20 In accordance with the 2003 reform, judges' monthly salary was linked to the gross average monthly salary of employed persons in the state in the previous year multiplied by a coefficient of 4.5. The transitional provisions were introduced to ensure gradual introduction of the new system. Thus, until the beginning of 2006, a judge's salary was calculated on the basis of the monthly gross average (MGA) salary of 2001 and in 2003 (60 per cent), 2004 (70 per cent) and 2005 (80 per cent) of the calculated salary was paid. In 2006, amendments were introduced providing that the MGA of 2001 should be also taken as a basis for calculating the 2006 salaries of judges, provided that the monthly salary of judges in 2007 and 2008 would be calculated taking into consideration the MGA of 2005 and in 2009 the MGA in 2006, and that the coefficient 4.5 would remain unchanged. In November 2008 amendments were adopted to link salaries in 2007, 2008 and 2009 to the 2005 MGA keeping the coefficient of 4.5. In June 2009, further amendments were introduced to retain the 2005 MGA as a basis until the end of 2010; additionally, from June 2009 to 31 December 2010, only 85 per cent of the salary was paid. Again, in December 2009 the system of remuneration was amended. The new regulation provided that the MGA of 2005 with a coefficient of 4.5 would be taken as a basis for 2010 and 2011 salaries and shortened the period during which 85 per cent of the salary to be paid to 31 December 2009, and from 1 January 2010 to 31 December 2011 set the amount of remuneration to be paid to judges to 73 per cent. It further introduced a ceiling on the amount of salary to be paid to judges by the amount of the remuneration of the prime minister.

2003, then, for example, in 2010 the base salary of a district court judge should be calculated taking into consideration monthly gross average salary (MGA) in 2008 multiplied by 4.5. Following numerous amendments, the legislator adopted a system where the base salary of a district court judge in 2010 was to be calculated based on (MGA 2005 × 4.5) × 0.85. In real numbers, if the new system of calculation were applied, then the base salary of the district court judge would equal only 38 per cent of what judges may have lawfully expected if the system introduced in 2003 were to be fully implemented.[21]

The first complaint, joined by 243 applicants, concerned the constitutionality of the national law stipulating a decrease in judges' remuneration,[22] while the second complaint, joined by 257 applicants, challenged the decrease in remuneration (for a different period) and a maximum ceiling on the remuneration of a judge set by the amount of the Prime Minister's salary.[23]

In the first case, the applicants argued that legislative amendments freezing judges' salaries for three years infringe the principles of legal certainty, legal stability and independence of courts.[24] The Saeima, on the contrary, claimed that legislative changes were necessary to tackle economic recession and meet the requirements of international donors to downsize state spending. Therefore, in the opinion of the legislator, the legislative amendments do not violate the principle of independence of courts.

Faced with this uneasy task, the Constitutional Court in a lengthy judgment provided a detailed analysis of the principles of the division of powers and independence of the courts. First, the court – based on the provisions of the Constitution – established its own jurisdiction to examine the constitutionality of a decision adopted by another branch of power even in cases involving the interests of the judiciary.[25]

Secondly, the court discussed that remuneration must correspond to the responsibility linked to the significance of the office and the workload of the judge[26] and found that remuneration falls within the content of the principle of

21 Case 2009-11-01, para 27.

22 Constitutional Court of Latvia Case 2009-11-01 of 18 January 2010.

23 Constitutional Court of Latvia Case 2009-11-01 of 22 June 2010.

24 Constitutional Court of Latvia Case 2009-11-01 of 18 January 2010, para 2.

25 Constitutional Court of Latvia Case 2009-11-01 of 18 January 2010, para 5. 'One of the fundamental principles of a democratic state enshrined in Article 1 of the Satversme is the principle of the division of power, which includes the control of the judiciary over the legislator and the executive power. Not a single legal provision or an action of the executive power can stay outside the control of the judiciary, if it infringes the interests of any person. [see: Judgment of 9 July, 1999 by the Constitutional Court in the case 04-03(99) para 1 of the Concluding Part]. The judiciary as a whole and the Constitutional Court as part of it has to ensure as complete control of the two other branches of power as possible (see: Judgment of 22 February, 2002 by the Constitutional Court in the case 2001-06-03 para 1.2. of the Concluding Part)' (official English translation).

26 Ibid., para 9.

independence of judges.[27] This principle guarantees effective realization of human rights,[28] safeguarding the rule of law in the interests of society and the state,[29] and implementation of the principle of division of powers.[30] Discussing principles of independence of judges and division of powers, the court extensively relied on international law and principles as well as jurisprudence of other Constitutional Courts.[31]

Third, the court stated that the principle of independence of judges, protected under Article 83 of the Constitution, also includes a prohibition on decreasing the remuneration of judges during their term in office.[32] However, this prohibition is not absolute. Under special circumstances such as the presence of serious, socially justifiable reasons, temporary derogations are allowed provided, however, that those derogations comply with the Constitution.[33] The court then found that although the derogations adopted by law had a legitimate aim, the legislator did not comply with the principle of solidarity and did not consider the possible consequences and risks following from the restriction imposed on judges not to hold another job.

Thus, the court concluded that the contested legislation breached the principle of independence of judges and is incompatible with the Constitution.[34] By adopting the contested provision, the legislator violated the principle of division of power.[35]

---

27 Ibid., para 8.2.

28 Ibid., para 7.1.

29 Ibid., para 7.2.

30 Ibid., para 7.3.

31 The Constitutional Court in addition to the national Constitution also refers to international law instruments including: The United Nations Basic Principles on the Independence of the Judiciary; Procedures for the effective implementation of the Basic Principles on the Independence of the Judiciary, UN ECOSOC resolution 1989/60 of 24 May 1989; International Covenant on Civil and Political Rights, Article 14, General Comment No. 32; The Council of Europe Committee of Ministers Recommendations No. R (94)12 Principle III 'Proper working conditions'; The Consultative Council of European Judges Opinion No 1 on standards concerning the independence of the judiciary and the irremovability of judges, European Charter on the Status of Judges and the Universal Charter of Judge adopted by the International Association of Judges. The Court also refers to the judgment of 14 July 2005 by the Constitutional Court of the Czech Republic in case Pl. US 34/04) and judgment of 12 July 2001 by the Constitutional Court of the Republic of Lithuania in case No. 13/2000-14/2000-20/2000-21/2000-22/2000-25/2000-31/2000-35/2000-39/2000-8/01-31/01, judgment of the European Court of Human Rights in the case of Campbell and Fell v. The United Kingdom 78. §, judgment in the case of Langborger v. Sweden, judgments of the European Court of Human Rights in the case of Bryan v. The United Kingdom 37. § and judgment in the case of Coeme and others v. Belgium). See paras 7–9 Constitutional Court of Latvia Case No. 2009-11-01 of 18 January 2010, para 7.3.

32 Case 2009-11-01 of 18 January 2010, para 10.2.

33 Ibid., para 10.3, 11.4.

34 Ibid., para 25.

35 Ibid., para 24.

In the second case, the two central questions were whether the legislator, by proportionally decreasing judges' base remuneration to 73 per cent[36] and setting a restriction on the remuneration of judges by the amount of salary of the Prime Minister, had violated Constitutional provisions.[37] The Saeima, as well as invited parties, argued that in a situation of deep economic recession neither a temporary reduction of judges' remuneration nor a link to the Prime Minister's salary should be considered as unconstitutional. The applicants disagreed. In addition to arguments challenging reduction of the salary (similar to what was put forward in case No. 2009-11-01) the applicants also argued that the provision stipulating that judges' remuneration may not exceed the Prime Minister's remuneration is incompatible with the principle of equality that follows from Article 1 of the Constitution.[38]

After intensive discussion of the principle of legal equality that the court derives from Article 1 of the Constitution,[39] the Court pointed out:

> The setting of any salary paid from the state budget falls within the jurisdiction of the legislator, and, to a certain extent, it is always a political decision. However, the Satversme sets limitations also upon political decisions; therefore, the Saeima's scope of discretion in adopting decisions concerning the remuneration of the Prime Minister and of judges is different. It is admissible that the Prime Minister's remuneration is set freely, without assessment. However, setting of judges' remuneration in this way, based only upon the legislator's political will, is contrary to the principle of the division of power and the principle of the independence of courts. If the legislator were given an unlimited right to influence the salaries of judges in accordance with its political will, the concept of judicial independence would become meaningless.[40]

The court then concluded that setting a ceiling on judges' base salary by the remuneration of the Prime Minister is incompatible with Article 1 of the Constitution.[41]

Concerning the decrease of judges' remuneration, the court first pointed out that restrictions for a limited time that pursue a legitimate aim are in general admissible if they do not violate constitutional principles. However, after examining the decrease of judges' remuneration against the constitutionally protected right to receive remuneration commensurate with work done (Article

36 For details see n. 20.

37 Articles 1, 83 and 107 of the Constitution.

38 For discussion, see Constitutional Court of Latvia Case 2009-111-01 of 22 June 2010, para 11.

39 Article 1 of the Constitution: 'Latvia is an independent democratic republic.'

40 Case 2009-111-01 of 22 June 2010, para 14 (official translation); See also para 11.3.

41 Ibid., para 15.

107 of the Constitution)[42] and the principle of legal certainty (Article 1 of the Constitution), the Court concluded that:

> As the result of the decrease in percentage of judges' remuneration, the coefficient applied in calculating a judge's salary is lowered from 4.5 to 1.7. Thus, the remuneration for work, upon which judges could lawfully and justifiably rely, actually is decreased by 62 per cent. Thus, the decrease in percentage of judges' remuneration set by the contested provisions, even though it is temporary, cannot be regarded as proportional and does not comply with the principle of legal certainty.[43]

The court further continued that considering the interests of society with regard to ensuring stability of the basic budget of the state and with respect to fair and independent courts, as well as the time necessary for the legislator to adopt legislative amendments, a temporary reduction of judges' remuneration for one year should be allowed. This reduction is allowed only if the reduction is set in the amount of 73 per cent of the previous year's MGA and in accordance with the principles provided in case 2010-11-01. Thus, the court found that the reduction of judges' base remuneration by 27 per cent instead of 62 per cent for a duration of one year is in accordance with the Constitution.[44]

In this series of 'remuneration cases', the Constitutional Court showed a strong institutional character by setting limits on legislative discretion in relation to the remuneration of judges. The step was warmly welcomed by the judicial branch, which is repeatedly confronted with the legislator's discretion.

Disputes on institutional competences of courts and other political actors

Following discussion of the general transformation and current problems of judicial systems, below I analyse the relationship between national courts and other political actors, and the relationship between the Supreme Court and national courts specifically in EU law-related matters. In Estonia, in terms of institutional competences the most central are the European currency (Euro), the request for an opinion from Parliament and a local election case that involved the Chancellor of Justice. Both cases, discussed in detail below, ultimately test the extent of institutional competences assigned to specific institutions in the context of changed institutional structures following EU accession.

---

42 Article 107 of the Constitution of the Republic of Latvia 'Every employed person has the right to receive, for work done, commensurate remuneration which shall not be less than the minimum wage established by the State, and has the right to weekly holidays and a paid annual vacation.'

43 Constitutional Court of Latvia Case 2009-111-01 of 22 June 2010, para 27.

44 Ibid., paras 29–32.

In the Euro case, Parliament requested an opinion from the Supreme Court on the constitutionality of introduction of the Euro in Estonia. The Supreme Court has no consultative function for cooperation with legislative or executive powers and consequently Estonian law does not provide a procedure for the Parliament to request an opinion from the Supreme Court before adopting certain legislation. In spite of the lack of the necessary procedure, the Supreme Court accepted the request for an opinion and stated its position approving introduction of the Euro.

However, in another high-profile case (the local elections case), the Chancellor of Justice brought legal proceedings to declare the Political Parties Act unconstitutional because, *inter alia*, it was in conflict with EU law (under Estonian law only Estonian citizens can be members of political parties).[45] The Supreme Court, in an *en banc* decision relying on textual-linguistic arguments, found that under Estonian law the Chancellor of Justice has no formal ground to contest conformity of Estonian law with EU law. Justice Laffranque in her dissenting opinion criticized this position of the Supreme Court, arguing that instead of narrow linguistic arguments the Court should have analysed the issue in the broader legal context in which the current legal rules exist. Laffranque started by acknowledging that textual interpretation of existing legal provisions does not provide legal competence to the Chancellor of Justice to contest conformity of national law with EU law.[46]

It is within the scope of the legislative authority to establish the competences of other political actors, including the Chancellor of Justice. Lack of *expressis verbis* competence of the Chancellor of Justice to contest conformity of national law with EU law goes against his duties and functions in applying national law. In fact, lack of this competence makes it impossible to fulfil the functions of Chancellor of Justice provided by law:

> … the Chancellor of Justice as a person applying law has to take into account the supremacy of application of EU law, irrespective of whether Estonian law grants him pertinent competence or not. In a situation where the great bulk of Estonian legislation originates in the institutions of the European Union, it is inevitable for the Chancellor of Justice to review the conformity of Estonian law with EU law.[47]

Laffranque continues by developing the argument of 'indirect competence', that is, a national procedural avenue showing how the competence of the Chancellor of Justice could be indirectly derived. She argues that under national law the Chancellor of Justice can petition for unconstitutional national legislation of

45 Dissenting opinion of justice Julia Laffranque to the judgment of the Supreme Court *en banc* in case 3-4-1-1-05, joined by Justices Tõnu Anton, Peeter Jerofejev, Hannes Kiris, Indrek Koolmeister and Harri Salmann.

46 Dissenting opinion Laffranque para 2.

47 Dissenting opinion, Laffranque, 3-4-1-1-05, para 3.

general application to be declared invalid by the Supreme Court. The Political Parties Act contested in this case is such a national legislative act of general application. Thus the Supreme Court *en banc* should have examined the petition of the Chancellor of Justice and reviewed the constitutionality of the Political Parties Act considering its conformity with EU law.[48]

The Estonian Supreme Court, as the highest court in the national jurisdiction, plays a central role in the court system. The case law of the Supreme Court, *de jure*, is not acknowledged by the national legislator as a binding authority on lower courts or even the Supreme Court itself. However, as a matter of practice, the jurisprudence of the Supreme Court is closely followed by the lower courts.[49]

The Estonian Supreme Court in several cases has encouraged national lower courts to be active in resolving EU-related disputes. First, the Supreme Court has pointed out that national courts of all instances must, if necessary on their own initiative, review the connection of applicable national law with EU law.[50] Secondly, in a concrete case, each court may set aside national law if it is in conflict with EU law but without necessarily initiating a constitutional review procedure.[51] The court has explained that the principle of supremacy upon application, as developed by the ECJ, means that it is sufficient to set aside a conflicting national law provision in a concrete case.[52] The court has pointed out that ultimately it is for the national legislator to decide whether a procedure should exist to declare national law invalid if it is in conflict with EU law.[53]

The Administrative Chamber has provided guidance on how national lower courts should approach EU law-related cases. National administrative courts applying or interpreting national law that flows from EU law must start by monitoring conformity of national law with EU law provisions.[54] In analysing the compatibility of national law with EU law, it is recommended to go beyond the applicable EU legal act and if necessary look at EU law in a broader sense.[55] It is necessary to analyse whether Estonian law, and if needed applicable EU secondary law, is in conformity with EU primary law, EU law general principles and fundamental principles recognized in the European Union, including respect for fundamental rights and freedoms.[56] If necessary, for help with this conformity analysis, national courts should turn directly to the ECJ with a reference for a

48 Ibid., para 4.

49 See, however, the case where the lower court judge refused to adopt the Supreme Court's position in the pensioners' discrimination case.

50 3-4-1-5-08, para 42.

51 3-3-1-33-06, para 32; see also 3-3-1-85-07, judgment 7 May 2008, para 38; 3-4-1-5-08, para 32.

52 3-4-1-1-05 paras 49–50; 3-3-1-33-06, para 32; the court has referred to C-10/97 kuni C-22/97: *Ministero delle Finanze vs. IN.CO.GE. '90*, EKL 1998, lk I-6307.

53 3-4-1-1-05 paras 49–50; 3-3-1-33-06, para 32.

54 3-3-1-85-07 of 7 May 2008, para 38.

55 Ibid., para 38.

56 Ibid., para 38.

preliminary ruling.[57] The national court does not need to turn to the Supreme Court to formulate a preliminary reference. Based on the factual and legal circumstances involved in a given case, the adjudicating court in the frame of the main substantive proceedings is better placed to formulate a preliminary reference request and thus provide the ECJ with all necessary factual and legal information:[58]

> Because for the decision to request a preliminary ruling it is necessary that the court submitting a request for preliminary reference determines the factual and legal circumstances of the case in order to give the European Court information necessary for a decision, in the given case the Administrative Chamber of the Supreme Court cannot decide on the necessity to submit a preliminary reference. This must be decided by the administrative court that holds a substantive hearing on the subject matter of the case.

National Courts and the ECJ (trans-judicial dialog) 2004–10

This section analyses the relationship between national courts and the ECJ. I concentrate on the understanding of institutional competences between national and EU level and the activity of national courts *vis-à-vis* European courts.[59]

Estonia: Delimitation of competences ECJ – National courts

The Estonian Supreme Court has discussed in detail and clarified in several judgments the division of competences between national and European courts in application of EU law. Thus, according to the jurisprudence of the ESC, Estonian courts have no right to question the validity of EU primary legislation. [60] The ESC has explained that disputes related to the conformity of EU secondary legislation with EU primary law must be settled by the ECJ or CFI to guarantee uniform application of EU law.[61] In relation to secondary EU law, national courts have no competence to declare EU law invalid. Therefore, a national court must consider EU regulation as valid until the ECJ finds it partly or entirely invalid.[62] As to review of conformity of EU legislation with the national Constitution, the ESC has stated that national courts including the Supreme Court have no competence to review conformity of EU legislation with the national Constitution:

---

57 3-4-1-5-08, paras 31–2

58 3-3-1-74-05 of 25 April 2006, Administrative Law Chamber, para 23.

59 For analysis of the cases from new MSs in the ECJ see Harbaceviča Solvita, 'Eiropas Kopienu tiesa un jaunās dalībvalstis' (The European Court of Justice and the new Member States), in *Eiropas Savieniba un tiesiska valsts: Latvijas pieredze* (European Union and the rule of law: experience of Latvia), Rīga, Rīgas Juridiskā augstskola, 2009.

60 3-3-1-74-05 of 25 April 2006, Administrative Law Chamber, para 12.

61 Ibid., para 12.

62 Ibid., para 13.

> … the European Court of Justice has held that the validity of measures adopted by the Community institutions can only be judged in the light of Community law, and the validity of a Community measure or its effect within a member state cannot be affected by allegations that it runs counter to either fundamental rights as formulated by the constitution of that state or the principles of a national constitutional structure.[63]

Only Estonian legislation that is partly based on EU law may be subject to constitutional review and only in parts that are not based on EU law provisions.[64] In exceptional cases, Member States in implementing EU law are bound by national constitutional provisions and principles (that could be subject to constitutional review) when EU law and ECJ case law provide a Member State with a discretion in transposition and application of EU law.[65] Additionally, constitutional review may be carried out by a national court to evaluate the formal legality of a national law implementing a EU law provision.[66] However, the ESC stresses that according to the law the national Supreme Court has competence and constitutional review cannot be excluded in cases of future reforms of EU primary law that would, for example, include amendments to the provisions on delegation of additional competences to the EU.[67]

Turning to the competences of national courts, the ESC noted that considering the place of the Constitutional Amendment Act in the national hierarchy of norms, legal conflict between the Estonian Constitution as supplemented by the Constitutional Amendment Act and EU primary law currently in force is not possible.[68] In a dispute that challenges conformity of national law with the Estonian Constitution and EU law, the court adjudicating the matter must first review conformity of Estonian law with EU law.[69] If the court finds that a national provision is contrary to EU law, then the court must set aside the national provision without even considering if the national provision is also contrary to the Estonian Constitution.[70]

The ESC explicated that national courts have an obligation to review the conformity of national law with EU law provisions. The fact that in legal proceedings the European Commission did not challenge conformity of national provisions with EU law does not preclude national courts in a concrete case from establishing that national law is contrary to EU provisions.[71] Based on ECJ case

---

63 3-3-1-87-07, para 42.
64 Ibid., para 39.
65 Ibid.
66 Ibid.
67 Ibid.
68 3-3-1-74-05 of 25 April 2006, Administrative Law Chamber, para 12.
69 3-4-1-5-08, para 31.
70 3-3-1-33-06 of 5 October 2006.
71 3-3-1-74-05 of 25 April 2006, Administrative Law Chamber, para 12.

law, the national court in determining whether national law is contrary to an EU law provision must take into consideration criteria established by the ECJ.[72] Moreover, according to ECJ case law, national courts as a general rule must carry out the proportionality test in determining conformity of national law (in the specific case sanctions for violation of EU law) with EU law.[73]

Estonia: Preliminary reference procedure

As to the preliminary reference procedure, the ESC has importantly noted that all national courts have a right to request a preliminary reference from the ECJ in cases of doubt.[74] The highest national courts have not only a right but also an obligation to request a preliminary reference. This obligation according to Article 267 TFEU (ex 234 TEC) para 3 as interpreted by ECJ case law is subject to two exceptions: *acte éclairé* (the European Court has already clarified in its early court practice the meaning of the norm), and *acte clair* (the legal norm is sufficiently clear and precise).[75] The ESC has provided detailed guidance on *when* to request a preliminary reference. Thus, the national court must request a preliminary reference when it is in doubt regarding the validity of EU law, conformity of EU secondary law with EU primary law,[76] or whether a national implementing measure is in conformity with an EU regulation.[77] However, it is necessary to stress that an Estonian court cannot ask the European Court whether Estonian law is in conformity with EU law but rather can request an interpretation of EU law.[78]

However, if the national court does not have doubts regarding the validity of EU secondary law, or if the ECJ has already confirmed the validity of a contested provision but the national court is in doubt regarding conformity of national law with EU law, then the question regarding conformity of national law with an EU law provision must be resolved on the basis of ECJ case law or if necessary by requesting a preliminary reference regarding interpretation of EU law.[79] The national court must check if a request for a preliminary ruling concerning the same issues has already been received by the ECJ or if proceedings are pending in the ECJ or CFI concerning the validity of the EU law provision concerned. If this is the case, the national court has to decide whether it is necessary to stay the national proceedings and request a preliminary reference.[80] If a national court has reasonable doubts regarding the validity of a EU law provision, it must stay

72 3-3-1-6-09, para 14.

73 3-3-1-80-08, para 15.

74 3-3-1-74-05, of 25 April 2006, Administrative Law Chamber, para 21.

75 3-3-1-79-08, para 13.

76 3-3-1-85-07 of 7 May 2008, para 38.

77 3-3-1-74-05, para 13.

78 3-3-1-88-07, para 37.

79 3-3-1-85-07 of 7 May 2008, para 38.

80 3-3-1-74-05, para 14.

national proceedings and request a preliminary reference, even if a similar request is already pending before the ECJ.[81]

The ESC has explained that a request for a preliminary reference may be necessary even if the ECJ has already declared a similar provision invalid. With reference to ECJ case C-461/03 *Gaston Schul*, the ESC stated:

> … even in cases which at first sight are similar, careful examination may show that a provision whose validity is in question is not comparable to a provision which has already been declared invalid because, for instance, it has a different legal or factual context, as the case may be … It is important to note in that regard that a reference for a preliminary ruling on validity constitutes, on the same basis as actions for annulment, a means of reviewing the legality of Community acts.

The sole fact that the validity of a EU provision under consideration is challenged by one of the MSs does not give a sufficient ground to question the validity of the EU law provision and suspend the national court proceedings.[82]

The ESC has also stipulated *how* national courts should request a preliminary reference. The obligation to review conformity of national law with EU provisions, including the possibility to request a preliminary reference if necessary, entails that the national court must analyse and justify why in its opinion a ground exists to question the validity of EU law.[83] To ask for a preliminary reference the national court must determine the relevant factual and legal circumstances in order to provide the ECJ with the necessary data.[84] The request for a preliminary reference must be formulated in the form of a question requiring interpretation of the EU law provision concerned and not in the form of a question on the validity of the national provision.[85]

In the practice of the ESC, the decision of the ESC in case 3-4-1-1-05 not to request a preliminary reference was criticized by Justice Laffranque in her dissenting opinion. Laffranque argued that if the Supreme Court has doubts on the content of the pertinent EU law provisions, it should suspend the proceedings and ask the ECJ for a preliminary ruling:[86]

> According to the case-law of the European Court of Justice, the relevance of the question on which a preliminary ruling is sought is an issue to be decided primarily by a national court, and therefore the European Court of Justice has

81 Ibid., para 22.

82 3-3-1-74-05, of 25 April 2006, Administrative Law Chamber, para 21.

83 Ibid., para 21.

84 'Kuivõrd Euroopa Kohtult eelotsuse taotlemise küsimuse otsustamiseks on vajalik, et eelotsust taotlev kohus määraks kindlaks probleemi faktilised ja õiguslikud asjaolud, et anda ka Euroopa Kohtule otsustamiseks vajalikud andmed', ibid., para 23.

85 3-3-1-88-07, para 37.

86 3-4-1-1-05, para 11, Dissenting Opinion, Laffranque.

> also accepted referrals for interpretation of EU laws which are the objects of abstract norm control in national proceedings.[87]

The position of the ESC was also criticized in an academic article by Estonian ECJ Judge Lõhmus (2007), who stated:

> Were the arguments to the contrary less significant? What should have been done in such a case? Such a situation justifies – and in the case of the Supreme Court obliges – asking for a preliminary ruling. The response of the European Court could have influenced the decision in a complicated yet fundamental court case.

Practice of Estonian lower courts indicates that national courts relatively well understand the preliminary reference procedure and request a reference if necessary.[88] However, in some cases the basis for refusal to request a preliminary reference is doubtful. Thus in a case concerning a decision of the Citizenship and Migration Board to expel an individual from Estonia, the Tallinn Administrative Court stated

> … for the purposes of interpretation and uniform application of Article 6 para 1 of the EC Reunification Directive it may be necessary to ask the position of the European Court. However, because the administrative court must review the Citizenship and Migration Board request during a limited time, the national court of first instance cannot request a preliminary reference.[89]

In this case, national procedural rules were considered by the court as an obstacle and a valid justification for refusal to submit a request for a preliminary ruling. Considering the jurisprudence of the ECJ, this approach is problematic for the uniform application of EU law.[90]

In conclusion, national law and national Supreme Courts provide procedures and clear guidance on when and how to request a preliminary reference from the ECJ. However, some examples from the ordinary courts indicate that in certain cases national courts fail to request a preliminary reference based on the constraints of national procedural rules. From the institutional coherence point of view, this could be problematic.

---

87 Ibid.

88 See Table 3.3 for list of preliminary rulings.

89 3-07-1513 of 31 July 2007, para 12.

90 There is established case law of the ECJ on suspension of enforcement of a national provision based on a Community regulation in proceedings pending before a national court; see for example, Joined cases C-143/88 and C-92/89, Zuckerfabrik Süderdithmarschen AG v Hauptzollamt Itzehoe and Zuckerfabrik Soest GmbH v Hauptzollamt Paderborn [1991] ECR-415; C-432/05 Unibet (London) Ltd and Unibet (International) Ltd v Justitiekanslern [2007] ECR I-2271.

Table 3.3 Estonia – preliminary rulings 2004–2012 (by date and court lodging reference)[91]

Case no.	Parties	Date of lodging preliminary reference	Court lodging preliminary reference	Date of ECJ judgment
C-241/07	JK Otsa Talu OÜ v PRIA	21 May 2007	Supreme Court (third instance)	4 Jun. 2009
C-560/07	Balbiino v TCB	18 Dec. 2007	Tallinn Administrative Court (first instance)	4 Jun. 2009
C-56/08	Pärlitigu OÜ v TCB	13 Feb. 2008	Tallinn Administrative Court (first instance)	16 Jul. 2009
C-140/08	Rakvere Lihakombinaat v TCB	7 Apr. 2008	Tallinn Administrative Court (first instance)	29 Oct. 2009
C-249/09	Novo Nordisk A/S v Ravimiamet	7 Jul. 2009	Tartu Circuit Court (second instance)	5 May 2011
C-523/09	Rakvere Piim AS, Maag Piimatööstus AS v Veterinaar- ja Toiduamet	15 Dec. 2009	Tartu Circuit Court (second instance)	7 Jul. 2011
C-146/11	AS Pimix v Maksu- ja Tolliameti Lõuna maksu- ja tollikeskus, Põllumajandusministeerium	25 Mar. 2011	Supreme Court (third instance)	Pending

Latvia: Preliminary reference procedure

Latvian procedural codes provide detailed regulation on situations where national courts should refer to the ECJ.[92] The Administrative Procedure Act states that national courts should request a preliminary reference regarding the interpretation or validity of European Union legal norms.[93] Similarly, Section 5.1 of the Civil

91 This table and the discussion in this chapter covers cases as of 01.03.2012.

92 Latvian Administrative Procedure Act Section 104.1, Latvian Civil Procedure Section 5.1.

93 'A court in the cases provided for by European Union (Community) legal norms, shall assign matters to the European Court of Justice regarding the interpretation or validity of European Union (Community) legal norms for the rendering of a preliminary ruling.'

Procedure Act provides 'A court in accordance with European Union legal norms shall assign matters to the European Court of Justice regarding the interpretation or validity of legal norms for the rendering of a preliminary ruling.' If the national court decides to refer to the ECJ for a preliminary ruling it has a duty to stay the proceedings[94] until the date when the preliminary ruling of the ECJ comes into effect.[95]

In a number of rulings, the Senate of the Supreme Court of Latvia has had the opportunity to lay down fundamental understandings and national procedure for requesting a preliminary ruling.[96] In 2006, in a case related to compensation for imprisonment, the Senate discussed the legal nature of a preliminary ruling in the context of national procedural law:

> According to article 5.1 of the Civil Procedure Act the preliminary ruling procedure is an instrument with the assistance of which national court of the Member States may in the European Court of Justice obtain preliminary clarification regarding issues of the European Union, the answers to which are necessary to hear a legal dispute as to its substance (see *S. Gatawis, E. Broks, Z. Bulle Eiropas tiesības (Europe Law). Riga, 2002.y., 149.p.*).[97]

In 2008, in a VAT deductibility fraud case,[98] the applicant, arguing that third-party transactions vitiated by fraud cannot undermine his right to a VAT refund, requested the Regional Court of Administrative Cases to submit a preliminary reference.[99] The Regional Court without discussing the grounds or reasons for not applying EU law provided the following reasoning for rejecting the request for a preliminary ruling:[100]

> Based on the aforesaid [The court discusses in the preceding paragraphs only the Latvian tax penalty system] the Regional Court denies the argument of the applicant requesting an ECJ preliminary ruling on the issue whether the SRS had grounds to lay the obligations of bad taxpayers on the claimant as ungrounded.

Section 104.1 'Assigning of Matters to the European Court of Justice', Administrative Procedure Act.

94 Article 214 sec. 4.1, Latvian Civil Procedure Act; Article 273 sec. 5, Latvian Administrative Procedure Act.

95 Article 275 sec.7, Latvian Administrative Procedure Act; Article 216 sec. 4, Latvian Civil Procedure Act.

96 As of September 2010, Latvian courts requested preliminary ruling eight times.

97 Supreme Court of Latvia, case SJC-2 judgment of 14 June 2006.

98 For discussion, see Part III 'Jurisprudence of Ordinary Courts'.

99 Regional Administrative Court, case A42117404 judgment of 20 June 2008, para 7.

100 Case A42117404 para 11.4 (see n. 92).

The reasoning of the court unfortunately does not provide clear guidance why the application for a preliminary reference is ungrounded.[101] The grounds for rejecting the applicant's request for a preliminary ruling were better explained in Supreme Court decision SKA-175/2009.[102] In this case concerning the minimum length of validity of a travel document,[103] the Supreme Court denied a preliminary ruling on the basis of the *acte claire* doctrine:[104]

> The European Court of Justice has admitted that a national court whose judgments may not be appealed has no obligation to file a preliminary ruling if it is decided that the issue is not relevant for hearing the case or the Court has already provided an interpretation of the relevant legal act or Community law is so clear that it does not provide any reasonable doubts (283/81, *Srl CILFIT and Lanificio di Gavardo SpA v. Ministry of Health*). The norms of the previously mentioned directives regarding its period of validity are apparently clear.[105]

The Supreme Court also relied on the *acte claire* doctrine in a case related to dismissal of a woman after maternity leave.[106] The applicant, Mrs Preisa, after return from maternity and parental leave, found a hostile working atmosphere and a negative attitude from her manager and other colleagues, who without any

101 Although I agree with the court that in the present case general references to EU law by the applicant are ungrounded, the court nevertheless could have paid more attention to explaining differences between the European Court of Human Rights and the European Court of Justice. The arguments of the applicant suggest that he probably intended to ask for review of his case in the light of the human rights jurisprudence of the ECHR and not the ECJ.

102 Supreme Court of Latvia, SKA-175/2009 of 05 March 2009.

103 Three individuals, a parent and two children, appealed the decision of the district court of administrative cases. The applicants requested first, to reverse the decision of the Latvian Office of Citizenship and Migration Affairs (OCMA) and secondly, to compensate damages. A national regulation provided that children who are younger than age 5 may receive passports with a maximum validity of one year. Validity of a travel document may be longer than one year if the estimated travel time exceeds one year or if a parent specifically requests a longer validity period. EU law, Council Directive 68/360/EEC and Council Directive 73/148/EEC, provide: 'where a passport is the only document on which the holder may lawfully leave the country, its period of validity shall be not less than five years.' Similarly, a five-year period is provided under Directive 2004/38/EC. Common OCMA practice was, if not expressly requested for a longer period, to issue passports for children with a validity period of one year. The applicant argued that national practice is contrary to EC law and asked the Supreme Court to request a preliminary ruling with two questions: (1) whether the national norm is contrary to EC Directive 2004/38 and (2) whether MS may deviate from the obligation provided under the directive on the grounds of public order and safety?

104 Case 283/81 Srl CILFIT and Lanificio di Gavardo SpA v. Ministry of Health.

105 SKA-175/2009 of 05 March 2009 para 16.

106 Supreme Court of Latvia, case SKC-383/2009 of 20 May 2009.

reason rejected her requests for information and cooperation.[107] Among other things, Preisa was assigned duties that she did not fulfil before her maternity leave and that were not in accordance with her initial employment contract.[108]

The employer took a number of formal steps to remove her from office.[109] Those steps eventually led to her dismissal based on breach of contractual obligations by the employee. All steps for dismissal taken by the employer were in accordance with formal procedural rules provided under labour law. However, Mrs Preisa argued that she was subject to gender discrimination, psychological terror and unjustified difference in treatment, and finally unlawful unjustified removal. The court of the first level dismissed the applicant's claim. The appeal court dismissed the applicant's claim for unlawful dismissal but satisfied Mrs Preisa's claim for moral damages for her suffering at work.

Mrs Preisa filed a cassation complaint. She argued that her dismissal, *inter alia*, violated the provisions of EU law prohibiting gender discrimination and the principle of equal treatment and asked to submit questions on interpretation of EU law to the ECJ.[110] The court, after examining the principle of discrimination and the constitutional right to work provided under national law, turned to discussion of EU law. The court explained:

> The case law of the ECJ concerning special protection of women during pregnancy and maternity establishes two basic principles: 1) any worse treatment because of pregnancy or maternity constitutes direct discrimination on grounds of sex (Case 177/88, Elisabeth Johanna Pacifica Dekker v Stichtig Vormingscentrum voor Jong Volwassen (VJV-Centrum) Plus, (1990) ECR Page I-03941, C-207/98, Silke-Karin Mahlburg and Land Mecklenburg-Vorpommern, ECR 2000 I-549), 2) special working conditions related to pregnancy and maternity time can not provide for any employment disadvantage (Case C-136/95, Caisse nationale d'assurance des travailleurs salariés 'vieillesse' (CNAVTS) v Evelyne Thibault, ECR 1998 I-022011).[111]

Based on the provisions of national law as well as the jurisprudence of the ECJ, the Senate annulled the decision of the appellate court and returned the case

107 During her absence on maternity leave, another employee was hired. Upon her return, he was promoted to the managing position and in fact became her immediate superior.

108 The amount of assigned duties was so large and complex that she could not meet delivery times. Unable to fulfil the assigned work, she turned to her supervisor for the appointment of assistants, as well as a review of her work in accordance with her position, but the request was ignored (para 6).

109 The employer gave Presia notice that she did not fulfil her tasks on time which resulted in a loss for the company, requested explanations for her bad relationship with colleagues, and so on.

110 Para 19.2.

111 Para 14.2.

for reconsideration to the appeal level. The court did not explicitly discuss the applicant's request for a preliminary ruling but *de facto* applied the *acte claire* doctrine to resolve the case without turning to the ECJ.

The Senate requested a preliminary ruling in a 2008 tax-related dispute, challenging amendments to the national law on VAT that introduced a time limitation of three years during which a taxable entity can request an input VAT refund.[112] In this case, the Supreme Court Senate was in doubt whether national law providing for a limitation period for a VAT refund is in conflict with EU law that does not specify such a limitation period.[113] Confronted with this legal matter the Senate stayed the proceedings and requested a preliminary reference:[114]

> … the Senate is of the opinion that there exist doubts regarding the interpretation of Article 18 (4) of the Sixth directive and an interpretation is crucial for deciding this case. Therefore, according to Section 104.1 of the Administrative Procedure Act a question should be asked to the European Court of Justice.[115]

---

112 Before adoption of amendments to the national VAT law in March that entered into force on 1 July 2005, national law did not provide any time limitation during which a taxable entity could reclaim input VAT. Applicants who had not submitted a VAT refund claim during this period lost a substantial amount of money, challenged the introduction of the three-year limitation on two main counts: first, that a three-year limitation is contrary to the constitutionally protected right to property and the EC VAT Directive that does not establish a limitation period and secondly, that the transition period between adoption of the amendments imposing a time limit on VAT refunds was not long enough to give concerned taxable entities sufficient time to adapt to the new regulation.

113 SKA-459/2008 of 23 October 2008. The essence of the case deals with a VAT refund and the Latvian law restriction which provides a statute of limitations for repayment of overpaid taxes. The applicant argued that 'The relevant institution should have applied Article 18 (4) of the EC VAT Directive. In the applicant's view this provision does not provide a limitation period, therefore, the limitation period of three years stipulated in section 16 (10) of the Law on Direct and Indirect Taxes is not applicable' (para 2). After detailed discussion of the Latvian tax laws, the court addresses the EU law aspect: 'Taking into consideration that article 18.4 of the Sixth directive stipulates the rights of a tax payer to request refund of the overpaid tax but does not provide any conditions as to the term during which the tax payer may exercise this right, it may be considered that the applicant's right is restricted on the basis of article 16.10 of the Taxes and Duties Act which provides for such term' (para 2). Although the facts of the case took place prior to 1 May 2004, the court did discuss the case in 'pre-accession language' similar to, for example, the judgment in SKA-1/2006 where the court admitted that grammatical interpretation should pre-empt teleological interpretation in a pre-accession situation.

114 Case C-472/08, Alstom Power Hydro v Valsts ieņēmumu dienests, judgment of 21 January 2010.

115 Paragraph 9.

Interestingly, in a similar case[116] adjudicated seven months later (at the time when the ECJ decision in *Alstom* was still pending) and challenging exactly the same national provision on the limitation period of the VAT refund, the Senate did not stay the proceedings and rendered its decision.[117] The applicant had specifically requested the Senate to stay the proceedings and submit a request for preliminary ruling but the court did not do so. The Senate addressed the arguments of the applicant related to EU law but did not explain why a request for preliminary ruling was rejected nor provided any mention of the pending ECJ case in *Alstom Power Hydro*.

Thus, contrary to the position in SKA-459/2008 where the court openly acknowledged interpretational difficulty and requested a preliminary ruling in case SKA-108/2009 the Senate found itself a solution to this interpretation difficulty. Relying on the arguments by the applicant that referred to ECJ case law in support of its position the Senate (adopting a decision against the applicant) reasoned as follows:

> From the cassation application it appears that the European Court of Justice in case C-62/00 paras 38–40 has indicated that for reducing the period within which repayment of VAT is made from six to three years it is necessary to provide a transition period which is equal to the previous repayment period. The Senate does not see in the previously mentioned decision, including paragraphs 38–40, a phrase that corresponds to the claimant's statements. The ECJ decision has not been translated into Latvian. In English, German and French with regard to the transition period are used respectively *adequate, angemessen* and *suffisant* which in Latvian means '*adequate', 'sufficient' and 'appropriate'*. Therefore, in the Senate's view the European Court of Justice has indicated that the transition period should be sufficient to enable taxpayers to file their requests.[118]

Concluding that *per se* a time limitation of three years is not contrary to national or EU law (a decision also reached later by the ECJ), the court dismissed the cassation application. The applicant, however, challenged the relevant Latvian law norms in the Latvian Constitutional Court and won the case.[119] The Constitutional Court approached the matter after the ECJ decision in *Alstom* that found that a three-year limitation period is not contrary to EU law.[120] The court carefully evaluated the

---

116 SKA-108/2009 judgment of 28 May 2009.

117 Judgment in the case of *Alstom* (see n. 114) was rendered by the ECJ only on 21 January 2010.

118 SKA-108/2009 of 28 May 2009, para 13.

119 2010-02-01. The judgment by the Latvian Constitutional Court of 19 June 2010 provides an excellent example of the high-quality legal argumentation that takes into consideration the complex legal relationship between national, EU and international law.

120 Here, unfortunately, it must be noted that the question formulated by the Senate of the Supreme Court was somewhat unfortunate or partial. It stated 'On a proper

reasoning of the ECJ but concluded that the national amendments nevertheless violated the applicant's rights.[121]

A preliminary ruling was also requested in a dispute related to dismissal of a pregnant woman.[122] In a case recently decided by the European Court of Justice, a woman was dismissed from the position of member of the management body of a capital company.[123] According to Article 224 of the Commercial Law, 'A member of the board of directors may be removed by a decision of the shareholders.' Removal of a member of the board as provided by Article 224 of the Commercial Law is outside the scope of protection provided to employees in case of dismissal. In this specific case, removal of a female member of the board, as acknowledged by both parties, was not conditioned on her pregnancy.[124] However, the fact remained that at the moment of removal Mrs Danosa was in the third month of her pregnancy. The court of first level and the appeal court dismissed her application and found that removal of a member of the board is outside the scope of protection provided by the labour law. Therefore, the courts of lower level found that Mrs Danosa cannot rely on the prohibition of removal of a pregnant employee provided under labour law.

The case reached the Senate of the Supreme Court, which intensively analysed the provisions of national law as well as the provisions of EC Directive 92/85/EEC prohibiting dismissal of workers during pregnancy and breastfeeding.[125] The Senate could not reach a conclusion whether Mrs Danosa should be regarded as a worker within the meaning of EU law and ECJ jurisprudence, even if under

construction of Article 18(4) of [the Sixth Directive], is it contrary to that provision for domestic legislation to lay down a limitation period of three years for the exercise of the right to recover sums of VAT overpaid (the difference between output tax and deductible input tax)?', see *Alstom*, para 13. Thus the question, as later also pointed out in the decision of the Constitutional Court in case 2010-02-01, did not cover to a sufficient extent the complexity of the national situation and only addressed the lawfulness of the three-year period for repayment as such.

121 The court, following the arguments of the applicant, distinguished a legal question related to the 'three-year limitation' itself and the procedure for introduction of this limitation into the legal system. The court concluded, following *inter alia* the reasoning of the ECJ, that a three-year limitation is not in itself contrary to constitutional principles or EU law. However, the introduction of this limitation at short notice without due consideration of the rights of individuals that may be affected by the amendments is contrary to national law and ECJ case law.

122 Case SKC-383/2009 of 20 May 2009; SKC-88/2009 of 13 May 2009.

123 Supreme Court of Latvia case SKC-88/2009 of 13 May 2009; European Court of Justice case C-232/09 Dita Danosa v. LKB Lizings SIA.

124 Supreme Court of Latvia case SKC-88/2009 of 13 May 2009, para 5.

125 Council Directive 92/85/EEC of 19 October 1992 concerning the implementation of measures to encourage improvements in the safety and health of pregnant workers, workers who have recently given birth and women who are breastfeeding (tenth individual directive within the meaning of Article 16(1) of Directive 89/391/EEC).

national law the services of a member of the board are outside employment protection.

Under these circumstances (that is, removal of a pregnant woman), the Senate had doubts on interpretation of Article 224 para 4 of the Commercial Law in the light of Article 10 of EC Directive 92/85/EEC and ECJ case law. The Senate considered that it was important for the current dispute resolution to establish whether a member of the board of a corporation is to be considered a worker (employee) within the meaning of EU law and whether the fact that Article 224 para 4 of the Commercial Code allows removal of a member of the board without restrictions, including pregnancy, is not contrary to Article 10 of Directive 92/85/EEC and ECJ case law. Based on the above conditions the Senate needed to request a preliminary ruling from the ECJ.[126]

126 Supreme Court of Latvia case SKC-88/2009 of 13 May 2009, para 5.6.; The Senate referred the following two questions: '1) Are the members of the managerial body of a capital company to be regarded as being covered by the concept of worker laid down in Community law? And 2) Do Article 10 of Directive 92/85/EEC[1] and the case-law of the Court of Justice of the European Communities preclude Article 224(4) of the Komerclikums, which provides that the members of the board of directors of a capital company may be removed without any restrictions, in particular, in the case of a woman, irrespective of the fact that she is pregnant?' See ECJ case C-232/09 Dita Danosa v. LKB Lizings SIA [2010] ECR I-0000. The ECJ in its judgment of 11 November 2010 concluded that '1. A member of a capital company's Board of Directors who provides services to that company and is an integral part of it must be regarded as having the status of worker for the purposes of Council Directive 92/85/EEC if that activity is carried out, for some time, under the direction or supervision of another body of that company and if, in return for those activities, the Board Member receives remuneration. 2. Article 10 of Directive 92/85 is to be interpreted as precluding national legislation, such as that at issue in the main proceedings, which permits a member of a capital company's Board of Directors to be removed from that post without restriction, where the person concerned is a 'pregnant worker' within the meaning of that directive and the decision to remove her was taken essentially on account of her pregnancy.'

Table 3.4 Latvia – preliminary rulings 2004–2012 (by date and court lodging reference)[127]

Case no.	Parties	Date of lodging preliminary reference	Court lodging preliminary reference	Date of ECJ judgment
C-16/08	Schenker v. SRS	15 Jan. 2008	Regional Administrative Court (second instance)	11 Jun. 2009
C-93/08	Schenker v SRS	28 Feb. 2008	SC Senate	12 Feb. 2009
C-472/08	Alstom v SRS	23 Oct. 2008	SC Senate (third instance)	21 Jan. 2010
C-199/09	Schenker v SRS	4 Jun. 2009	SC Senate (third instance)	2 Dec. 2010
C-232/09	Dita Danosa v LKB Līzings SIA	25 Jun. 2009	SC Senate (third instance)	11 Nov. 2010
C-248/09	Pakora Pluss v. SRS	7 Jul. 2009	SC Senate (third instance)	29 Jul. 2010
C-382/09	Stils Met v. SRS	28 Sept. 2009	SC Senate (third instance)	7 Oct. 2010
C-294/10	Andrejs Eglītis and Edvards Ratnieks v Ekonomikas Ministrija	15 Jun.2010	SC Senate (third instance)	12 May 2011
C-348/10	Norma and Dekom v. Ludzas novada dome	9 Jul. 2010	SC Senate (third instance)	10 Nov. 2011
C-619/10	Trade Agency Limited v Seramico Investments Limited	29 Dec. 2010	SC Senate (third instance)	Pending
C-263/11	Ainārs Rēdlihs v Valsts ieņēmumu dienests	26 May 2011	SC Senate (third instance)	Pending
C-454/11	Gunārs Pusts v Lauku atbalsta dienests	1 Sept. 2011	SC Senate (third instance)	Pending
C-470/11	SIA Garkalns v Rīgas dome	14 Sept. 2011	SC Senate (third instance)	Pending
C-471/11	SIA Cido Grupa v Valsts ieņēmumu dienests	14 Sept. 2011	SC Senate (third instance)	Pending
C-487/11	Laimonis Treimanis v Valsts ieņēmumu dienests	22 Sept. 2011	Regional Administrative Court (second instance)	Pending
C-525/11	SIA Mednis v Valsts ieņēmumu dienests	17 Oct. 2011	SC Senate (third instance)	Pending
C-527/11	SIA Ablessio v Valsts ieņēmumu dienests	10 Oct. 2011	SC Senate Administrative Department	Pending
C-558/11	SIA 'Kurcums metal' v Valsts ieņēmumu dienests	7 Nov. 2011	SC Senate (third instance)	Pending
C-563/11	SIA Forvards V v Valsts ieņēmumu dienests	9 Nov. 2011	SC Senate Administrative Department	Pending
C-650/11	Ilgvars Brunovskis v Lauku atbalsta dienests	19 Dec. 2011	SC Senate (third instance)	Pending

127 This table and the discussion in this chapter covers cases as of 01.03.2012

Chapter 4
Argumentative Coherence: Justifications, Values and Legal Culture

Although the primary focus of this book is on law and legal principles, a full analysis of national adjudication of EU law would be incomplete without assessment of institutions and legal methods. Robert Alexy, in his well-known *Theory of Legal Argumentation* (2010) arguing for the theory of 'rational legal discourse', convincingly claims that rules, or limiting conditions of legal discourse, *per se*, say nothing about how delimitation of relevant principles occurs in practice.[1] To assess practice 'it will be necessary to determine in more detail both the rules according to which the limiting conditions are to be taken into account and the actual forms of argument in which reference may be made to them' (Alexy 2010: 19). In the context of the three-dimensional coherence framework advanced in this book, this entails that, in addition to the substantive dimension that focuses on legal rules and principles it is also necessary to assess the actual forms of justifications that courts use in order to refer to or apply EU law and principles in practice.[2]

Therefore, this chapter of the book considers the argumentative dimension of coherence in more detail. For the coherence argument advanced in this book, by argumentative dimension I understand a system of meanings of legal texts as conveyed by national courts through legal reasoning.[3] Under the analytical approach of this book, three dimensions of coherence are interconnected but analytically distinct, and all three are necessary. The substantive dimension is about norms and legal principles (that is, the substance of law that helps to sustain coherence). The institutional dimension is about institutional arrangements that help to sustain

1 Legal discourse is subject to the requirements of legal rules and procedural regulations. Alexy contends 'rules of discourse lay down how one may arrive at well-founded normative statements from this starting point but without fully prescribing every step.'

2 In this context, I also find very appealing the claims of the Social Theory of law that argues that application of law is not only 'rationalization' of law but also 'realization in law' through society-wide acceptance, see for example, Teubner (1997). Another well-known approach that further (but from another perspective) develops the idea of acceptance is a 'dialectic approach' argued by Aulis Aarnio. Aarnio (1997), by connecting the concept of 'acceptability' with the concept of 'audience', builds a normative argument that legal interpretation is an activity justifiable in relation to an audience. The research design of the present book does not allow investigation of those claims in more detail.

3 The implicit presupposition and hidden meanings that may inform judgments of national courts lies beyond the scope of this analysis. With due respect to the reach of social science and jurisprudence scholarship on hermeneutics, my reference to this concept is modest.

coherence. Finally the focus of this chapter, the argumentative dimension, is on legal methodology – that is, legal techniques and justification structures – that helps justify and sustain coherent application of legal norms and institutional interactions.

In other words, in this chapter I focus primarily on how national courts, through legal argumentation and justification, communicate a meaning and a need to apply EU legal norms in the national legal context. Therefore, my main units of analysis are the types of argumentation and justification structures that national courts use in order to reach their legal *dicta*.[4] Specifically, considering the Soviet law background that was strongly biased toward textual positivism and formalism, assessment of legal interpretation and argumentation style is central in assessing the possible continuing impact of Soviet legal culture and value preferences on the current practice of national courts. As Andris Guļāns, Chief Justice of the Latvian Supreme Court, pointed out, 'the hardest and the most revolutionary battles [during post-Soviet transformation of the judicial system] had to be won in our own minds' (2005: 8).

The coherence framework proposed in this book builds on scientific approaches in political science and law that underline the importance of communication.[5] Against this background, I conceptualize jurisprudence both as context-dependent and context-productive.[6] Courts and judges as a part of the wider socio-political system are inevitably influenced by the broader context, that is, legal and political culture along with social and political values. However, courts as part of the system also influence the broader context. I argue that coherence of application of EU law is enhanced through analytical-persuasive communication by courts that brings to the fore underlying values, institutional and social interactions (contested issues) and renders meaningful legislation adopted through political power-struggle processes at EU and national levels, while conversely coherence is undermined by technical-mechanical justifications that are mostly concerned with the legality rather than the legitimacy of legal pronouncements.

Acknowledging the importance of in-depth analysis of legal discourse, empirical studies on types, logical structure and rationale of legal arguments, the present enquiry is limited in its scope by a rather aggregated approach to legal argumentation.

4 For the analysis of the justification structures in the German higher courts see for example Albers (2012).

5 The semiotic or narrative approach to law is a vast field of scientific inquiry with divergent theoretical positions. The central idea of this approach is that law provides a framework for human action – a framework of communication. In this perspective, adjudication is understood in terms of a communicative process rather than of traditional models that focus on power relations. Legal systems are never closed systems but provide room for communication. Analysis of communication is crucial for the understanding of a legal system and the legal reality it generates.

6 To put this plainly, jurisprudence is not only an *object* of analysis that is better explained by contextual factors (addressed in Part I) but is also itself a *subject* that defines the wider context-dependent normative system (Part III of the book). On normativity of jurisprudence as context-dependent and context-productive, see Walker (2008: 7) and Habermas (1997: xi).

I broadly distinguish two types of argumentative style of the courts: analytical-persuasive and technical-mechanical. The aim is not to analyse the logical structure or rationality of the judgment in itself, but rather, to assess through the types of arguments used by courts the methodological avenues through which courts settle competing legal claims. In other words, the main focus is on the types of justification courts rely on to solve conflicting normative claims following from the plurality of authority characterising application of EU law in national legal orders.

In developing my argument why 'analytical-persuasive' arguments should be preferred over 'technical-mechanical', I find it helpful again to refer to Robert Alexy (1998: 41) who argues, 'a coherent set of propositions should comprise as many and as different propositions as possible.'[7] Therefore, I understand coherent argument in jurisprudence as an argument that is not only narrowly consistent with technical linguistic interpretation of legal norms but also more broadly rationally coheres with legal norms in the social context and higher universal legal principles. This does not suggest rejection of the centrality of the positivist nature of law but rather argues that by supplementing linguistic arguments with systemic, evaluative and transcategorical arguments, the overall argument and justification advanced by the court becomes analytically stronger and more persuasive.

The legal skill and practice by courts of relying on a variety of legal arguments going beyond strict textual positivism cannot be taken for granted in the post-Soviet legal context. Kühn, comparing the development of legal methodology in western European Member States and post-Communist newcomers, has claimed that

> While Western European legal systems face the problems of how to make their legal culture more open and substantive, and contribute in this way to the ongoing process of making 'an ever-larger Union', the post-communist judicial methodology is much closer to the narratives of the European legal culture that prevailed in the nineteenth century, before the first wave of the European anti-formalist movements. (2004: 532)

Kühn refers to Central European courts as 'empires of mechanical jurisprudence' where 'judges view their activity as primarily mechanical; their decisions even in actual cases resemble exercises in deductive logic, based solely on the binding force of written domestic law' (2005).

Following a similar line of reasoning, the Chief Justice of the Supreme Court of Latvia Justice Andris Guļāns, in a speech in 2005 on Latvian judicial reform, pointed to the difficulties that Latvian judges faced (and still face) in developing legal argumentation skills and practices going beyond technical-mechanical application of legal texts:

---

7 Different theoretical arguments have been put forward by legal theorists how a legal-argumentative complexity can be addressed to produce rationality coherent outcome. Habermas emphasizes 'communicative rationality' with locus on deliberation, Alexy stressed 'discursive rationality' putting emphasis on procedural elements.

> The basic problem of judges in those days, and partly also today, is the lack of a respective judicial school and knowledge. This has objective reasons as the judges were educated in the Soviet era when there were no other opinions. Along with performing the duties of judges, they had now to study new principles of applying law, to develop judicial consciousness. It was a unique process which took place in the course of court reform. (2005: 2)

In Estonian legal scholarship, Raul Narits strongly advocates developing national jurisprudence based on normative value-based communication:

> It seems that the debate can only be fruitful if we can avoid so-called legist thinking and understanding of law. It is the legist position that treats law as the product of the state (its power, discretion, even arbitrariness). Law is reduced to its formal sources, so-called positive law. Law is identified with legislative texts in their broad sense. It seems that such an approach no longer meets today's needs. (2002: 13)

Furthermore, not only the legal argumentation style of courts but also the extent of development of national analytical scholarship in post-Soviet legal systems distinguishes newcomers from Western European MS. If, for instance, the German judicial system 'is heavily oriented on legal science, which, at least formally, apart from precedents, is the main source of German courts' perception of law' (Kühn 2004: 537 citing Kötz 1990), then the Latvian and Estonian judicial systems can only to a limited degree benefit and build on still developing analytical academic legal scholarship.[8]

I agree with Reich (1999: 156), who argues that 'courts should decide cases but not publish encyclicae'.[9] However the importance of analytical-persuasive arguments in deciding EU law cases by national courts, especially in post-Soviet legal systems, must not be underestimated. Estonian scholar Marika Linntam (2002: 52), analysing national jurisprudence points regarding the role of judges and interpretation techniques, notes:

> It has to be highlighted that, in a period of transition and rapid reforms which Estonia is now passing through, the broader concept of interpretation of legal norms becomes especially necessary, as legislation cannot always keep up with the pace of real changes. In a new democracy like Estonia there are also unfortunately

---

8 In the Estonian context, the legal academic journals *Juridica* and *Juridica International*, especially recently, provide an increasing number of high-quality publications on issues of EU law. In Latvia, after suspension of publication of *Likums un Tiesības*, the leading legal journal is *Jurista Vārds*. However, the overall extent of national debate and depth of analysis is still hardly comparable, for example, to German legal scholarship.

9 Reich is a review article of the Slaughter et al. book *The European Courts and National Courts* (1998).

> more gaps in the law that cannot also be filled with analogy and need an alternative approach. Judges also have to make decisions in these circumstances, and one guarantee of a value judgement in this setting would be teleological interpretation, which takes into account the objectives of legal acts and the legal system as a whole of which the idea of justice forms an immanent part.

Legal rules define how the judge may arrive at a prescribed normative statement but without defining every step of this process (Alexy 2010: 17–18). These steps are methodological tools that judges rely on in adjudicating a case. Neil MacCormick (1999) argues that structured analysis of legal reasoning, argumentation and justification structures utilized by the courts help to yield a deeper understanding of the normative legal order envisaged as validly in force in the given jurisdiction.

Building on the premise that the Estonian legal order is a part of continental European legal culture, Raul Narits argues that Estonian constitutional discourse should focus more rigorously on analysis of development of the national constitution based on considerations of values and value structures of modern law and society.[10] He points out that although in Estonia 'there are signs that we wish to reach the level of a modern value-oriented structure of legal thinking … in some cases there are problems with cognising valid value scales in changed societal conditions' (2002: 13, see also Linntam 2002). Narits further underlines 'While the rest of the world switched over to value jurisprudence in the course of decades, we are facing a situation where we have to make the transition in a relatively short time' (2002: 13, citing Sildam and Mattson 1997: 10–13).

The legacy of a post-Communist legal culture heavily influenced by textual positivism, the novelty of the EU legal system for the professional legal EU and the general public, together with the state of development of national legal scholarship in Estonia and Latvia, are factors that potentially could distort or at least slow down application of EU law in the daily practice of national courts. Thus, the methodological skills of judges, the argumentative dimension, are central to analysis of application of EU law in national courts. This dimension of coherence is closely linked to other dimension discussed (substantive and institutional) but is analytically distinct, requiring separate tools of analysis.[11]

To distinguish between 'analytical-persuasive' and 'technical-mechanical' argumentative styles of national courts, I rely on the commonly accepted typology distinguishing between four types of legal argument: linguistic, systemic, teleological, and transcategorical (MacCormick and Summers 1999).

10 Narits refers to MacCormic, Krawietz and Alexy.

11 Even with the existing framework of legal texts and principles (substantive dimension of coherence) as well as institutions and procedures (institutional dimension) of application, the weakness of argumentative dimension has a potential to lead to incoherent application of EU law in the practice of national courts.

Table 4.1 The eleven argument types (based on MacCormick and Summers 1999)

Type of arguments to resolve incoherence	
Linguistic	1. Ordinary Meaning 2. Technical Meaning
Systemic	3. Contextual Harmonization 4. Argument from precedent 5. Arguments from analogy 6. Logical Conceptual 7. General principles of law 8. History
Teleological/Evaluative	9. Purpose 10. Substantive reasons
Transcategorical	11. Argument from intention

Application of EU Law in National Pre-accession Jurisprudence

In the period from 1994 to 1 May 2004, the Estonian Supreme Court referred to EU law provisions or principles in 28 cases. Prior to accession, EU law was not legally binding and in most cases the Estonian Supreme Court did not discuss EU law in substance. However, in a number of cases the Supreme Court relied on EU law principles as a non-obligatory persuasive authority.[12] Thus, EU law in the pre-accession period performed two functions: first, as an argumentative tool for consistent interpretation of domestic law with EU law, especially after entry into force of the Association Agreement and increasing harmonization of national law with the *acquis communautaire*.

For example, on 18 December 2002 in the *Eesti Telefon* case,[13] the Estonian Supreme Court, in applying for the first time the provisions of the Europe Agreement, relied on EU-conforming interpretation in order to interpret the provisions of national competition rules in conformity with EU competition law. The Supreme Court reasoned:

> It is necessary to interpret the Competition Act in the light of the Association Agreement (Europe Agreement) between the Estonian Republic and European Community member states. Article 68 and 69 of the Europe Agreement provided that Estonia endeavours gradually to ensure that Estonian legislation including

12 There was, for example, the so-called '2002 Local Government Election Case I' where the Chancellor of Justice extensively relied on EU law but the Supreme Court did not discuss or refer to EU law.

13 Supreme Court of Estonia, case 3-3-1-66-02 of 18 December 2002.

> in the competition field is compatible with EU law. In accordance with Article 82 of the EC Treaty (previously 86) paragraph 1 abuse of a dominant position that may have an impact on inter state trade is prohibited and according to paragraph 2 imposition of unfair purchase or selling prices is considered to be an abuse regardless of whether such an abuse disadvantages undertakings or consumers. The EC Treaty is not applicable in Estonia; however, the Supreme Court assumes that Riigikogu [Parliament] adopted the 1998 Competition Act taking into consideration obligations following from the Europe Agreement.[14]

Secondly, in interpreting domestic law that at the time was subject to constant amendments and inconsistencies, the Supreme Court relied on general principles of EU law as developed through ECJ jurisprudence to primarily fill gaps and develop national legal doctrine.[15]

As early as 1994, in adjudicating a case involving the Law of Property Act, the Estonian Supreme Court referred to the general principles of EU law:

> When creating the general principles of Estonian law the general principles of law developed by the institutions of the Council of Europe and the European Union should be taken into consideration alongside the Constitution. These principles have their origin in the general principles of law of the highly developed legal cultures of the member states.[16]

The reference to EU general principles of law was further developed by the ESC in a 1997 case related to naturalization requirements for acquisition of Estonian citizenship.[17] The ESC first repeated the wording of the 30 September 1994 judgment cited above and then continued 'The principle of equal treatment in the practice of the European Court of Justice is considered as one of the general principles of the European Union law. It is necessary to recognize this principle as a general principle of Estonian law.'[18]

In the pre-accession period, the main function of EU law in the Latvian Constitutional Court was an argumentative supporting authority in cases related to

---

14 Ibid., para 15.On discussion of the Europe Agreement see for example, Laffranque 2000; Albi 2001.

15 References of the Supreme Court to EU law was fuelled by Article 123 of the Constitution that allows direct application of international law norms.

16 Judgment of the Constitutional Review Chamber from 30 September 1994, III–4/A–5/94, available at www.nc.ee.

17 In case 3-4-4-1-96 related to the Law on Non-for-profit association, the President of the Republic of Estonia relied on general principles of EU law and the Europe Agreement.

18 3-3-1-5-97; However, see for example, in case 3-4-1-4-98 of 28 May 1998 (Rait Maruste separate opinion); a case involving differential treatment between a seaman with Estonian citizenship, stateless persons and citizens of foreign countries. See also cases 3-4-1-1-03 and 3-1-3-10-02 where the ESC relied on the Charter of Fundamental rights as an interpretive tool.

protection of individual human rights.[19] Among other international human rights instruments to which the Latvian Constitutional Court conventionally extensively refers, the Court also relied on the authority of the EU Charter of Fundamental Rights.

In a 2002 case concerning a decrease of pension payment to pensioners who choose to continue to stay in employment, the Constitutional Court, *inter alia*, referred to the EU Charter of Fundamental Rights:

> In its turn Article 25 of the EU Charter of Fundamental Rights determines that the Union admits and observes the right of older persons to an adequate standard of living, to independence and participation in public and cultural life *[Vildbergs H.J., Feldhūne G. Salīdzinošās konstitucionālās tiesības (Comparative Constitutional Rights). Riga: University of Latvia, 2001, p.92]*. The Charter was signed in Nice on December 7, 2000.[20]

Similarly, in a 2003 case concerning the retirement age of professors of higher academic institutions, the Constitutional Court, among other international and foreign law sources, also relied on the European Charter of Fundamental Rights and the EU age-discrimination directive:

> In compliance with Article 21 of the European Charter of European Union Fundamental Rights, any discrimination on the basis of old age is forbidden. Besides, the European Council November 20, 2000 Directive 2000/78 EC establishes that up to December 2, 2003 the Member States of the European Union shall pass all acts necessary for implementation of the Directive. Its Article 2 determines prohibition of direct and indirect discrimination. In conformity with the first part of Article 6 differences of treatment on the grounds of age shall not constitute discrimination, if, within the context of national law, they are objectively and reasonably justified by a legitimate aim, including legitimate employment policy, labour market and vocational training objectives and if the means of achieving that aim are appropriate and necessary.[21]

The provisions of EU law and the EU Charter of Fundamental Rights were most intensively addressed by the Constitutional Court in a case challenging the constitutionality of amendments restricting the pool of eligible legal counsel

19 See, however, for example, case 2001-09-01 of 21 January 2002 where the court was confronted with national law aiming at harmonization with EU requirements on production of sugar.

20 Case 2001-12-01 of 19 March 2002 On Compliance of Paragraph 26 of the State Pension Law Transitional Provisions with Articles 91 and 109 of the Satversme (Constitution).

21 Case 2002-21-01 of 20 May 2003.

representatives in criminal proceedings to sworn advocates.[22] The court addressed the challenged restriction in the context of the general right of a person to a fair trial and in relation to the obligation to provide legal aid assistance in criminal matters.

The Constitutional Court started its analysis by conventionally relying on EU law as a non-obligatory persuasive authority through the single-argument form of reference to the relevant EU law provision. Thus, analysing national rules regulating representation in court proceedings in the context of the right to a fair trial, the Constitutional Court also emphasized that additionally 'it is necessary to analyse the provisions included in international instruments, namely the Covenant, the Declaration, and the European Charter of the Fundamental Rights as well as other legal acts of the European Union.' The court then referred to Article 47 of the European Charter of Fundamental Rights providing that 'everyone has the right to receive legal advice and the right to defence and representation.'[23]

Then the court for the first time developed a complex contextual harmonization argument relying on the general aim of the right to free movement of workers facilitated and protected by EU law.[24] The court first recalled that Latvia is in the process of approximation of its national legal system with the norms of the European Union. Thus,

> The legislator, when taking a decision on securing due, accessible and qualitative legal aid in several types of processes, including that of the criminal process, should take into consideration the requirements of the European Union. This is necessary so that after the new Member States join the Union, efficient implementation of the legal system of the European Union is secured.

The court then developed its argument further by contextualizing the challenged national provisions against EU free movement of person and services provisions:

> When Latvia becomes a full-fledged member of the European Union, one of the freedoms of the European Union – free movement of persons and services,

---

22 Case 2003-08-01 of 6 October 2003 On the Compliance of Article 96 (the first sentence of the second part) of the Criminal Procedure Law of Latvia with Articles 89 and 92 of the Republic of Latvia Satversme (Constitution).

23 Ibid., para 1.2.

24 Ibid.; see also case 2003-21-0306 of 9 February 2004 challenging amendments to the Guarantee Fund of Mandatory Civil Liability Insurance for Owners of Road Transport. The amendments aimed at harmonization of national law with EC Second Council Directive 84/5/EEC of 30 December 1983 on the approximation of the laws of the Member States relating to insurance against civil liability in respect of the use of motor vehicles and Directive 2000/26/EC of the European Parliament and of the Council of 16 May 2000 on the approximation of the laws of the Member States relating to insurance against civil liability in respect of the use of motor vehicles and amending Council Directives 73/239/EEC and 88/357/EEC and case 2003-12-01 of 18 December 2003 challenging the civil service retirement age differences between men and women.

> will refer to our State. Thus Latvian advocates and other practising lawyers will be able to compete in the service market of the European Union. This sector is regulated by several secondary legal acts of the European Union. Very important are two directives. One is Council Directive 77/249/EEC of 22 March 1977 to facilitate the effective exercise by lawyers of freedom to provide services, which regulates short period provision of legal services in another Member State of the European Union. The other is Directive 98/5/EC of the European Parliament and of the Council of 16 February 1998 to facilitate practice of the profession of lawyer on a permanent basis in a Member State other than in which the qualification was obtained.[25]

Furthermore the court discussed how the challenged provision of national law may potentially impact access by Latvian lawyers to the EU internal market:

> After joining the European Union advocates from Latvia will have extensive possibilities to operate. They will experience the possibility of being employed in public institutions or private enterprises as well as to practice in other Member States of the European Union. Thus there should be such legal regulation in a state which allows Latvian advocates and practising lawyers to render legal services in other Member States of the European Union on the basis of the principle of equality. Legal regulation in Latvia must not differ from that of the other Member States of the European Union, otherwise inequality and deformation of competition may arise and that can become an obstacle in implementing free movement of persons. Economic and professional requirements envisage that lawyers will render legal services throughout the European Union and create different professional associations, which can be joined by lawyers of one or several states.[26]

Finally, the court pointed out that Latvia, by closing accession negotiations on the Chapter on free movement of persons, agreed to adopt a number of legislative acts aiming to implement the *acquis communautaire* in the sector of free movement of persons, *inter alia* related to the regulated profession of advocates. However, this obligation was at the time of the court hearing implemented only partially.

Thus, building a complex form of cumulative argument, the court concluded that 'it is necessary to amend the regulation of the right to legal aid in such a way that it corresponds to the requirements of the European Union.'[27] And in relation to the contested provisions of national law the court ruled:

> … to declare Article 96 (the first sentence of the second part) of the Latvian Criminal Procedure law as unconformable with Article 92 of the Satversme and null and void from March 1, 2004 if the legislator does not amend legal

25 2003-08-01, para 6.

26 Ibid., para 6.

27 Ibid., para 6.

> regulation of the performance of advocates so that it complies with the standards of the European Union and the European Council and guarantees the right to a fair trial in the full range.[28]

In conclusion, in pre-accession jurisprudence of Estonian and Latvian higher courts, EU law played only a very minor but important normative role as compared to other international treaties, for example, the European Convention of Human Rights. In Estonia, EU law has been mostly relied on to provide additional support arguments for harmonious interpretation of national law with EU law standards and to fill gaps in developing national legal doctrine. In Latvia, the Constitutional Court has mostly relied on the provisions of the European Union Charter of Fundamental Rights. Patterns of justification that both the Estonian Supreme Court and the Latvian Constitutional Court have mostly relied on to refer to EU law are non-independent single-argument types of justification that have been added to other international law arguments. However, cumulative forms including evaluative and contextual harmonization arguments have also been invoked by the courts in pre-accession references to EU law.

In Estonia, the EU legal materials referred to by the courts included provisions of the EC Treaty (now TFEU) and of the European Union Association Agreement, as well as general principles of EU law developed through ECJ jurisprudence. In Latvia, the main legal material of reference was the Charter of Fundamental Rights. The European Association Agreement was invoked rarely and only in a dissenting opinion.[29]

Application of EU Law in National 'Transitional Period' Jurisprudence

The transitional period includes cases where the facts of the case took place before formal accession to the European Union but the court adjudicated the dispute after accession. In this type of transitional case, national courts do not have a strict binding obligation to apply EU law provisions. However, Association Agreements signed in 1998 included a provision on gradual approximation of national legislation with EU law.[30] The Supreme Court of Latvia explained that national courts should not directly apply EU law to facts that occurred prior to accession. However, in interpreting national law adopted on the basis of EU law that entered into force before EU accession, the national court if necessary may rely on the relevant interpretation of an EU norm provided by the ECJ:

28 Ibid., the Substantive Part of the judgment.

29 See dissenting opinion in case 2000-03-01.

30 Article 68 and 69, Europe Agreement establishing an association between the European Communities and their Member States, of the one part, and the Republic of Estonia, of the other part, OJ L 68/3 (09.03.1998).

> EU law does not directly apply to acts that occurred prior to its accession to the European Union, while the court can rely on ECJ case law for interpretation of national law whose wording is similar to European Union law … Consequently, EC Regulation 2912/92 … was not directly applicable to the facts that occurred prior to Latvian accession to the European Union … ECJ case law on Regulation 2912/92 may be relied on for interpretation [if required] only to the facts, after 1 July 2002, [when a national provision analogous to EC law entered into force].[31]

Similarly, the Supreme Court relied on the Association Agreement in case SKA-397/2007 to argue that although formally EU law prior to accession did not have binding force, ECJ case law nevertheless may be relied on by the national court as a source of authority:

> As the Senate of the Supreme Court Department of Administrative Cases indicated in its decision of 13 September 2006 in case No. SKA-287/2006, according to the Europe Agreement establishing an association between the European Communities and their Member States, of the one part, and the Republic of Latvia (in force since 1 February 1998) Latvia has undertaken to achieve the approximation of its laws with the laws of the European Communities. The fact that the circumstances of the relevant case took place prior to the accession of Latvia to the European Union does not mean that the case law of the European Court of Justice case law is not applicable as the 2001 edition of the Value Added Tax Act was aimed at its approximation with the requirements of the laws of the European Union. It is relevant also to the interpretation of the Sixth Directive.[32]

The Supreme Court of Latvia in general adopted an EU law-friendly approach and relied on EU law provisions even where it was not a legally binding source of authority.[33] Thus, the Supreme Court has relied on linguistic arguments invoking EU secondary law and ECJ jurisprudence. In cases involving VAT disputes, the court accepted references to ECJ authority as a valid argument:[34]

31 SKA-405/2009 of 17 December 2009, para 11.

32 SKA-0397/2007, pra 14.1. The Regional Court of Administrative Cases also followed a similar argument in several of its cases, see for example, C27084604, C30483103, A42032104, A42077704, C27136403.

33 In a number of cases see for example, SKA-293/2006, SKA-422/2006, SKA-441/2006, SKA-22/2007, SKA-496/2008, SKA-62/2009, SKA-166/2010 the Senate of the Supreme Court Department of Administrative Cases relied on EU law as an interpretive tool even through the disputed events took place prior to EU accession.

34 Through a complex cumulative argument, the court however distinguishes the facts of the disputed case from the facts of ECJ cases to which the applicant refers and thus rejects the doctrine developed in ECJ case law.

> The Regional court in its judgment refers to the judgment of the European Court of Justice dated 12 January 2006 in joined cases C-354/03, C-355/03 and C-484/03 which concludes that each transaction in a chain of transactions must therefore be regarded on its own merits and the character of a particular transaction in the chain cannot be altered by earlier or subsequent events (see paragraph 47 of Judgment of the European Court of Justice of 12 January 2006 in joined Cases C-354/03, C-355/03 and C-484/03 regarding reference for a preliminary ruling in Optigen Ltd, Fulcrum Electronics Ltd and Bond House Systems Ltd v Commissioners of Customs & Excise cases).[35]

Likewise, the Regional Court of Administrative Cases, again in a number of VAT decisions, follows the example of the Supreme Court:[36]

> The Regional Court of Administrative Cases concludes that the claimant has correctly referred to the judgments of the European Court of Justice which sets case law on tax cases, which provides that a VAT payer who carries out such transactions cannot be affected by the fact that in the chain of supply of which those transactions form part another prior or subsequent transaction is vitiated by value added tax fraud, without that taxable person knowing or having any means of knowing.[37]

The Supreme Court also relied on systemic arguments from contextual harmonization to interpret national law in the light of the EU secondary legislation:

> … in order to interpret legal norms and to reach a just result which corresponds to the system of legal acts, in the view of the Senate the norms of the Sixth Council Directive of 17 May 1977 on the harmonization of the laws of the Member States relating to turnover taxes – Common system of value added tax: uniform basis of assessment (77/388/EEC) are also usable.[38]

Similarly, the Regional Court of Administrative Cases relies on a systemic argument:[39] 'The Regional Court of Administrative Cases is of the opinion that the views expressed in the decisions of the European Court of Justice regarding application of legal principles should be taken into consideration in the application of Latvian legal acts.'[40]

---

35 Paragraph 11 of SKA-293/2006.

36 C27228403, A42411406, A42117404, A42277905, A42290506, A 42200104, C27194702.

37 Paragraph 11 of A42411406.

38 Paragraph 10 of SKA-146/2009.

39 C39130603-166/04, A42088904.

40 Paragraph 16 of A42088904.

In some cases the Supreme Court also allowed references to teleological/evaluative arguments, although rejecting them in others:[41]

> Taking into consideration that the legal norms of the European Communities concerning deduction of VAT are similar to Latvian legal norms, the decisions of the European Court of Justice in which the relevant legal norms are interpreted could be used for interpreting Latvian legal norms under the teleological interpretation method.[42]

The Supreme Court, however, rejected teleological arguments based on EU law where national pre-accession law was in direct conflict with EU law. In case SKA-1/2006 adjudicated by the grand panel of the Senate of the Supreme Court Department of Administrative Cases, the court ruled that a grammatical interpretation of national law must prevail over teleological arguments based on EU law. The court first pointed out that until the date of accession the national legislator had a right to maintain legal regulations that might differ from EU law provisions; [43] and then continued:

> … not on all occasions is it necessary to use all interpretation methods. If, by interpreting a legal norm by the grammatical method it is concluded that the legal norm, as it is in the present case, is very precise and obviously determines [the meaning] the cassation application argument regarding the necessity for the court also to use the teleological method of interpretation is then ungrounded.[44]

The court justified its rejection to take into consideration teleological arguments based on the following reasoning:

> Legal literature suggests that one of the oldest lessons of legal thinking is that law is to be observed, even if it does not fully satisfy the requirement of justice. In the interest of legal certainty a person should be subject to such law even if she herself considers it to be unfair … Positive (written) law must be respected in order to guarantee legal certainty and the functioning of the legal system (see: Horns N. Introduction to science and philosophy, *Likums un Tiesības*, December, 2000, p. 354) … neither the court nor the authority can refuse to apply the law in force if preconditions for application have occurred (see: Case Nr. SKA-330/2005, 11).[45]

41 SKA-1/2006

42 Para 5.8 of A42336805. The argument was also used in A42231905.

43 Latvian legal norms could contain a different legal regulation, para 10, until their complete approximation with the legal norms of the European Communities.

44 SKA-1/2006, paras 9–10.

45 SKA-1/2006, para 11.

The Estonian Supreme Court has also actively referred to EU law and ECJ case law and adopted a conforming interpretation approach to cases based on facts that took place prior to accession. However, if national pre-accession legal provisions were in direct conflict with EU law, the Estonian Supreme Court similarly to the Latvian Supreme Court, applied the national law provision:[46]

> Estonia had the obligation to bring national law into accordance with EC law even before accession and it was advisable to interpret and apply national law accordingly. However, national law valid before accession to the EU cannot automatically be interpreted on the basis of EU law without taking into account the facts of a concrete case and treaties regulating relations between Estonia and the European Union (e.g. Association Agreement). EU law conforming interpretation of national law became legally binding only after accession to the EU. This position is supported by ECJ case law [reference to *Ynos* and *Lakep* judgments].[47]

Conclusions

In Estonia, EU law is placed on the highest normative level, main EU law doctrines are well explained and justified by the Supreme Court and access to court judgments is open and transparent. However, certain concerns may be noted in relation to institutional coherence, specifically very high court fees, limited access to legal aid, and procedural limitations related to the competences of the Chancellor of Justice. The Latvian context is more complex and less coherent. In Latvia, EU law does not explicitly enjoy the highest normative status. The main legal principles of EU law are introduced to the national legal system through code-specific and in certain respects not fully consistent national regulations. Although Latvian highest courts apply EU law and EU law principles, they provide only limited analytical-persuasive justifications. Further characteristics of the legal system that contribute to incoherence include weakly developed legal scholarship, extreme difficulties and expenses related to access to case law, and alleged political influence on the judicial system.

46 See for example, cases 3-2-1-103-06 of 8 November 2006 and 3-3-1-57-06 of 23 October 2006.

47 3-3-1-57-06 of 23 October 2006 para 16.

Table 4.2 National constitutional structures – impact on coherence

Factors	*Estonia*	*I.*	*Latvia*	*I.*
I. Substantive Coherence				
Constitutional norms	Constitutional Amendment Act as interpreted by ESC includes provisions on transfer of powers and places EU law on the highest level in the hierarchy of national norms. ESC has elaborately explained the nature of constitutional amendments	+++	Constitutional amendments include transfer of power provisions. Place of EU law in the national hierarchy of norms is not regulated at the Constitutional level. LCC is relatively passive and did not explain the nature of EU law-related constitutional amendments.	+
Doctrine of supremacy	Regulated at the constitutional level; Unconditional acceptance, EU norms above national constitutional provisions. ESC applied and explained the nature of the principle	+++	Regulated in national procedural codes; Conditional, EU norms are placed under national constitutional provisions. LCC and LSC applied but did not explain the nature of the principle.	+
Doctrine of direct effect	ESC applied and explained the nature of the principle. Ordinary courts apply consistently.	+++	LSC and LCC applied the principle. Ordinary courts apply with some instances of confusion between direct effect and direct applicability of EU Directives.	+
Doctrine of harmonious interpretation	ESC applied and the nature of the principle explained. Ordinary courts apply consistently.	+++	LSC and LCC and ordinary courts apply the principle in practice but do not discuss or explicitly refer.	++
II. Institutional Coherence				
Preliminary reference (procedure)	Until 2006, procedure for stay of proceedings for submission of preliminary reference to ECJ was lacking. This has been corrected by legislative amendments and extensively explained by the ESC. National ordinary and highest courts submit references to ECJ.	++	Provided for under procedural codes; the practical procedure for requesting a preliminary ruling is little explained by the LCC or LSC. Court of first instance hesitant to refer questions for preliminary ruling.	++
Court system	No major problems related to corruption or independence of courts	+++	Several high-profile scandals related to corruption of judges and appointments to the highest judicial positions.	-

Access to information	Comprehensive and free-of-charge database of legal judgments is available online	+++	Comprehensive and free-of-charge database of legal judgments is not available online. Commercial database is expensive.	-
Access to Courts	Concerns have been raised regarding access to legal aid provisions and high state fees.	+	Legal aid is also limited but state fees are reasonable; long backlog of pending cases.	++
Inter-court cooperation	Active and open cooperation between national and EU courts.	+++	Active and open cooperation between national highest courts, but not yet of ordinary courts.	++
Intra-court cooperation		+++		+++
Legal scholarship	A number of regularly published, well-established and internationally recognised legal journals in Estonian and English.	+++	Legal journals are limited and only in Latvian.	+
III. Argumentative				
Legal culture (openness to supranational norms)	Open. Constitutionally protected principle of primacy of international law.	+++	Constitutionally protected principle of primacy of international law.	+++
Legal interpretation	In explaining main EU legal doctrines and principles, ESC has relied on a variety of legal justifications including systemic and teleological arguments as well as on a variety of legal sources including ECJ jurisprudence.	+++	LCC is an example of argumentative excellence. LSC and national ordinary courts are still lagging behind. However, reference to ECJ jurisprudence is common at all court levels.	++

Note: Impact on coherence: '+++' = strongly positive; '++' = positive; '+' = rather positive (but with important constraints); '---' = strongly negative; '--' = negative; '-' = rather negative.

PART III
Adjudication of EU Law by the National Ordinary Courts

Chapter 5
Comparative Overview of National Case Law

Part III of this book is the second step in empirical analysis of the national jurisprudence of Estonian and Latvian courts. Following discussion of the three-dimensional framework of coherence (Part I) and application of this analytical framework to the jurisprudence of the highest courts (Part II), Part III examines application of the three dimensions of the principle of coherence to the jurisprudence of *ordinary courts*. The analysis of Part II reveals that Estonian constitutional structures provide a more coherent system of application of EU law than in Latvia.[1]

Building on the analysis of Part II, I assess how constitutional structural principles, institutional constraints and interactions, as well as argumentative practices of higher courts, are translated into the daily jurisprudence of ordinary courts. In other words, I assess to what extent positive and negative issues identified under the three dimensions of coherence at the constitutional level define and impact application of EU law by ordinary courts.

The analysis of the jurisprudence of ordinary courts does not aim to provide detailed legal analysis of all legal matters and nuances of national law involved in the cases discussed. This is not necessary for the coherence argument and in fact would be nearly impossible, given the number of cases under analysis. To advance the main argument of this book, I concentrate primarily on interactions between EU and national law.

National case law of ordinary courts is organized into groups based on the main legal subject-matter.[2] Within each group of cases, which includes if applicable jurisprudence of all levels of courts, I first consider how national ordinary courts define and reconcile conflicting norms of national and EU law (the substantive coherence dimension). Secondly, I analyse whether conflicts or disagreements emerge between levels of national courts on application of EU law principles; under what conditions and at what level of the national judicial system courts request a preliminary reference from the European courts, and if other institutional factors impact adjudication of EU law (the institutional coherence dimension). Finally, I examine argumentation patterns that national courts adopt to justify application of EU law (the argumentative coherence dimension).

1 For summary see Table 4.2: National constitutional structures – impact on coherence.

2 See Table 5.1.

National Case Law of Ordinary Courts

The total number of cases both in Estonia and Latvia that refer to EU law, ECJ case law, or principles of EU law is over 1,800.[3] What does this number indicate? Close analysis of cases shows that in a large number of these, especially during the first two years following accession, EU law provisions or ECJ case law are only referred to by one of the parties or the court without substantive consideration of the relevant legal provision. Thus, EU law is mentioned as an additional authoritative normative source, without developing a full argument indicating how a cited EU law provision is directly relevant to the facts of the concrete case or how a cited provision reinforces the legal argument. This 'use' of EU law may be explained on the one hand by generally high attention to the EU in the accession period and on the other hand by relatively little specialized knowledge of EU law.

Consider as an example a Tallinn Administrative Court case involving a public tender for purchase of public transportation network buses.[4] The applicant challenging the decision of the Public Procurement Office argued that an ISO certificate should be taken into consideration and weighted more as an evaluation criterion in the tender evaluation criteria. In support of its position, the applicant referred to ECJ jurisprudence: 'The quality management certificate is used in other EU MS as one of the assessment criteria for the public procurement tenders for bus services (see e.g. ECJ judgment C-513/99 *Concordia Bus Finland*).'[5] In this case, the argumentation strategy of the applicant is built on the provisions of national law, with ECJ case law and the experience of other EU MSs used to additionally strengthen the argument. The court, however, in this specific case did not consider in substance a reference either to the experience of other EU MSs or the ECJ *Concordia Bus* judgment referred to by the applicant.

Similarly, in a dispute involving tax payment in the Riga Administrative District Court the applicant argued that a decision of the national tax authority to withhold value-added tax was contrary to national law as well as the EU 6th Directive. The national court, however, did not consider application of the EU 6th Directive to the dispute and built its reasoning solely by reference to national law.[6] Another more recent example is from the Latvian Regional Administrative Court. The court, discussing whether a national administrative decision was well reasoned, first relied on the case law of the Latvian Supreme Court that explained the criteria that an administrative decision must meet. The court then pointed out that similar criteria are also applied by the European Court of Justice, for example, in case T-168/01.[7]

3 See also Annex 1.

4 Case 3-06-113 of 22 May 2006, Tallinn Administrative Court.

5 Ibid.

6 Case Nr.A42030304 judgment from 5 May 2005, Administrative Court of Appeal.

7 In the relevant paragraph of the case of the European Court of First Instance, the CFI discusses the obligation to state reasons in decisions adopted by the European Commission.

Consequently, the large number of cases that refer to EU law, especially during the first two years following accession, is partly explained by the tendency to use EU law as an additional supportive reference in legal disputes in the ordinary courts. This tendency is increasingly diminishing, and as will be analysed below, the argumentation of the parties and reasoning of the courts in recent cases has become more elaborate. This is most likely the result of increasing knowledge and experience of applying EU law among legal professionals.[8]

Another observation that applies to all national case law is that a large number of cases does not equate with the diversity of legal conflicts settled in the national courts. In other words, national case law is structured not as diverse single cases but rather as a large group of cases that share very similar fact patterns. In Estonia, the main groups of cases that substantively analyse EU law provisions or apply ECJ case law include structural fund subsidies cases, surplus stock fee (sugar) cases, and discrimination in entitlement to pension and residence rights of third-country nationals. In Latvia, the main groups of cases include value added tax, consumer protection, competition and labour law cases.

Those large groups of national cases emerged as a result of (1) transitional measures adopted after EU accession (sugar cases in Estonia); (2) complex regulation of new fields that had not regulated before EU accession (for example, structural fund subsidies cases in Estonia); (3) introduction of new rules or harmonization of existing national legislation with EU law (VAT cases in Latvia; pension and residence permit cases in Estonia) that concerned a large number of national companies or individuals.[9]

The main groups of cases that emerged in national jurisdictions 2004–09 are summarized in Table 5.1 overleaf.

8 For the purpose of analysis of the substantive coherence dimension that examines normative inconsistencies between national and EU law, as well as legal principles used by courts to settle normative incoherencies, national cases that merely point to EU law are not central and therefore are not analysed in detail.

9 Notably, within the group, cases share very similar fact patterns, involve similar contested national and EU law provisions and as a result very similar argumentative patterns by courts. Thus, for example, most cases in the group of Estonian structural fund subsidies cases are brought by farmers contesting an administrative decision for agri-environmental support, the applicant is often represented by the same lawyer and the national agency is also represented by the same lawyers from the responsible department. Consequently, the judgments of the court also follow a nearly identical line of reasoning.

Table 5.1 Comparative overview of case law of ordinary courts (by main subject matter/country)

	Economic freedoms and market integration	**Equality, justice and social integration**
Estonia	surplus stock fee payment structural fund subsidies intellectual property	discrimination in pension and residence rights
Latvia	VAT competition intellectual property	consumer protection labour law

Chapter 6
Jurisprudence of Estonian Courts

Structural Funds Subsidies

Structural funds subsidies comprise the largest group of cases, including 89 cases at first instance, 42 cases at second instance, 12 cases in the Supreme Court[1] and one case in the ECJ.[2] Structural funds cases are very technical in nature.[3] The legal dispute is often centred on specific details of national law regulating the procedure for determination of funds, measurement, or eligibility criteria. The large number of administrative cases involving structural subsidies cases is explained by three main reasons: first, the complexity and novelty of the legislative framework regulating grant of structural funds assistance; secondly, limited capacity and resources of administrative agencies, and third, lack of adequate knowledge of the new legislative framework and administrative procedure by applicants.

From the point of view of legal doctrine, beyond a narrow circle of specialists working with structural funds, those cases provide only a limited interest for EU lawyers. The importance of those cases was, especially in the immediate post-accession period, and remains in the methods of interpretation and application of EU law. This includes understanding by national lower courts of the novel and complex EU regulations of structural funds and the ability to rely on EU legal

1 Cases: 3-3-1-95-06; 3-3-1-96-06; 3-3-1-11-09; 3-3-1-19-09; 3-3-1-80-08; 3-1-81-08; 3-3-1-79-08; 3-3-1-75-08; 3-3-1-64-07; 3-3-1-27-07; 3-3-1-28-07; 3-3-1-26-07.

2 C-241/07 JK Otsa Talu.

3 During the period 2004–06, structural support was allocated from four funds: the European Regional Development Fund; the European Social Fund; the European Agricultural Guidance and Guarantee Fund; the Financial Instrument for Fisheries Guidance. On a EU level, in the period from 2004–06, 18 EC regulations laid down general provisions and each structural fund specific regulations. On the national level, the main legislative framework act regulating the grant of structural assistance is the Structural Assistance Act (SAA) (perioodi 2004–2006 Sturktuurtoetuste Seadus (RT(1) I 2003, 82, 552) The SAA provides 'bases for preparations to grant structural assistance and for the processing of applications, as well as the rights and obligations of the subjects involved in granting or using structural assistance and the procedure for supervision.' The SAA also stipulated that proceedings concerning applications for structural assistance and for the grant of assistance are subject to the Administrative Procedure Act. (Article 1(2) of the 2004–2006 Struktuuritioetuste Seadus). Fund and measure-specific regulations are provided by Regulations of the Minister of Agriculture.

sources and principles.[4] This also means the craft of justifying application of EU law instruments through a variety of interpretive methods. The interplay between national and EU law is the focus of the analysis that follows below.

The general legal framework of structural funds cases is summarized in Table 6.1 below.

Table 6.1 Structural fund cases – legal framework

Issue: Community support for development		
	EU level	National level
Rule	Reg. 1257/1999 Reg. 1260/1999 Reg. 796/2004	Law on implementation of the common EU agricultural policy Estonian Rural Development Plan Vabariigi Valitsuse 22.12.2006 määruse nr 278 'Toetuse tagasinõudmise ja tagasimaksmise ning toetuse andmisel ja kasutamisel toimunud rikkumisest teabe edastamise tingimused ja kord'
Administrative Agency		PRIA – Estonian Agricultural Registers and Information Board
Application (main problems)	• compatibility of specific eligibility/exclusion criteria and administrative formalities provided under national law with EU Regulations • limits of administrative discretion and principle of good administration of national institution administering EU-supported funds	

In the series of structural funds cases, applicants contest administrative decisions of the PRIA.[5] The most contested legal issues include compatibility of various

4 Structural assistance between 2004 and 2006 was implemented through four European Union structural funds: the European Social Fund, the European Regional Development Fund, the European Agricultural Guidance and Guarantee Fund and the Financial Instrument for Fisheries Guidance. The legal framework regulating distribution of structural support was and is a complex mixture of EU regulations, national legislative acts and national-sector specific orders. During the period 2007–13, structural support is allocated from three funds, which are the main sources of support in the regional policy of the European Union. These are the following: the European Regional Development Fund, the European Social Fund and the Cohesion Fund.

5 Structural fund cases developed in two waves. The factual and procedural background of the first wave of cases is as follows: the applicant applied to the Office for area payments (national implementing agency) in order to obtain financial support (that is, area subsidy, agri-environmental subsidy). Support for agri-environmental subsidy is part of the European Agricultural Guidance and Guarantee Fund. The application was rejected by the director of the Office.

eligibility and exclusion criteria provided under national implementing legislation as well as established administrative practice with applicable EU regulations.[6]

EU law, Regulation No 1257/1999, sets the aims, methods and objectives regarding agriculture, the environment and welfare of farm animals (Article 22) in relation to agri-environmental or animal welfare; defines the minimum years of commitment that a farmer must undertake (Article 23), and establishes general rules on how agri-environmental commitment will be granted and calculated (Article 24 (1)).[7] It also provides that measures supported by the rural development fund must comply with EU law and be consistent with other EU policies. However, Member States may lay down further or more restrictive conditions for granting EU support, provided that such conditions comply with EU law principles as well as meeting the objectives and requirements of this policy field.

National law adopted to provide more detailed regulation for the grant of rural development support in connection with the Common Agricultural Policy provides that the Minister of Agriculture determines the kinds of available support and the allocation of budgetary resources among various support fields,[8] and establishes specific requirements[9] and procedural rules for obtaining rural development support.[10]

Based on the type of contested incoherencies between national and EU norms, national case law may be clustered into three main groups: cases that contest conformity of conditions and eligibility criteria under national law with the general objectives and aims of EU law; cases that challenge conformity of national procedural rules and administrative practices with EU law and principles of good administration, and cases that question the conformity with EU rules of national rules on the requirements and conditions for full or partial return of EU support (see Table 6.2).

6 In most cases, unless procedural rules were manifestly violated (for example, measurement of land was not conducted correctly, or the Office failed to provide reasons for refusal of the subsidy), the court dismissed the application. In 42 cases, the applicant brought an appeal before the court of second level and following dismissal in twelve cases, the applicant brought an appeal on a point of law before the Supreme Court.

The two main grounds for rejections include: eligibility criteria are not met; support was not available in a given calendar year due to limited resources. The applicant brought proceedings before the administrative court of first level for annulment of the specific provisions of the decision of the director of the Office and seeking an order for payment of the support in question. The second wave of cases concerned disputes related to the conditions and procedures under which the recipient of support was requested to return a certain amount of funds. In this series of cases, the Office sent notification to the applicant requesting return of the subsidy already paid on the ground that the applicant failed to meet the conditions attached to grant of the support payment.

7 Regulation No 1257/1999 establishes the framework for Community support for sustainable rural development.

8 Regulation No 51 of the Minister for Agriculture of 20 April 2004, para 42.

9 Ibid., para 3.

10 Ibid.: 'Detailed requirements for obtaining agri-environmental support and detailed rules for applying for support, treatment of applications and payment of support.'

Table 6.2 Structural fund cases – type of legal incoherence

	Group of cases	Type of incoherence
1	Cases that contest conformity of conditions and eligibility criteria under national law with the general objectives and aims of Community law	Specific national norm/ general EU norm
2	Cases that challenge conformity of national procedural rules and administrative practices with Community law and principles of good administration	National practice/national and EU principles of good administration
3	Cases that question conformity with EU rules of national rules on the requirements and conditions for full or partial return of Community support	Conformity of national norm with EU norm

Conformity of national law with the general objectives and aims of EU law

This group of structural fund cases[11] involved issues mainly related to eligibility criteria and grounds for refusal in determining eligible support. Applicants contested the criteria related to measurement (GPS measurement techniques);[12] quality of eligible land (that is, what land is to be considered as land in good agricultural order, how many trees and bushes are allowed, etc.),[13] as well as the pool of eligible recipients for support (large farm/small farm subsidies, economic sustainability of the applicants[14] and conditions under which eligible recipients may be restricted).[15] Considering the relationship between EU and national norms, the contested form of incoherence is between national specific norms implementing EU policy and EU structural funds provisions in specific policy fields (see Table 6.3).

National rules regulating the procedure and grant of structural fund support did not explicitly provide an evaluation of the economic sustainability of the project as part of the eligibility criteria. On this ground, for example, in case 3-05-1191, the applicant argued that by rejecting his structural fund project application on the basis of a negative expert opinion on the sustainability of the proposed project the administrative agency had violated the applicant's rights. Thus, the applicant in this case suggested that the courts should interpret the provisions of national law narrowly, only relying on the text of the Minister of Agriculture Regulations.

11 Over 30 cases, 2005–08.

12 See for example, 3-07-130; 3-06-422; 3-06-422; 3-06-1316; 3-06-1448; 3-06-472, 3-06-511; 3-06-1857.

13 See for example, cases 3-07-2211; 3-07-53, 3-06-1448; 3-06-1368, 3-07-107.

14 Case 3-05-1191 (3-558/05) of 22 February 2006, Tartu Administrative Court.

15 3-06-2067; 3-06-2489; 3-06-2068.

Table 6.3 Incoherence – specific national norm/general EU norm

Specific		*General*	
National rule on eligibility criteria	**National Structural Funds regulation**	**EU Regulation**	**EU Structural Funds**
Art. 12 and 13 of the Minister of Agriculture Regulations	National Development Plan for Implementation of EU Structural Funds		

The administrative agency disagreed. The PRIA argued that the Minister of Agriculture Regulations is national implementing legislation adopted to enforce the National Structural Funds Regulation and EU Structural Funds Regulation. Thus, a narrow linguistic reading of the specific national implementing law is insufficient. National law must be applied in the systemic-contextual framework of the more general objectives provided under EU law that national law aims to implement.

The courts of first instance upheld the arguments of the PRIA and explained, relying on the jurisprudence of the Supreme Court of Estonia, that

> In analysing sustainability one cannot rely solely on the criteria established in Articles 13 and 14 of Regulation Nr. 36. Based on Article 12 of Regulation Nr. 36 it is necessary also to control the criteria and procedures related to the application and the applicant. Consequently, the PRIA controls information submitted by the applicant based on Article 18 and 19 of the Structural Funds Regulation, his previous economic activities and the economic prospects of the proposed project in accordance with Article 18 of the Structural Funds Regulation and Regulation Nr. 36.[16]

The court pointed out that what takes place is not a narrow linguistic-mechanical reading of national law, but rather an interpretation is necessary that takes into consideration objections to EU law provisions.[17] Similarly, in another case, the court additionally explained that the national administrative agency is obliged in reviewing applications for structural fund support to check the economic sustainability of the applicant and of the submitted project proposal with national law as well as the Estonian National Development Plan for Implementation of EU Structural Funds.[18] Thus, in both cases, the courts concluded that by undertaking

16 Case 3-05-1191 (3-558/05) of 22 February 2006, Tartu Administrative Court.

17 Ibid., Tartu Administrative Court, see below under teleological method of interpretation, p. 238.

18 Case 3-05-1181 (3-557/05) of 28 February 2006, Tartu Administrative Court; also confirmed by the judgment of the Tartu Circuit Court (appeal court) decision of 25 May 2006.

additional inquiry into the economic sustainability of the applicant and ordering an expert opinion on the sustainability of the project proposal (actions that are not specifically listed in the eligibility criteria of the national regulation), the administrative agency not only acted in conformity with national law but also importantly fulfilled its obligation to ensure that national law is applied in conformity with national and EU general policy objectives.[19]

In another case concerning an application for investment support for agricultural holdings, the court had to decide whether the administrative agency had correctly refused to grant support.[20] The case concerned an application for renovation of a piggery. Two undertakings belonging to the same concern (the main company and its subsidiary) each applied for renovation of the same piggery. Both companies submitted a duly completed application that met all the necessary requirements for the maximum amount of available financial support, claiming that each company would be responsible for half the costs of necessary renovation works. The question was whether the double-maximum amount of financial support for the same building would be justified and in conformity with national and EU law regulating distribution of structural fund support.

In order to resolve the issue, the national administrative agency submitted a question to the European Commissioner for Agriculture asking whether providing support in a given case is permissible and if such support would not be contrary to the financial interests of the Community. In reply, the office of the Commissioner stated that the quantitative limits established by the programme for each applicant aim to avoid concentration of support and gaining competitive advantage through state aid to one applicant. What mattered was not only the strictly legal status of the applicant undertaking but also the economic point of view. If between undertakings there are strong economic ties, especially if decisions are taken by the same natural person, then it may be concluded that from the economic point of view it is one and the same undertaking.

In considering the reply by the European Commission for Agriculture and the provisions of national law on state aid and competition, the court concluded that although both undertakings had met all legal requirements provided under national law regulating the grant of investment support for agricultural holdings, it was correct, in view of the aims of the structural fund support regulations and competition law considerations, to grant financial support to only one of two economically closely related undertakings.

Therefore, in the cases contesting incoherencies between national implementing legislation and general objectives provided under Community law, national courts have consistently held that narrow linguistic interpretation of national law is not enough. It was repeatedly explained by the courts that implementing legislation must be applied taking into consideration EU law. This was carefully applied by the national judges against the complexities of the highly regulated issues of

19 Case 3-05-1191 (3-558/05) of 22 February 2006, Tartu Administrative Court.

20 Case 3-05-1317 of 21 March 2006, Tartu Administrative Court.

structural fund subsidy payments, often against the claims of individual applicants (farmers) to rely exclusively on the provisions of the national law.

Conformity of national procedural rules and administrative practices with EU law principles and conformity of national norm with EU norm

The second group of cases contesting incoherencies between national and EU law concern refusal of the implementing agency to grant support due to insufficient budgetary resources allocated to the specific field. In order to ensure sustainable management of funds for the whole programming period, the Minister of Agriculture had amended legislation regulating eligibility for agri-environmental support. The pool of eligible applicants for 2005 was limited to farmers who had already undertaken an agri-environmental commitment for 2004.[21] Consequently, according to national law, only existing recipients of agri-environmental support could apply in 2005, to the exclusion of new applicants. Applicants relying on EC Regulation 1257/1999/EC, Article 24 (1)) that states 'Support in respect of an agri-environmental or animal welfare commitment shall be granted annually ... ' argued that amendments adopted by the Minister of Agriculture 1) violate administrative discretion and 2) directly conflict with EU law.

Addressing those two issues, national courts have essentially been faced with the question what 'annual granting of the subsidy' required under EU law means. Whether it should be understood as an obligation on national authorities to administer each year a new open call available to all interested recipients, or alternatively, national authorities have discretion, under certain circumstances, to limit the pool of applicants eligible for the subsidy in a given year. This question of interpretation ultimately submitted by the Supreme Court of Estonia reached the ECJ in the *JK Otsa Talu* case.

First, Tartu Administrative Court (the court of first instance) found that the Minister of Agriculture acted within the scope of his administrative discretion. The restriction of otherwise eligible recipients adopted by the Minister of Agriculture by Regulation No. 51 was within the administrative discretion provided under EU law and national legislation:

> Minister of Agriculture Regulation No. 51 with amendments to the Regulation of the European Union's Common Agricultural Policy Implementation Act, § 43 subsection 2 and § 44 subsection 2 and in accordance with European Union Council Regulation 1257/1999/EC European Agricultural Guidance and Guarantee Fund (EAGGF) support for rural development, and certain Regulations to amend the declaration and the introduction of Art. 44 approved

21 Minister of Agriculture Regulation nr. 51, Article 82 sec. 7: 'In 2005, a person may apply for support for an environmentally-friendly production activity if a decision was made in 2004 granting the applicant support for an environmentally-friendly production activity and the applicant has entered into the commitment specified in Paragraph 3(1)(3).'

> pursuant to subsection 2 of the Estonian Rural Development Plan 2004-2006, therefore, Minister of Agriculture regulations has a necessary delegation norm.[22]

The restrictive measure adopted by the Minister of Agriculture is objectively justified: 'The Court agrees with the applicant that the country can provide a variety of benefits in accordance with its capabilities and financial resources, taking into account both the allocated European Union financing and state co-financing',[23] and this measure is proportionate:

> The adoption of § 82 subsection 7 of the Regulation No. 51 did not violate the principle of equal treatment in relation to the applicant. Violation of the principle of equal treatment of the applicant can take place if he is treated differently from other applicants in the same circumstances and with same expectations. Equal treatment must be guaranteed in the same circumstances. Violation of equal treatment takes place if the same situations are treated differently without reasonable grounds.[24]

Secondly, the applicants challenged conformity of national law (Minister of Agriculture Regulation nr. 51, Article 82 sec. 7) with EU law (EC Regulation 1257/1999/EC, Article 24 (1)). The applicants argued that the decision of the Minister of Agriculture not to grant agri-environmental support to new applicants[25] violated the EC regulation providing that 'support in respect of an agri environmental commitment shall be granted annually'.[26]

The courts of both first and second instance disagreed with the applicant that there is incoherence between national and EU law. The court explained:

> Regulation No 51, § 82 subsection 7 does not conflict with Article 24 p. 1 of EU Council Regulation 1257/1999/EU. Under the referred provision, agri-environmental commitments are allocated each year. Equally, under Regulation No 51, § 82 subsection 7, it was possible to apply for environmental friendly farming support if the applicant was already granted environmental friendly support in 2004 ... This means that in case of the existence of already undertaken environmental friendly commitment the applicant also had a right to apply for support.[27]

22 3-06-250 judgment of 28 April 2006, Tartu Administrative Court.
23 3-06-253, 24 April 2006, Tartu Administrative Court.
24 3-06-250 judgment of 28 April 2006, Tartu Administrative Court.
25 Minister of Agriculture Regulation nr. 51, Article 82 sec. 7.
26 Article 24 (1), EC Regulation 1257/1999/EC.
27 3-06-253 of 14 September 2006, Tartu Circuit Court.

Thus, the courts found that the restriction adopted by Regulation No. 51 of the Minister of Agriculture was consistent with obligations under EU law. This position was subsequently upheld by the ECJ in its 2009 *JK Otsa Talu* judgment.[28]

However, in a number of cases, the decisions of the administrative agency PRIA were nevertheless annulled by the court.[29] The main ground for annulment was failure by the administrative agency to provide detailed reasons for refusal of assistance, thus violation of the principle of good administration led to annulment of the contested decision to the satisfaction of the claim by the applicant.[30] Similarly, the Supreme Court found that although the implementing agency had correctly applied the law, failure by the agency to sufficiently explain its decision was a valid ground for annulment of the decision.[31]

However, in other cases also concerning refusal on the ground of insufficient budgetary resources (but in another field) which did not involve violation of the principles of good administration, the courts upheld the regulation of the Minister of Agriculture and decisions of the implementing agency.[32]

The principle of good administration and limits of administrative discretion were rigorously stressed by the courts not only in the agri-environmental 2005 restriction cases discussed above but also in other structural funds cases. For example, in a case related to determination of a single area payment for less-favoured land, the responsible agency did not consider an application for support because the applicant made a mistake in the annex attached to the correctly and timely submitted application. The court supported the applicant, who claimed that the agency should have taken into consideration Article 19 of EC Regulation 796/2004 'Adjustment of obvious errors', which provides that 'an aid application may be adjusted at any time after submission, in cases of obvious errors recognized by the competent authority.'[33] Under national law, Article 7 section 3 subsection 1 of the Minister of Agriculture Regulation nr. 49, the administrative agency has a right to give an applicant time to remove obvious errors from an application or other supporting documents. Subsection 2 of the same provision stipulates that if the applicant fails to remove an error within the given period, the administrative

---

28 C-241/07 JK Otsa Talu [2009] ECR-I 4323.

29 See for example, cases 3-08-531/14; 3-07-2155 of 31 December 2008, Tallinn Administrative Court.

30 Case 3-07-2155 of 31 December 2008, Tallinn Administrative Court; Case 3-07-298 of 28 May 2007, Tartu Administrative Court.

31 3-3-1-80-06 of 19 December 2006.

32 See for example, case 3-06-253 of 24 April 2006, Tartu Administrative Court; 3-06-250 of 28 April 2006, Tartu Administrative Court; case of 14 September 2006, Tartu Circuit Court.

33 Commission Regulation (EC) No 796/2004 of 21 April 2004, laying down detailed rules for the implementation of cross-compliance, modulation and the integrated administration and control system provided for in Council Regulation (EC) No 1782/2003, establishing common rules for direct support schemes under the common agricultural policy and establishing certain support schemes for farmers.

agency need not consider the application. In the given case, although the applicant had corrected its mistake in due time, the agency nevertheless did not satisfy the application.

The court in annulling the administrative decision stated that

> The head of the department correctly applied Article 7 section 3 of Minister of Agriculture Regulation nr. 49 that provides in accordance with Article 19 of EC Regulation 796/2004/EC a right of the PRIA to set a deadline for correcting obvious errors in applications or supporting documents ... Because the applicant in due time removed the error ... PRIA did not have a legal ground to apply subsection 2 of Article 3 section 3 ... .

Similarly, the court annulled the decision of the administrative agency in a case contesting the procedure and practice by PRIA for on-the-spot checks and report for determination of the area payment.[34] The applicant argued that by conducting on-the-spot checks without prior notification and by failing to communicate non-compliance found to the farmer, the PRIA had violated the provisions of EC Regulation 796/2004/EC and the principles of good administration. The court, considering the facts of the case and Article 48 (1) and (2) of Regulation 796/2004/EC providing a list of points that must be included in the control report as well as an obligation to notify the farmer of any non-compliance found during the check, concluded that the PRIA had violated the principles of good administration. The court concluded that by failing to notify the applicant, and thus by denying the possibility to the applicant to submit its position and reasoned objections, the PRIA had violated the obligation under Article 48 (2) of the EC regulation as well as the right to be heard that is a constitutionally protected general principle of law.

Administrative discretion cases indicate that courts are careful to point out that agencies must not only rely on correct EC law provisions but also sufficiently justify their decisions. Failure to provide sufficient reasoning is a solid ground to annul the decision of the administrative agency. Moreover, in applying EU law, administrative agencies must take procedural rights and obligations seriously.

The judicial practice of national courts on EC law application in general is consistent across court levels. However, in some areas, the position of courts of first and second levels on application of EU law diverges. An example of the divergent positions of courts of the first and second levels is a series of cases related to refusal to grant investment support to eligible applicants on the basis of lack of sufficient budgetary resources allocated for the specific supported field. In those cases, the applicants challenged a decision of the Minister of Agriculture and the implementing agency to refuse to grant support for applicants who had met all the eligibility criteria. Motivated by lack of necessary financial resources and with approval of the Minister of Agriculture, the national implementing agency elaborated an evaluation system for identifying the best project proposals. On the

34 Case 3-07-298 of 28 May 2007, Tartu Administrative Court.

basis of this points-based evaluation system, among 18 applicants who met all eligibility criteria only the top five applications received support. Other applicants were notified by decision of the implementing agency that they had met all the requirements for the grant of support but their application was refused due to insufficiency of budgetary resources.

A number of unsuccessful applicants brought proceedings to the courts requesting annulment of the implementing agency's decision as not sufficiently motivated. The applicants argued that a mere statement that there are not sufficient resources to meet all applications is not a sufficient ground to refuse otherwise eligible applicants.

The courts of first instance[35] found that the decision of the implementing agency was reasonable and although laconic, sufficiently motivated. However, the appeal court disagreed and annulled the decision of the lower courts:

> Both the Supreme Court and ECJ through their well established court practice consider the obligation to justify as important and find that it is desirable to provide reasons and relevant facts in the court opinion itself. The obligation to motivate and reason administrative decision must ensure a correct and fair decision and is related to the possibility to control of the act. An administrative act motivation must be based on the reasonableness, if the rational grounds are not provided in the administrative act itself, then accordance with APA § 56 subsection 1 second sentence it must be in provided in the document accessible to the participants in the proceedings, which are cited in the administrative act. Thus, if in the disputed regulation the presentation of the all reasons would be disproportionate, at least the main reasons have to be explicated and references to other documents where detailed motivation is made should be provided ... PRIA in its decision has ignored those requirements. PRIA in addition to indicating lack of funds would have had to explain the points the applicant has received as a result of substantive analysis of his application, the ranking of the application and how many applications have been satisfied.[36]

Another example where courts of first and second instances applied EU law provisions differently concerns cases related to reduction of agri-environment support.[37] An applicant who undertook an agricultural agri-environmental commitment and who held a large stock of agricultural livestock grazed only some of the animals on the land subject to the environment subsidy. The national implementing agency, following an on-the-spot check, reduced the amount of environment friendly support on the ground that not all the animals were grazed on the eligible land. The applicant contested the decision of the PRIA and brought proceedings to the administrative court.

35 See for example, cases 3-06-2067 and 3-06-2068 of Tartu Administrative Court.

36 3-06-2067, para 6.

37 Case 3-07-1186.

The court of first instance, with reference to national law implementing EC Regulation 1257/1999/EC, stated that based on national law, it was clear that if animals are not grazed on the land subject to agri-environment obligation then the subsidy must be reduced by 20 per cent. According to the PRIA and the court of first instance, the obligation to graze animals means that all the animals belonging to the applicant must be grazed on the land.

The applicant and the appeal court disagreed with this narrow linguistic understanding of national law. The appeal court stressed with reference to Articles 2, 5 and 22 of EC Regulation 1257/1999/EC that one of the aims of the EC Regulation is to promote preservation and promotion of high natural value and sustainable agriculture respecting environmental requirements so that support should be granted to agricultural holdings which comply with minimum standards regarding environment, hygiene and animal welfare. Support for agricultural production – according to the EC regulation designed to protect the environment and to maintain the countryside – should contribute to achieving EU policy objectives regarding agriculture and the environment. This type of EU support promotes an environmentally favourable extension of farming and management of low-intensity pasture systems. The support is annual and calculated on the basis of the following elements: income foregone, additional costs resulting from the commitment given, and the need to provide an incentive. Based on those provisions of the regulation, the appeal court concluded that support for agri-environmental commitment is area-based support.

The court further analysed the provisions of EC Regulation 817/2004 to conclude that, based on EU law, it is wrong to reduce support for an agri-environment commitment if not all the animals belonging to an undertaking are grazed during the determined period. National law should not be read narrowly to mean that only if *all* the animals belonging to an agricultural holding are grazed is the agri-environment commitment of land fully met. Taking into consideration the objectives of EU policy, it is sufficient that land subject to an agri-environment commitment is in good agricultural order and grazed by animals.[38]

In resolving incoherence claims between national and EU law, national judges have justified their reasoning by relying on linguistic, systemic and teleological arguments. The linguistic arguments referring to the ordinary meaning as well as arguments from technical meaning were the first step in the courts' justification patterns. However, systemic arguments as well as justifications supported by references to the general principles and purpose of EC law have been equally prominent.

Linguistic: plain-language meaning of EC law provisions

Thus the courts have often cited relevant EC law provisions as, for example, in judgment 3-07-107 of the Tallinn Appeal Court. The court explained the applicable EU law provision:

38 Case 3-07-1186 of 14 January 2008, Tartu Circuit Court.

> According to Article 28 (1) Regulation 796/2004/EC every on-the-spot check shall be the subject of a control report which makes it possible to review the details of the checks carried out. The report shall indicate in particular: ... [list of conditions]... [Contested] Control report is in accordance with the requirements of Article 28 (1) Regulation 796/2004/EC.[39]

Under other factual circumstances, in a case challenging administrative proceedings by the PRIA in determining eligible land and the amount of assistance, the court overruled the decision of the PRIA on the grounds that administrative actions by the PRIA had violated Article 28 (1) and (2) of Regulation 796/2004/EC and principles of good administration.[40] As in case 3-07-107, the court started with a reference to the plain-language meaning of the EC regulation. In addition to the list of conditions that must be included in the control report provided in Article 28 (1), the regulation in Article 28 (2) provides that 'The farmer shall be given the opportunity to sign the report to attest his presence at the check and to add observations. Where irregularities are found the farmer shall receive a copy of the control report.' The court also stressed that the same principle that the farmer must be informed on the spot is also provided in Article 48 of the same regulation:

> In this case, the complainant received control report on 21.12. 2006, four months after the actual control took place. The inspection report signed on the spot by K. Tikku cannot be regarded as a control report within the meaning of Article 48 para 1 of European Commission Regulation No 796/2004/EC. The report submitted to K. Tikku on the spot for signing was without annexes, meaning without actual control lists. The control lists contain the most relevant information, the results of on-the-spot inspection. In the control report, the actual situation is determined which is then taken as a ground for determining the subsidy.[41]

Similarly,

> In accordance with Article 30 para 2 of Commission Regulation (EC) No 796/2004, the total area of an agricultural parcel may be taken into account provided that it is fully utilized in accordance with the customary standards of the Member State or region concerned. In other cases the area actually utilized shall be taken into account. As on-site inspection found that fields No. 21 and No. 22 are overgrown and abandoned thus not corresponding to the above obligations and therefore according to Article 30 subsection 2 of the Commission Regulation (EC) No 796/2004 are not measured.

39 Case 3-07-107 of 29 May 2007, Tartu Circuit Court.

40 Case 3-07-985 of 13 September 2007, Tartu Administrative Court.

41 Ibid.

Linguistic: Comparing various language versions of the text

In addition to the ordinary and technical meaning of the official EC legal texts in the Estonian language, the courts, in cases of uncertainty, have also relied on comparative assessment of legal texts in other EC official languages. An example is a case related to revocation of a training grant financed through the Structural Fund, where the dispute concerned definition of eligible expenses. The applicant was granted a training grant to undertake a course. Following the end of the financing period, the applicant submitted proof of expenses. The documents submitted indicated that the invoice and bank transfer took place a few months before the actual starting date of the project approved and financed through the training grant. On that ground, the administrative agency considered the documents submitted as ineligible expenses and consequently demanded repayment of the financial transfers received by the applicant from the agency. The applicant disagreed and argued that the system of accounting that the company uses as well as the definition of eligible expenses under Community law allows to take into consideration 'actual expenses' related to the grant. In this context, the court had to determine the meaning of the definition of eligible expenses. In order to understand the meaning of the contested definition, the court compared different official language versions of Community legislation:

> Structural assistance is financial support that the state grants to an individual or an undertaking with the assistance of European Union structural funds. The grant of assistance is regulated both by EU and national legal acts. EU Council Regulation 1260/1999/EC of 21 June 1999 sets general provisions related to structural funds. Article 30 subsection 2 of the above mentioned Regulation in the Estonian language translation is worded as follows 'Kulutused ei ole kõlblikud saama fondidelt toetust, kui lõplik abisaaja on need tegelikult teinud enne abitaotluse komisjoni jõudmise kuupäeva. Kõnealust kuupäeva loetakse kulutuse abikõlblikkuse alguskuupäevaks'.[42] Translations of this provision into other official languages of the Community use constructions like '*Expenditure ... has been paid*', '*Une dépense ... a été effectivement payee*', '*die Zahlung ... tatsächlich geleistet hat*', etc. that refer directly to making payment. In addition, in all translations the word 'actual' refers to the factual date of payment and not to the legal or accounting meaning of expenditure.[43]

Systemic arguments are also often invoked by courts. These include arguments from contextual harmonization, precedent and analogy.

---

42 Expenditure may not be considered eligible for a contribution from the Funds if it has actually been paid by the final beneficiary before the date on which the application for assistance reaches the Commission. That date constitutes the starting-point for the eligibility of expenditure.

43 Case 3-05-2006 of 29 May 2006, Tallinn Circuit Court, para 12.

Systemic: Contextual harmonization of national law provisions with EU law provisions

For example, in judgment 3-05-2006 discussed above, the court, following consideration of the various language versions of the relevant Community law provision, stressed:

> Article 30 subsection 2 of Council Regulation 1260/1999/EC was not applicable in the present case to the issue of the contested administrative act. The above mentioned provision regulates the submission of applications to the European Commission and not to the national implementing agency. The contested procedure at issue was regulated by the national Structural Assistance Act and regulation nr. 154. Nevertheless, it is necessary to take into consideration the argument by the respondent that in development of national norms applicable to the grant of assistance Estonia relied on the same principles as Community acts. Thus, the term 'expenditure' within the meaning of national regulation nr. 154 art. 4 must be interpreted similarly to the one provided under Article 30 subsection 2 of the Regulation 1260/1999/EC.[44]

Systemic: Argument from precedent – reference to ECJ case law and argument to analogy

The ECJ has consistently held that the undertaking can rely on the legitimate expectation in the legality of aid only when the aid was granted in accordance with the procedure laid down in Article 93 EC Treaty (see C-24/95 Alcan Deutschland ECR I-1591, para. 25; recently C-346/03 and C-529/03 Atzeni, not yet published para 64.) The Circuit Court finds, that although in the present case the aid does not constitute state aid in the meaning of Article 93 EC Treaty, a similar duty of care applies to the applicant of training grant in application of Article 4 para 4 of the Regulation nr. 154.

Systemic: Argument from general principles of law

This is well illustrated, *inter alia*, by the judgment of the court of first instance in case 3-07-2155.[45] The court not only cited the jurisprudence of the Supreme Court but, importantly, quoted[46] and reinforced the argument that national procedures for distribution of structural fund subsidies must take into account the general principles of EU law and make sure that the effectiveness of EU law is preserved while applying national procedural law.[47] In support of this argument, the court

44 Ibid., para 12.

45 Case 3-07-2155 of 31 December .2008, Tallinn Administrative Court.

46 Supreme Court of Estonia case 3-3-1-80-06 of 19 December.

47 Case 3-07-2155 of 31 December 2008, Tallinn Administrative Court.

of first level relied on the jurisprudence of the Estonian Supreme Court that thoroughly analysed the requirement to rely on general principles of EC law in national administrative practice.[48]

Kanger (2007), based on assessment of structural funds support cases from 2004 to July 2006, has criticized national lower courts for their lack of self-initiative to analyse substantively the interplay between EU law and general principles and national law and to specifically identify which law applies to what issue. This criticism can be only partly supported by analysis of the 89 decisions of structural fund cases at first instance.

It is correct that a limited number of early (2005–06) cases focused on technical/procedural aspects related to the division of competences between national and EU level and not on substantive provisions of EU law. However, increasingly, national courts provide substantive assessment of EU law provisions and reference to EU law principles. By way of further example is a decision of 11 June 2008 by Tartu Administrative Court. The court, before turning to the specific facts related to the case concerning determination of the eligible parcel for a single area payment for less-favoured land, explained:

> The Supreme Court held in decision 3-3-1-26-07 of 20.06.2007 that to control whether XXX farm meets the established requirements for receipt of support, it is necessary to consider EU legislation, particularly EC Regulation 796/2004 which is directly applicable in Estonia and that provides in Article 8 para 1 that a parcel that contains trees shall be considerate as eligible for support provided that agricultural production can be carried out in a similar way as in parcels without trees in the same area. Additionally the interpretation provided in EC Commission working document AGRI 60363/2005 of 09.03.2005, according to which as a general rule a land parcel with more than 50 trees on one hectare is not eligible for support, should be taken into consideration. Furthermore, the Supreme Court referred to EC Regulation 796/2004, Article 30 para 2, which allows Member States to consider the total area of an agricultural parcel provided that it is fully utilized in accordance with the customary standards of the MS or region concerned. Otherwise the area actually utilized shall be taken into account.
>
> Also in decision 3-3-1-26-07 the Supreme Court concluded that based on national law provisions it is necessary to rely on the Minister of Agriculture Regulation No. 51 from 20.04.2004 Article 3 according to which support may be applied for farmland in good agricultural order, grassland or for land temporarily out of

48 Supreme Court of Estonia case 3-3-1-80-06 decision of 19 December. The Supreme Court by referring to ECJ case law on the principle of good administration, the EU Charter of Fundamental Rights and the European Code of Good Administrative Behaviour concluded that national civil servants although not direct addressees of the European Code of Good Administration must nevertheless take good European administrative practice into account when applying EU law or applying an EU law implementing national provisions.

> agricultural use ... Estonian legislation does not specify the concrete conditions with which a 'parcel in good agricultural condition' must comply.[49]

After analysing the specific facts and expert opinions and considering the above mentioned criteria, Tartu Administrative Court concluded:

> ... for both contested parcels it is not possible to graze animals similarly to parcels not covered by trees ... Both parcels are not in good agricultural condition ... according to local agricultural custom ... both parcels are mostly covered by trees with coverage of over 60% and in some places reaching 90%, which according to European Commission working document AGRI 60363/2005 must not exceed 50 trees per hectare ... Experts consider that neither of the parcels can be considered in total as eligible for support ... and the size of the eligible parcel must thus be determined on the basis of the actual area utilized.

Although in its concluding part the court does not specifically refer to the provisions of the EU Regulation, it is rather clear from the wording and the reasoning of the court that assessment of the factual circumstances was conducted with due consideration of EU law. Considering the structure and the logic of the opinion, it was not necessary to repeat references to EU law provisions in every part of the decision.

Similarly, the court of second instance considering an analogous case explained:

> The decision, whether XXX met the requirements established for the recipients of the support, must be based on Article 8 p. 1 of European Commission Regulation No 796/2004, taking into account respective interpretations provided in the 9 March 2005 European Commission Working Document AGRI 60363/2005, as well as based on Article 30 p. 2 second sentence of Regulation No 796/2004, that provides that for the purpose of the subsidy the actually utilized area must be considered. In addition it is necessary to rely on the obligations of the Minister of Agriculture 20th April 2004, the requirements of Regulation No 51, that at the time of submission of application and factual control of the land was in force.[50]

Another example is a Tallinn Administrative Court case from 6 November 2009 concerning Regulation of the Minister of Agriculture No. 44 excluding small and medium-size enterprises (SMEs) from the pool of eligible beneficiaries for technology investment subsidy. In this case, the court of first instance analysed the compatibility of national rules with EC Regulation 1628/2006 and the principle of equal treatment:

> In itself it is correct that EC Regulation 1628/2006 article 1 para 2 does not exclude SMEs from the scope of application of this Regulation in the agricultural

---

49 3-07-2216; similarly see 3-07-2211.

50 3-07-2216.

> sector. It is also correct that in various legal acts support for SMEs through structural funds is considered important. It is also necessary to agree that to leave agricultural sector SMEs out of technological investment subsidies would be in breach of the principle of equal treatment and general principles following from the EC Regulation. However, in the present case SMEs are not left without technological investment subsidies. Investment technology subsidies are supported by Ministry of Agriculture Regulation No. 31 of 10 April 2008 … that applies only to SMEs. [the court then quotes the number of funds distributed to SMEs based on Regulation No. 31 and the amount of funds distributed to large enterprises based on Regulation No. 44]. Thereby, in the given cases the principle of equal treatment is not violated. The complainant does not have a subjective right to request subsidy simultaneously from multiple funds – the obligation to unconditionally support all activities from one measure does not follow from EC Regulation 1628/2006. According to the Structural Funds Act Article 13 para 4, within the conditions related to the specific measure it is possible to stipulate a specific activity, region, eligible pool of applicants or part of the budget.[51]

Teleological/evaluative: Argument from substantive reason

Teleological-evaluative justifications based on arguments from substantive reasons played a central role in structural funds cases. The governing idea in this type of argument is that the specific purpose or goal of the policy is fundamentally important. Thus, the contested statute must be interpreted favouring achievement of this specific purpose. In structural funds cases, the courts have considered the purpose and aims of EC structural funds regulations as fundamentally important goals that national administrative agencies must advance in applying EC law. National law must be compatible with and secure the aims of EC regulations (see Table 6.4).

Surplus Stock

The most vividly discussed and publicly visible cases related to EU law were the surplus stock fee cases (surplus stock).[52] The surplus stock cases emerged as a result of transitional measures adopted by the European Union to avoid disruption

---

51 3-09-814 of 6 November 2009, Tallinn Administrative Court.

52 In May 2005, the European Commission found that the Estonian Republic must be fined €46 million for 91,464 tons of excess sugar stocks at the time of accession. Commission Regulation (EC) No 832/2005 of 31 May 2005 on the determination of surplus quantities of sugar, isoglucose and fructose for the Czech Republic, Estonia, Cyprus, Latvia, Lithuania, Hungary, Malta, Poland, Slovenia and Slovakia. According to the EC Commission, as of May 2005, Estonia had 91,464, Cyprus 40,213, Latvia 10,589, Malta 2,452 and Slovakia 10,225 tonnes of surplus sugar stocks.

Table 6.4 Structural fund cases – summary and conclusions

Coherence Dimension	
Substantive	Incoherence – specific national norm/general EU norm Incoherence – national practice/national and EU principles of good administration Incoherence between national norm and EU norm Incoherencies resolved through (1) principle of harmonious (consistent) interpretation and (2) reference to general principles and purpose of EU law.
Institutional	Preliminary reference was requested in case *JK Otsa Talu*
Argumentative	Types of arguments: *(a) Linguistic: plain language meaning of EU law provisions* *(b) Linguistic: comparing various language versions of the text* *(c) Systemic: contextual harmonization of national law provisions with EU law provisions* *(d) Systemic: argument from precedent – reference to ECJ case law* *(e) Systemic: argument from analogy* *(f) Teleological/evaluative: argument from substantive reaso*n

of the market following accession of new MSs.[53] Based on obligations flowing from EU Regulation 1972/2003/EC and other sector-specific EU regulations, in April 2004 Estonia adopted the Surplus Stock Charges Act (2004 Surplus Act).[54] The 2004 Surplus Act established conditions and procedures for determining and

53 EC Regulation 1972/2003 (general regulation) and EC Regulation No 60/2004 (specific to the sugar sector) 'The objective which the Commission was pursuing by means of the charge at issue was not solely to prevent the build-up of stocks of the products at issue for speculative purposes arising from trade, but quite simply to prevent the build-up of surplus stocks, that is to say, stocks which were not part of the usual reserves found in the new Member States.' Case T-257/04 The agricultural situation in the new Member States was radically different from that in the old Member States since, before enlargement of the European Union in 2004, those two categories of traders were subject to different rules, quotas and production support mechanisms. Moreover, although the Community institutions could prevent the build-up of surplus stocks within the Community by methods specific to the common organization of agricultural markets, they could not prevent the build-up of surplus stocks in the territory of the future Member States. It is for that reason that Annex IV, Chapter 4, paragraphs 1 to 4, to the abovementioned Act of Accession imposed an obligation on the new Member States to eliminate their surplus stocks at their own expense without imposing a parallel obligation on the old Member States. Since the agricultural situation in the new Member States was different from that in the old Member States, no discrimination could result from the mere application of different rules to traders in the new Member States, on the one hand, and to traders in the old Member States, on the other (see paras 128–30, 199–200).

54 Üleliigse Laovaru Tasu Seadus.

imposing charges on companies for excess stocks of selected products. Accordingly, national handlers of agricultural products should have submitted a declaration on the amount of agricultural stocks to the Ministry of Agriculture.[55] Then, the Ministry of Agriculture by decision determined the amount of surplus stock and the Estonian Tax and Customs Board, based on the procedure established by the Taxation Act, administered enforcement of the Ministry of Agriculture decision.[56]

Therefore, following the procedure established in the 2004 Surplus Act, the Ministry of Agriculture determined the amount of the surplus stock of agricultural products for each individual company.[57] As a result, companies holding surplus stock of agricultural products received a tax notice indicating the amount of the surplus stock charge. The Estonian Tax and Customs Board issued tax notices in the total amount of 549 million Estonian kroons (~€35.3 million).[58] The applicants brought proceedings against the decision of the Ministry of Agriculture and tax notice to the administrative courts. The total amount of tax notices contested in the courts by 31 companies was 407 million kroons (~€26.2 million).[59] This triggered not only public attention but also resulted in litigation by the companies represented by the best commercial law offices (see Table 6.5).

Table 6.5 Surplus stock cases – legal framework

Issue: Surplus Stock Charge for excess amounts of agricultural products		
	EU level	National level
Rule	Reg. 1972/2003 Reg. 60/2004	Constitution of the Republic of Estonia Constitutional Amendment Act Surplus Stock Act
Administrative agency	Ministry of Agriculture Estonian Tax and Customs Board	
Application (main problems)	• the legal basis of the procedure for determination of surplus stocks • method for determining surplus stocks (mathematical coefficient)	

55 Article 10 para 1 of the Surplus Act.

56 Article 15 para 1 of the Surplus Act.

57 Article 6 (2) of EC Regulation No 60/2004 provides that quantities of sugar exceeding the quantity considered as being normal carry-over stock at 1 May 2004 have to be eliminated from the market at the expense of the MS.

58 Only 35 million kroons, that is, less than 10 per cent of the total amount have been paid by 70 national companies. The largest enterprises, the total debt of which was determined as 514 million kroons refused to pay and contested tax notices and procedure for determination of the surplus stock fees in courts. Information available (in Estonian) online at the European Union Information Centre's website http://elik.nlib.ee/?id=7268&showSearch=1 (last accessed 01 November 2011).

59 European Union Information Centre.

The factual and legal background of the surplus stock cases is complex and developed in multiple stages. Below is a short overview of how litigation in national courts developed in the period between 2004 and 2010.

The Surplus Act was passed for the implementation of Commission Regulations No 1972/2003/EC (on transitional measures to be adopted in respect of trade in agricultural products) and No 60/2004/EC (establishing transitional measures in the sugar sector).

According to Article 6 (1) of the Surplus Act, carryover stock is the stock of agricultural products in the possession of a handler on 1 May 2004. The amount of carryover stock is calculated as the average of stocks available as of 1 May of the four preceding years, to be multiplied by 1.2. Carryover stock is used for calculating overstock, which is subject to charge.

Pursuant to the procedure established by the 2004 Surplus Act, the Ministry of Agriculture determined the amount of surplus stocks of handlers. Based on the decision of the Ministry of Agriculture, the Estonian Tax and Customs Board issued tax notices ordering the applicants to pay additional tax on their surplus stock.[60]

The applicants (national companies) challenged two administrative decisions: (1) decisions of the Ministry of Agriculture and (2) ETB tax notices in national courts requesting annulment of the tax notices and suspension of application of Articles 6 para 1, 6 para 2, and 10 para 2 of the 2004 Surplus Act. The applicants, *inter alia*, argued that the provisions of the Surplus Act were contrary to EC Regulations 1972/2003 and 60/2004 and the Estonian Constitution.[61]

National lower courts (see, for example, the decisions of the Tallinn Administrative Court 3-2562/2004 and 3-2587/2004) dismissed the applications of the traders and upheld decisions of the contested administrative agencies. The procedure for determination of the surplus stock charge, including the coefficient of 1.2, was considered by national lower courts to be in accordance with EU law.

The Supreme Court of Estonia in case 3-3-1-74-05 of 25 April 2006 for the first time discussed the procedural issues related to surplus stocks. The Supreme Court addressed the issue of stay of proceedings and procedure for requesting a preliminary reference from the European Courts. The Supreme Court upheld the decision of the Tallinn Circuit Court[62] annulling the decision of the Tallinn Administrative Court granting a stay of proceedings in the pending case until the decision of the CFI in a Polish case challenging the validity of the 1972/2003/EC Regulation.

The Administrative Law Chamber of the Supreme Court upheld the ruling of the Circuit Court, but significantly amended the reasoning. After discussing the legal nature of the EU regulation, the Supreme Court nevertheless stated that under certain circumstances, such as in the cases of the 2004 Surplus Act, a review of the national act adopted to enforce certain regulations is necessary. It is a duty

60 Article 15 para 1 of the Surplus Act.

61 For discussion, see for example, Lõhmus 2007 (in Estonian); Ginter 2007.

62 3-04-414 of 2 May 2006, Tallinn Circuit Court.

of the national court in the event of any doubt to check whether national law complies with the regulation. If the national court has doubts on the validity of the EU regulation, it must stay the proceedings and request a preliminary reference. Provided that another Member State has already contested the validity of the same EU regulation, the national court has a right to stay the proceedings until the ruling of the European Court, or to submit a request for a preliminary reference. Stay of proceedings in cases of a pending case in the European Court must not be automatic and in itself it is not sufficient ground to stay proceedings in national courts. The national court has a duty to explain and give reasons why it believes that the validity of EU law should be contested. The Supreme Court further explained under what circumstances and how national courts should submit a preliminary reference to the European Courts. The Supreme Court concluded that instead of stay of proceedings on the basis of the complaint for annulment submitted by Poland in a given case, the national court should have submitted directly a preliminary reference to the European Court.

The Supreme Court in case 3-3-1-33-06 of 5 October 2006 annulled the judgments of the lower courts, and satisfied the appeal of the traders to suspend application of Articles 6 (1), 7 and 10 (1) of the 2004 Surplus Act due to conflict with EU law. The Supreme Court found that the method of determination of surplus stock, specifically the coefficient 1.2, established in Article 6 (1) is not in conformity with Regulation 1972/2003/EC. The national rule does not directly follow from EU regulation, it is formulated overly rigidly, not allowing to sufficiently take into account special circumstances of individual traders and it is not proportionate to the aims to be achieved by Regulation 1972/2003/EC. The Estonian legislator should have adopted a more flexible and nuanced method for determining surplus stock and the relevant charges. Relying on the principle of *acte clair*, the Supreme Court did not submit a request for a preliminary reference.

Following the Supreme Court judgment in 3-3-1-33-06, the question emerged of the impact of the Supreme Court judgment in the specific case on other similar surplus stock pending cases in the lower courts. The lower courts adopted divergent practices. In some decisions of the Tallinn Administrative Court, for example, case 3-04-403 of 6 October 2006, the court, relying on the Supreme Court judgment, satisfied the claim of the applicant. Some companies referring to the 3-3-1-33-06 submitted appeals to the Circuit Courts, for example, an appeal submitted on 23 October 2006 by Svensky Kaubanduse AS in case 3-04-415. *Svensky Kaubanduse AS* in addition to the arguments presented in the court of first level relied on the Supreme Court decision to argue that determination of surplus stock based on the 1.2 coefficient is contrary to EU law.

In some cases, see for example, *Svensky Kaubanduse AS* 3-04-415, the Ministry of Agriculture and ETB, relying on the Supreme Court position, partly annulled the decision and tax notice determining surplus stock on the basis of the 2004 Surplus Act. The Circuit Court on the basis of the ETB application suspended court proceedings in the part related to the tax notice.

On 25 January 2007, the Parliament adopted amendments to the 2004 Surplus Act that entered into force on 16 February 2007 (2007 Surplus Act). The Parliament left Articles 6 (1) and 6 (2) of the 2004 Surplus Act unchanged. However, in the 2007 Surplus Act a new provision, Article 6 (3), was added and Articles 10 (2) and 23 (2) amended to provide a more flexible method and grounds for determining specific circumstances relevant for determination of surplus stock. In accordance with the Supreme Court reasoning in 3-3-1-33-06, the amendments adopted by the Parliament in the 2007 Surplus Act had a retroactive effect if applying 2007 amendments was to the benefit of the trader. However, a more preferential method of determining surplus stock could be applied retroactively only to traders that had challenged determination of surplus stock in the courts and in relation to whom until 5 October 2006 a final decision of the court had not entered into force.

In accordance with the 2007 Surplus Act, the Ministry of Agriculture again determined surplus stock and the ETB issued tax notices. The 2007 administrative decisions of the Ministry of Agriculture amending the 2004 decisions and tax notices on the basis of the 2007 Surplus Act have created substantial confusion. It was not clear what are the legal effects of the 2004 decisions and tax notices. The Ministry of Agriculture formally did not annul the 2004 decisions but adopted amendments. As some companies later litigated in the courts, this created situations where some companies effectively had two tax notices in two different amounts for the same surplus stock of agricultural products.

The 2007 decisions of the Ministry of Agriculture and tax notices created a new round of litigation in the national courts. In some instances, the legal proceedings challenging the 2004 decision and tax notice were still pending on appeal while companies submitted to the courts of first instance new legal complaints challenging the 2007 administrative decisions. In parallel, in some cases (for example, 3-07-881 of Tallinn Administrative Court), one of the parties requested a stay of proceedings in the pending case until decisions in similar cases by the ECJ in the *Balbiino* case.[63] This created a very complex legal situation when similar cases have been adjudicated by various courts at various court levels.

Tallinn Administrative Court in the *Balbiino* case by decision of 28 November 2007 decided to stay the proceedings and refer for the first time questions related to determination of surplus stock to the ECJ.[64] The court asked, *inter alia*, whether the national system of determination of surplus stock based on the 2007 Surplus Act, including the coefficient 1.2, is in accordance with EU law; and whether imposing surplus stock on the company that in practice had not obtained a real advantage in terms of price difference from marketing surplus stock after 1 May 2004 is in accordance with the aims of the EU regulation.

63 C-560/07 Balbiino AS v Põllumajandusminister and Maksu- ja Tolliameti Põhja maksu- ja tollikeskus [2009] ECR I-I-04447.

64 Tallinn Administrative Court submitted six well-formulated questions regarding the method of determining the amount of surplus stock and the charge imposed.

On 11 December 2007, the ECJ Grand Chamber adopted its decision in case C-161/06 *Skoma-Lux sro v Celní ředitelství Olomouc*[65] where the ECJ found that under certain conditions a EU regulation which is not published in the language of a MS is unenforceable against individuals in that state. The findings of the *Skoma Lux* judgment impacted national adjudication. Parties in pending cases in the national courts with reference to the *Skoma Lux* judgment argued that the Surplus Stock Act should be unenforceable against individual companies because on 1 May 2004 relevant EU legislation was not fully translated into the Estonian language.[66] This issue was taken up by national courts in a number of judgments in 2008–10.

The Supreme Court in cases 3-3-1-86-07 *AS Maag Piimatööstus* and 3-3-1-87-07 *OÜ Altromax Grupp* at length discussed the implications of the *Skoma-Lux* judgment on adjudication in Estonian courts.[67] The court was of the opinion that the regulation had not been properly published at the time of submission of the declarations serving as the basis for determination of surplus stock. Thus, the regulation could not have given rise to the individual obligation of the company to pay a charge. On this ground, the Supreme Court annulled the judgments of the lower courts and satisfied the claim of the applicant. Therefore, the *Skoma-Lux* judgment was a turning-point in the adjudication of the Estonian courts. It played a central role in Supreme Court reasoning and was instrumental for satisfying the claims of the applicant.

Shortly before the Supreme Court judgments applying the *Skoma-Lux* reasoning, Tallinn Administrative Court in case 3-07-845, *Rakvere Lihakombinaat AS*, stayed the proceedings and on 19 March 2008 submitted a reference to the ECJ.[68] In both the *Balbiino* and *Rakvere Lihakombinaat* cases the applicants attempted to rely on the *Skoma-Lux* reasoning, claiming that Regulations 1972/2003/EC and

65 C-161/06 Skoma-Lux sro v Celní ředitelství Olomouc [2007] ECR I-10841.

66 See for example, 3-05-617 AS Maag Piimatööstus.

67 3-3-1-86-07 of 7 May 2008 AS Maag Piimatööstus, paras 45–50; 3-3-1-87-07 of 7 May 2008 OÜ Altromax Grupp, paras 41–4.

68 C-140/08 Rakvere Lihakombinaat AS v Põllumajandusministeerium and Maksu- ja Tolliameti Ida maksu- ja tollikeskus [2009] ECR I-10533. The court asked, *inter alia*, the following questions: '(1) Does Article 4(1) and (2) of [Regulation No 1972/2003] preclude the ascertainment of the amount of [the] operator's surplus stock by automatically deducting … (… as transitional stock) the operator's average stock as at 1 May of the four years of activity preceding 1 May 2004, multiplied by 1.2? (2) If the answer is in the affirmative, would the answer be different if in determining the amount of the transitional stock and [the] surplus stock it were possible also to take into account the growth of the operator's production, processing or sales volume, the maturation period of the agricultural product, the time when the stocks were built up, and other circumstances independent of the operator? (3) Is it compatible with the objective of [Regulation No 1972/2003] to levy the surplus stock charge where the operator is found to have a surplus stock as at 1 May 2004 but the operator shows that he has not obtained a real advantage in terms of a price difference from marketing the surplus stock after 1 May 2004?'

60/2004/EC cannot be enforced against them in so far as, at the date of accession of Estonia to the Union, these regulations had not yet been published in Estonian in the Official Journal of the European Union.

After a long institutional history of adjudicating on the surplus stock cases in national courts, finally on 4 June 2009 the ECJ rendered a long-awaited decision in the *Balbiino* case. In reply to six questions submitted by the Tallinn Administrative Court, the ECJ found that the national system regulating determination of surplus stock is not contrary to EU law. This means that the national measure for determination of surplus stock based on the coefficient 1.2 is not *per se* in violation of EU law obligations. This is a notably different position from the one adopted earlier by the Estonian Supreme Court in case 3-3-1-33-06. In relation to the *Skoma-Lux* official language argument, the ECJ adopted a more refined approach, stating that

> ... the rule stated in Skoma-Lux does not preclude the enforcement against individuals of those of the provisions of Regulations Nos 1972/2003 and 60/2004 which were taken up in the ULTS [Surplus Act]. That rule might nevertheless remain of residual application if certain provisions of those regulations which were not implemented by the ÜLTS were relied on by the Estonian authorities against individuals before the official publication of the regulations in Estonian. As the Advocate General observes in point 40 of his Opinion, it will be for the national court, if necessary, to interpret the ULTS in order to ascertain whether such circumstances exist.[69]

Thus the ECJ pointed out that non-availability of the regulation in the Estonian language cannot be considered an 'automatic' ground for precluding enforcement of obligations flowing from the regulation against individuals.

In parallel to national litigation on surplus stock charges, Estonia challenged EU Regulation 832/2005 that determined the amount of surplus stock of sugar for new MSs, including Estonia. Estonia argued that it is contrary to EU law to include in the total amount of surplus stock of sugar (for Estonia 91,464 tons) those stocks held by households (42,732 tons). The Court of First Instance in its judgment of 2 October 2009 did not satisfy Estonia's claim to annul Regulation 832/2005.[70] The judgment of the CFI is currently being appealed by Estonia in the ECJ.[71]

---

69 Balbiino AS v Põllumajandusminister and Maksu- ja Tolliameti Põhja maksu- ja tollikeskus [2009] ECR I-I-04447, para 32.

70 T-324/05 Republic of Estonia v Commission of the European Communities [2009] ECR II-03681.

71 C-535/09 P: Appeal brought on 18 December 2009 by the Republic of Estonia against the judgment delivered on 2 October 2009 in Case T-324/05 Republic of Estonia v European Commission [pending].

The second surplus stock case, *Rakvere Lihakombinaat*, was decided by the ECJ on 29 October 2009.[72] In line with *Balbiino* reasoning, the ECJ stated in relation to the national methodology for determining surplus stock that the 1.2 coefficient does not undermine the objectives pursued by Regulation 1972/2003 and does not infringe the principles of proportionality and equal treatment. In relation to the language argument, the ECJ with reference to *Skoma-Lux* and *Balbiino* explained that the provisions of the regulation that were taken up in national legislation are enforceable against individuals even if the regulation itself has not been published in the Official Journal of the EU in the Estonian language. Only those provisions that have not been implemented by national legislation and that have not been published in the Official Journal of the EU cannot be relied on by national authorities to create obligations for individuals. It is for the national court to verify whether and to what extent national law took over the EU provisions at issue.

As a result of the reasoning and explanations provided by the ECJ in the *Balbiino* and *Rakvere Lihakombinaat* cases, Tallin Administrative Court on 13 November 2009 adopted an unusual 'collective' decision on all surplus stock cases pending before it. Specifically in relation to the language requirement, the court determined that the surplus stock charge cannot be imposed on 22 companies. In the opinion of the Tallinn Administrative Court, unavailability of the translation into Estonian language of the provisions of the regulation relevant for determination of the surplus renders the obligation to pay surplus stock charge unenforceable again individuals.[73]

The surplus stock saga, however, did not stop with the judgment of the Tallinn Administrative Court. In the opinion of the Tallinn Circuit Court in the *Pimix* case delivered on 29 January 2010, the obligation to pay surplus stock charge is enforceable against individuals. Following analysis on availability of the relevant provisions of EU law in the Estonian language, contrary to the court of the first level, the appeal court found that the applicant had an opportunity to learn about the requirements of the regulation in the Estonian language.[74]

National courts of all levels including the Supreme Court[75] as well as the ECJ have adjudicated cases related to surplus stocks. Arguments by the parities and

72 Case C-140/08 Rakvere Lihakombinaat AS v Põllumajandusministeerium and Maksu- ja Tolliameti Ida maksu- ja tollikeskus [2009] ECR I-10533, paras 59–62, 64.

73 See press release of 13 November 2009 of European Union Information Center at the Estonian National Library available at http://elik.nlib.ee/?id=7250&lightStr=laovaru (last accessed on 1 October 2011). This judgment unfortunately is not publicly available in the full text.

74 See press release of 2 Feburary 2010 of the European Union Information Center at the Estonian National Library available at http://elik.nlib.ee/?id=7482&lightStr=laovaru (last accessed on 1 October 2011). This judgment unfortunately is not publicly available in the full text.

75 The Supreme Court adjudicated ten surplus stock fee-related cases Case 3-3-1-86-07 of 07 April 2008 (AS Maag Piimatööstus); 3-3-1-87-07 of 07 April 2008 (Altromax

reasoning by the courts are well developed and elaborate. Judgments include a full range of legal arguments (linguistic, systemic, teleological and transcategorical) and techniques, and rely on a wide range of legal materials.

For example, one of the first judgments of the Tallinn Administrative Court (court of the first instance) from 28 December 2005 is 16 pages long.[76] In this case, the applicant developed nine lines of complex cumulative arguments arguing why the provisions of the Surplus Act should be inapplicable.[77] Likewise, the Ministry of Agriculture presented a strongly augmented position on why the application by the company must be dismissed and surplus stock charge paid in the full amount. In this sense, surplus stock cases are a blueprint for national adjudication involving EU law disputes. This includes the application of EU main legal principles and understanding of the legal meaning of EU law in the national context, as well as development of procedural rules regulating stay of proceedings and request for a preliminary reference.

In essence, companies refused to pay surplus stock charges claiming that (1) the legal basis, (2) procedure for determination of surplus stock, and (3) method for calculation of the charge is contrary to both constitutional and EU law. For example, in one of the first cases,[78] the applicant challenging the legal basis and national rules for determination of the amount of surplus stock, specifically in relation to EU law argued that:

1. it is within the competence of the national courts to set aside application of EU regulations if they are contrary to the provisions of the Constitution;
2. EU Regulation 1972/2003/EC does not impose an obligation on individual companies but rather on MSs. Thus, it is MSs that must carry the burden of the financial penalty imposed by the EU;

Grupp OÜ); 3-3-1-88-07 of 07 April 2008 (Svensky Kaubanduse AS); 3-3-1-85-07 of 07 April 2008 (OÜ Aiva Baltic); 3-3-1-49-07 of 13 November 2007 (Contimer OÜ); 3-3-1-68-07 of 13 November 2007 (Priva Shipping Company OÜ); 3-3-1-33-06 of 05 October 2006 (X AS) and 3-3-1-74-05 of 25 April 2006 (X OÜ).

76 3-2562/2004. The applicant was fined for surplus stocks of rice in the amount of 393 964 kroons (~€25,259). The applicant relied on nine legal grounds in challenging the directive of the Ministry of Agriculture. The court of first level did not satisfy the claim and left the amount of the tax notice unchanged. See also decision of the Tallinn Administrative court in case 3-2587/2004; see also judgments of the Tallinn Administrative Court 3-04-415; 3-05-272 of 14 June 2006.

77 See for example, 3-2562/2004 where the applicant argued that the Surplus Act violated constitutional provisions (Articles, 23, 29, 31, 32 and Article 123); general principles of law (principles of legitimate expectations, legal certainty, proportionality); EU law provisions (Accession Treaty between Estonia and the European Union, Regulations 1972/2003 and 60/2004) and aims (protection of competition at the internal market). Similarly 3-05-272 of 14 June 2006.

78 3-2562/2004.

3. the 2004 Surplus Stock Act by imposing a financial penalty on individual companies violates Constitutional principles and the aims of the EU Regulation 1972/2003/EC.

The applicant relied on linguistic arguments (references to national law); systemic arguments (place of the EU Regulation in the national legal system; general principles of national and EU law) and teleological arguments (aims of the EU Regulation 1972/2003/EC).

The Ministry of Agriculture argued that based on Article 249 TEC (now 288 TFEU), Regulation 1972/2003/EC has general application, is binding in its entirety and directly applicable in all MSs including Estonia. The 2004 Surplus Act by establishing conditions and procedures for determining surplus stock is not contrary to national law or EU law. Applicants should have been aware that following accession to the European Union, surplus stocks of agricultural products would be subject to the charge in accordance with the law. The fact that the applicant was not able to make a profit on resale of surplus stock is not decisive.

The Tallinn Administrative Court, in addressing the arguments of the parties, started with detailed explanations of the competences of national courts and the principle of supremacy in application of EU law:

> Although European Commission Regulation 1972/2003/EC is applicable to the present administrative dispute, the court lacks competence to suspend application of EU regulations due to conflict with national Constitution. The Code of Administrative Procedure allows suspension of application of only national acts and not of EU legal acts contrary to the Constitution. Also in accordance with the EU supremacy principle the court lacks competence to set aside application of the European Commission regulation due to possible conflict with the Estonian Constitution.[79]

The court further elaborated on the principle of supremacy of EU law flowing from the Constitutional Amendment Act adopted by public referendum and the *Van Gend en Loos* judgment of the ECJ. Next, relying on Article 10 TEC (now 10 TFEU), Article 249 TEC (now 288 TFEU), and the ECJ 33/76 *Rewe* judgment,[80] the court explained the direct effect of the EU regulation. Together, the principles of supremacy and direct effect demand that national courts apply the provisions of the EU regulation even if national law is contrary to EU regulation:

> In accordance with the EU principle of supremacy and direct effect of the Regulation all obligations following from the Regulation are applicable to the

79 3-2562/2004 of 28 December 2005, Judge Tiina Pappel, Tallinn Administrative Court.

80 33/76 Rewe-Zentralfinanz eG and Rewe-Zentral AG v Landwirtschaftskammer für das Saarland ECR [1976] ECR 1979.

> applicant even if the provisions of the Surplus Act for some reasons are not applicable. In a situation when there is a conflict between the Regulation and the Surplus Act, national courts following from EU law supremacy and direct effect, must apply the provisions of the Regulation or apply the provisions of the Surplus Act in accordance with the purpose and aims of the Regulation. Therefore, in the opinion of the court the central question in this administrative dispute is whether the provisions of the Surplus Act are in accordance with the Regulation, and not whether the Surplus Act is contrary to the Constitution.[81]

Next, the court provided a detailed analysis of compliance of the Surplus Act with the Constitution. Finally, the court analysed whether Article 4 of the Surplus Act is contrary to the aims of EU Regulation 1972/2003/EC. The court, referring to the preamble to EU Regulation 1972/2003/EC and analysing the effects on the price of rice following accession to the EU, concluded that 'determination of the surplus stock charge as provided in Article 4 of the 2004 Surplus Act is in accordance with the aim of the Regulation to impose a charge in order to avoid surplus stock and it is proportionate in order to achieve this aim.' The court specifically pointed out that the procedure for determination of the amount of surplus stock including the mathematical coefficient of 1.2 is reasonable and in accordance with the law. Thus, the court did not satisfy the claim of the applicant and left the decision of the Ministry of Agriculture unchanged.

Similarly, in the cases decided by Tallinn Administrative Court on 12 January 2006, the applicant, a producer of syrups, challenged the decision of the Ministry of Agriculture and tax notice of the TCB. The applicant challenged mainly the procedure for determination of surplus stock.[82] The applicant, *inter alia*, argued that the national regulation should be flexible in order to take into account also planned expansion of production after 1 May 2004. After elaborate analysis of the plain language of the regulation, as well as the aims of the regulation, the court concluded that planned expansion of the production cannot be taken as a ground for determining the amount of surplus stock. The court dismissed the application.

Notably, courts of first instance in the 2005–06 decisions did not consider submitting a preliminary reference to the ECJ, although those cases challenged the understanding and application of EU regulations. National courts seemed to be reasonably confident that elaborate analysis of EU law based on complex interpretation methods, including linguistic, systemic and teleological, is sufficiently clear to conclude that national law, the 2004 Surplus Act, is not contrary to EU law or principles.[83]

---

81 3-2562/2004 of 28 December 2005, Judge Tiina Pappel, Tallinn Administrative Court.

82 3-2587/2004 of 12 January 2006, Judge Tiina Pappel, Tallinn Administrative Court.

83 See criticism in Ginter 2007, on reluctance of national courts to submit a request for preliminary reference.

New developments in the national courts practice occurred when Poland brought an action before the court of first instance for annulment of Regulation 1972/2003/EC.[84] On the request of a trader holding surplus stocks, Tallinn Administrative Court in May 2005, granted stay of proceeding in adjudication of the pending national chase until a decision in the Polish complaint in the CFI. The Code of Administrate Procedure included a provision allowing stay of proceeding if judgment is pending in the European Courts. Tallinn Administrative Court relied by analogy on the national procedural rule allowing stay of proceedings until judgment in another case that may be relevant for adjudication of the present dispute. The Estonian Tax and Customs Board (TCB) supported by the Ministry of Agriculture successfully challenged the ruling of the Tallinn Administrative Court on stay of proceedings in the Tallinn Circuit Court (court of second instance) arguing that if the national court had doubts as to the validity of the regulation it should have submitted a reference for a preliminary ruling.[85] The Circuit Court annulled the ruling on stay of proceedings by the court of first instance. The trader appealed the decision of the Circuit Court further through cassation complaint to the Supreme Court. This resulted in the first 'surplus stock' case adjudicated by the Supreme Court.[86]

The Administrative Law Chamber of the Supreme Court upheld the ruling of the Circuit Court, but significantly amended the reasoning. After discussing the legal nature of the EU regulation, the Supreme Court nevertheless stated that under certain circumstances, as in the cases of the 2004 Surplus Act, review of the national act adopted to enforce certain regulations is necessary. It is a duty of the national court in the event of any doubt to check whether national law complies with the regulation. If the national court has doubts on the validity of the EU regulation, it must stay the proceedings and request a preliminary ruling. Provided that another MS has already contested the validity of the same EU regulation, the national court has a right to stay the proceedings until the ruling of the European Court or submit a request for a preliminary ruling. Stay of proceedings in cases of a pending case in the European Court must not be automatic and in itself it is not a sufficient ground to stay the proceedings in national courts. The national court has a duty to explain and give reasons why it believes that the validity of Community law should be contested. The Supreme Court further explained under what circumstances and how national courts should submit a preliminary reference to the European Courts. The Supreme Court concluded that instead of stay of proceedings on the basis of the complaint for annulment submitted by Poland

84 Case T-257/04 [2009] ECR II-01545 as subsequently appealed to the European Court of Justice in Case C-335/09 P.

85 3-04-414 of 2 May 2006, Tallinn Circuit Court.

86 3-3-1-74-05 of 25 April 2006; for discussion of this case specifically related to the competences of national courts and submission of the preliminary reference see Part II of the book.

in a given case, the national court should have submitted directly a preliminary reference to the European Court.

The Supreme Court decision 3-3-1-74-05 of 25 April 2006 was an important ruling in terms of procedural rules regulating adjudication of surplus stock cases. However, this case did not address in detail the substantive law issues related to determination of surplus stock and the methodology for calculating the charge. The central judgment of the Supreme Court that had significant impact on adjudication of surplus stock cases in the national lower courts was Estonian Supreme Court decision 3-3-1-33-06 of 05 October 2006. In this case, contrary to the cases in the lower courts discussed above, the Supreme Court satisfied the appeal of the company. The court suspended application of Article 6 (1) of the 2004 Surplus Stock Act due to conflict with European Union law. Specifically, the Supreme Court found that the method of determination of surplus stock provided in Article 6 (1) of the 2004 Surplus Stock Act does not directly follow from the EU Regulation. Moreover Article 6 (1) of the 2004 Surplus Stock Act does not sufficiently meet the violated principle of proportionality (see Table 6.6).

Table 6.6 Surplus stock charge – summary and conclusions

Coherence Dimension	
Substantive	SINC 1 – conflict between national norms and EU norm SINC 2 – conflict between specific national norm and general EU norm SINC 3 – conflict between specific national norm and general EU policy objectives Incoherencies resolved through: (1) principle of harmonious (consistent) interpretation, (2) reference to general principles and purpose of EU law, and (3) principle of direct effect of Regulations
Institutional	Preliminary reference was requested in the cases of *Balbiino* and *Rakvere Lihakombinaat AS*
Argumentative	Types of argument: *(g) Linguistic: ordinary meaning of EC law provisions* *(h) Systemic: argument from precedent (ECJ jurisprudence)* *(i) Systemic: logical conceptual (relying on general principles of law)* *(j) Teleological/evaluative: argument from substantive reasons*

Pension Rights of Third-country Nationals

In contrast to 'economic' cases related to structural funds and surplus stock litigated with representation by commercial lawyers, the two groups of 'citizenship' cases analysed below – pension rights and residence permit cases – are usually litigated by concerned individuals themselves. As a starting-point of analysis, it must also be noted that the role of EU law in 'citizenship' cases is markedly different. The EU has significantly less competencies in social fields while the margin of discretion left to MSs is broad.

The incomplete nature of EC law and wide discretion accorded to national law, *per se*, make arguments in the 'citizenship' cases based on EC law weaker that in 'economic cases'. This, however, does not suggest that EC law is void of legal significance. Although textual arguments may be not available, systemic and teleological interpretation of national law in the context of EC law objectives and principles may provide a new or more stringent standard of review of national law. However, this requires active national courts willing to develop and rely on complex methods of interpretation.

The series of pension cases challenges national provisions on eligibility to the old-age state pension. The applicants contested decisions of the Pension Department that suspended pension payments. Meeting all requirements established by law, including work experience in Estonia for more than 15 years, the applicants were granted an Estonian old-age pension for life. However, a few months later, the Estonian authorities stopped payment of old-age pension to the applicants on the ground that they were already receiving a military pension from the Russian Federation. This situation resulted in 60 court cases in Estonia[87] and three collective action complaints to the European Court of Human Rights.[88] The situation currently affects over 2,000 individuals. [89]

The Estonian state authorities argue that retired servicemen can receive old-age pension benefits in Estonia only if they renounce their right to a military-service occupational pension from the Russian Federation. The applicants disagree and claim that they legally reside in Estonia; they have paid compulsory contributions to the Estonian welfare system, meet the age and employment qualifying criteria and thus must be entitled to old age benefits from the state. The fact that they receive an occupational pension from the Russian Federation for their military service (the years that are not covered by the Estonian state pension) cannot be a legitimate ground to exclude their entitlement to old-age benefits in Estonia (see Table 6.7).

87 For a list of cases of administrative (courts of first instance) and circuit courts (second instance), see Annex 2. The Supreme Court of Estonia also addressed the issue in three judgments, 3-3-1-31-08 of 13 June 2008 (*Poolus* case); 3-3-1-32-08 of 13 June 2008 (*Malkov* case) and 3-3-1-1-08 of 28 April 2008 (*Kiris* case).

88 Tarkoev and others v. Estonia (application 14480/08) and Minin and others v. Estonia (application 47916/08) judgment of 4 November 2010.

89 Although the number of cases in the courts of first and second instance is substantial (60), the cases follow the same line of reasoning (if not provided otherwise) and are largely identical both in the arguments of the parties and justifications of the courts. A large number of cases were prepared by the lawyers of one NGO. The analysis below refers to the 'Applicant' as meaning applicants in all 60 cases; 'Pension Department' as meaning all pensions departments and 'Court' as all courts of first and second instance that considered the case.

Table 6.7 Position of the parties to litigation on the issue of entitlement to old-age pension benefits

Estonian state	Applicants	Current Situation
Must choose one pension!	**Can have two pensions!**	**Only one pension!**
(1) Pension for military service paid from RF budget	(1) Pension for military service paid from RF budget	(1) Pension for military service paid from RF budget.
OR	AND	
(2) Pension for civil service paid from EST budget	(1) Pension for civil service paid from EST budget	Estonia does not pay pension for years of civil service in Estonia

The applicants argued that the decision of the Pension Department to terminate and revoke old-age pension payments is unlawful and not grounded because it violates, *inter alia*, the principle of equality protected by the Constitution, EU law and international treaties (see Table 6.8).[90]

In relation to EU law,[91] the applicants relied on EU Directive 2000/43/EC (Race Equality Directive)[92] to argue that denial of an old-age pension constitutes

Table 6.8 Pension rights of third-country nationals – legal framework

Issue: Prohibition of discrimination based on ethnic origin		
	EU level	National level
Rule	EU Directive 2000/43/EC	Article 5 of the 1994 Agreement between the Russian Federation and the Estonian Republic on Matters Related to Social Guarantees for Military Pensioners of the Russian Federation on the Territory of the Republic of Estonia
Administrative Agency	Ministry of Social Affairs Pension Departments	
Application (main problems)	• understanding the scope of application of the Race Equality Directive • principles of indirect discrimination, unreasonable restrictions and proportionality within the meaning of the Race Equality Directive	

90 For detailed discussion, see Evas 2009 and Evas 2012.

91 The arguments of the parties based on the Constitution and international treaties will not be treated here in detail.

92 Council Directive 2000/43/EC of 29 June 2000 implementing the principle of equal treatment between persons irrespective of racial or ethnic origin.

discrimination and unequal treatment within the meaning of the Race Directive.[93] First, the applicants citied the provisions of the Race Equality Directive defining the principle of direct and indirect discrimination:

> Also this situation is contrary to European Union Directive 2000/43/EC. According to the EU anti discrimination directive a) direct discrimination shall be taken to occur where one person is treated less favourably than another is, has been or would be treated in a comparable situation on grounds of racial or ethnic origin; b) indirect discrimination shall be taken to occur where an apparently neutral provision, criterion or practice would put persons of a racial or ethnic origin at a particular disadvantage compared with other persons, unless that provision, criterion or practice is objectively justified by a legitimate aim and the means of achieving that aim are appropriate and necessary.[94]

The applicant then continued by defining the relevant group of differentiated treatment and argued for the reverse burden of proof:

> … except Russian military pensioners all other foreign country military pensioners have a right to receive at the same time Estonian pension and military pension of another state. The applicant finds that consequently Russian Federation military pensioners are treated less favourably than other foreign military pensioners in the same type of situation. Because equally foreign country military pensioners as well as Russian Federation military pensioners have paid taxes to the Estonian Republic, Russian Federation military pensioners are discriminated against. In accordance with Article 8 (1) of the Race Equality Directive when a person who considers herself wronged because the principle of equal treatment has not been applied to her establishes, before a court or other competent authority, facts from which it may be presumed that there has been direct or indirect discrimination, it shall be for the respondent to prove that there has been no breach of the principle of equal treatment.[95]

In a similar case, the applicant further developed the argument on the reverse burden of proof:

> Estonia should have transposed Directive 2000/43/EC by 1 May 2004 … According to the EU general principle, if a EU MS does not fully or incorrectly

93 Contrary to Section 12.1 of the Estonian Constitution, Article 2.2 of the UN Covenant of Economic, Social and Cultural rights, Article E of the Revised European Social Charter and Directive 2000/43/EC.

94 3-06-1506 of 24 April 2007, Tallinn Administrative Court.

95 Ibid.; similarly see for example, 3-06-1511 of 16 March 2007, Tallinn Administrative Court; 3-06-1516 of 4 May 2007, Tallinn Administrative Court; 3-06-1518 of 9 March 2007, Tallinn Administrative Court.

> transposes a directive on time, individuals can nevertheless rely on the provisions of the directive by submitting a complaint to the national court. Indirect effect of the directive in this situation requires that national courts should interpret national law as much as possible in accordance with the principles of the directive. Accordingly the applicant requests in considering his complaint to apply Article 8 of Directive 2000/43/EC Tartu Pension Department must prove that foreign military pensioners (except the Russian Federation) do not have a right to receive at the same time a pension from Estonia and a military pension from another MS. The Social Protection Department confirms that they [other foreign countries' military pensioners] have this right. Therefore, the Social Protection Department confirms the fact of discrimination.[96]

If the applicants referred to the Race Equality Directive in every case, then the Pension Department in submitting counter-arguments only in a few cases addressed the issue of application of the Race Equality Directive to the dispute. For instance, in the Tartu Circuit Court, the Pension Department somewhat strangely argued:

> Article 8 of EU Directive 2000/43/EC is not relevant because it deals with the Employment Guidelines 2000 agreed by the European Council meeting in Helsinki on 10.12.1999 and 11.12.1999 that stress the need to foster conditions for a socially inclusive labour market by formulating a coherent set of policies aimed at combating discrimination against groups such as ethnic minorities.[97]

It is striking that the Pension Department apparently confused Article 8 of EU Directive 2000/43/EC imposing a reverse burden of proof in discrimination cases with paragraph 8 of the Preamble to the Race Equality Directive. It is somewhat puzzling how, after arguments presented by the applicants in the court of first level in relation to the reverse burden of proof, the Pension Department, in the case at appeal level, presented a flawed argument based on an incorrect understanding of the concept of reverse burden of proof and the relevant Race Equality Directive provision. The Tartu Circuit Court, however, in its reasoning did not mention this flaw in the argumentation of the Pension Department.[98]

The courts dismissed the arguments of the applicants based on the Race Equality Directive. In a judgment by the Tallinn Administrative Court, the court explained:

> The applicant considers that he is subject to racial or ethnic discrimination because according to his claim other foreign armies' military pensioners are treated in Estonia differently than military pensioners of the Russian Federation. According to Article 1 of EU Directive 2000/43/EC the purpose of the directive is

96 3-06-1759 of 13 March 2007, Tartu Administrative Court.

97 3-06-1925 of 12 June 2007, Tartu Circuit Court.

98 Ibid.

> to lay down a framework for combating discrimination on the grounds of racial or ethnic origin, with a view to putting into effect in the Member States the principle of equal treatment. With that even if payment of pensions to other foreign countries' military pensioners would be regulated differently than in Article 5 of the bilateral Treaty concluded by the Estonian Republic, one cannot suggest from that, that unequal treatment based on ethnic or racial origin takes place.[99]

Unfortunately, the court did not deliver a more detailed or in-depth reasoning why it had concluded that the applicants *prima facie* do not fall within the scope of the Race Equality Directive. Considering that it is uncontested that the applicants challenging the pension decisions are of Russian ethnicity, thus clearly belonging to the Russian ethnic minority group residing in Estonia, it would be a welcome step if the court would elaborate on the concept of ethnic origin, which is not defined in the Race Equality Directive. Lack of definition of 'ethnic origin' in the Race Equality Directive is one of the solid grounds of criticism of application of the Directive in the MSs:[100]

> Ethnicity is an even more complex term to define. In UK law, the House of Lords identified two essential conditions for the existence of an ethnic group: first, a long shared history as a separate group and secondly a cultural tradition including family and social customs. Other features indicative of ethnicity are a common geographical origin, common language, literature or religion, and being a separate group within a larger community. (Chalmers, Davies and Monti 2010)

The scope of Directive 2000/43/EC combating discrimination on the grounds of race and ethnic belonging is broader than the scope of Directive 2000/78/EC combating discrimination based on the grounds of religion or belief, disability, age, or sexual orientation.[101] Thus, contrary to Article 3.3 of Directive 2000/78/EC that specifically excludes from the scope of application of the Framework Employment Directive 'payments of any kind made by state schemes or similar, including state social security or social protection schemes'. Article 3.1 of the Race Directive provides that this directive applies to 'all persons, as regards

---

99 3-06-1506 of 24 April 2007, Tallinn Administrative Court.

100 See for example, Guild 2000.

101 Council Directive 2000/78/EC of 27 November 2000 establishing a general framework for equal treatment in employment and occupation (Framework Employment Directive). According to Article 1 'The purpose of this Directive is to lay down a general framework for combating discrimination on the grounds of religion or belief, disability, age or sexual orientation as regards employment and occupation, with a view to putting into effect in the Member States the principle of equal treatment.' Specifically, recital 13 provides that 'This Directive does not apply to social security and social protection schemes whose benefits are not treated as income within the meaning given to that term for the purpose of applying Article 141 of the EC Treaty, nor to any kind of payment by the State aimed at providing access to employment or maintaining employment.'

both the public and private sectors, including public bodies, in relation to ... (c) employment and working conditions, including dismissals and pay ... (e) social protection, including social security and healthcare'. Thus, the scope of the Race Directive is significantly broader than the scope of the Framework Equality Directive and includes not only prohibition of discrimination in 'pay' related to employment but also importantly prohibits discrimination in social protection, including social security and healthcare.

In another judgment by the Tartu Administrative Court in reply to the arguments by the applicants on the provisions of the Race Equality Directive, the court, although rejecting the applicants' claims, developed another line of argument to the Tallinn Administrative Court:

> The Court acknowledges that non calculation of years worked in Estonia and non payment of Estonian old-age pension without the obligation to renounce a military pension from the Russian Federation may seem unjust, but this fact cannot be a ground for satisfaction of the applicants' claim. For comparison, the court refers to Article 196 (5) of the Military Service Act. According to this provision if an individual has a right to more than one type of pension provided by law he must choose one pension type. Thus, even Estonian military servicemen cannot receive double pension (old-age and military at the same time) even if they meet all the requirements. This means that also for individuals defending the Estonian Republic a part of the years worked may be lost. Based on that the court finds that XXX's right to receive pension is not violated, because in any case he is guaranteed a minimum pension and through that income not less than income of other pensioners residing in Estonia.

Thus, in contrast to other foreign army military pensioners, the judgment of the Tartu Administrative Court takes as a comparative group Estonian military servicemen retirees in Estonia.

Regrettably, the national courts in the context of pension cases did not discuss in detail the notions of direct and indirect discrimination, nor did they address the issue of the reverse burden of proof in discrimination cases explicitly highlighted by the applicants. The procedure of the reverse burden of proof is still largely unknown to the Estonian courts.

In contrast to the full range of arguments put forward by the courts in surplus stock cases, the argumentative patterns in pension cases are poor. Courts neither rely on the jurisprudence of other foreign courts or European courts nor attempt to interpret the current dispute in the light of the purpose and aims of the Race Equality Directive. The courts did not consider any statistical evidence available on the differences in the amount of pension payments between ethnic groups that may be indicative of indirect discrimination. The courts also did not discuss in detail the wider legal background of the pension cases and the fact that Estonia is the only former USSR country that denies the right of former Soviet retirees to two pensions. In all other countries, including Latvia, it was possible to find a reasonable political compromise for granting two pensions (Evas 2009). All in all, although the national court did not have a strict obligation to submit a reference to the ECJ, nevertheless the guidance of the ECJ on interpretation of the scope of Directive 2000/43/EC would have been a welcome step.

The applicants, unconvinced by the conclusion of the Estonian courts, submitted three collective complaints to the European Court of Human Rights in 2008. The complaints include three main arguments: first, the applicants argue that denial of a pension amounts to deprivation of possession in violation of Article 1 of Protocol 1 to the ECHR; secondly, Russian military pensioners are the only exception to the general rule on pension entitlements and thus this differentiated treatment amounts to discrimination, and finally, the applicants argue that the national courts lacked impartiality and undertook the role of the defendant's lawyer. The European Court of Human Right in its judgment of 4 November 2010 found no violation of the principle of discrimination in conjunction with the right to property protected under Protocol 1 to the ECHR (see Table 6.9).[102]

Residence Rights of Third-country Nationals

The EC Long-Term Residence Directive (2003/109/EC) also triggered intensive national case law, 48 cases, in courts of first and second instance. The complex and contested citizenship and migration policy adopted by Estonia in the 1990s[103]

Table 6.9 Pension, discrimination cases – summary and conclusions

Coherence Dimension	
Substantive	Conflict between national norms and EU norm Incoherence is not addressed by the court through EU law analysis
Institutional	Preliminary reference was not requested
Argumentative	Types of argument: *(a) Linguistic: ordinary meaning of EC law provisions* *(b) Linguistic: technical meaning*

102 Tarkoev and others v. Estonia (application no. 14480/08) and Minin and others v. Estonia (application no. 47916/08) judgment of 4 November 2010.

103 As of 2 October 2010, the total number of registered population of Estonia: 1,364,076; the number of Estonian citizens: 1,149,303, in addition, 61,574 Estonian citizens live abroad. The number of residents of undetermined citizenship: 97,718; the number of residents with the citizenship of another state: 117,055 (of these 95,271 citizens of the Russian Federation, 5,019 Ukrainian citizens, 3,525 Finnish citizens, 2,159 Latvian citizens, 1,667 Lithuanian citizens, 1,438 Byelorussian citizens). Source: Ministry of the Interior, Population Register, available at http://estonia.eu/about-estonia/society/citizenship.html.

resulted in a large number of administrative cases on the right of residence and citizenship. Conventionally, applicants contesting a decision of the Citizenship and Migration Board relied, in addition to the provisions of national law and constitutional principles, on the provisions of international treaties: most often, on Article 8 of the European Convention on Human Rights, protection of the right to respect for private and family life. After accession to the European Union and entry into force of the Long-Term Residence Directive (LTR Directive), the EU Family Reunification Directive (2003/86/EC) and the Race Directive (2000/43/EC), the applicants attempted to invoke arguments based on EU law provisions.

Before discussing the details of these national legal disputes, it is also relevant briefly to reflect on the scope of present European Union law regulating the status of long-term residents and the rights attached to it. The European Council's 1999 Tampere summit called for a 'more vigorous integration policy'. As a result, a number of recommendations and directives have been adopted, including the LTR Directive.[104] However, this newly adopted EU law does not contain a complete set of standards and rules. It defines general objectives that aim to diminish the gap between rights and protection of third-country nationals and nationals of the European Union. However, the language of rights and entitlements included in the LTR Directive is formulated modestly. Often the provisions of the LTR Directive do not enjoy direct effect because they are not precise and unconditional. Therefore, EU directives in the field of citizenship entitlement for non-nationals is considerably different in its legal scope and nature than, for example, in the 'economic cases' of surplus stock and structural funds discussed above.

In the series of third-country national cases litigated in the national courts, the applicants asked the court to interpret conditions and restrictions on the right to obtain long-term resident status narrowly while giving full effect to the objectives of the LTR Directive. The controversy emerged over a national law condition that provides that an individual applying for a long-term resident status must be not absent from the territory of the state for longer than ten months in a five-year period (the ten months rule). Estonian law, *expressis verbis*, does not provide an exception to the ten months rule. The ten months rule is also a standard included in the LTR Directive. However, the LTR Directive allows, but does not oblige (!), MSs to take into consideration reasonable grounds that may justify exceptions to the ten months rule.

The ten months national rule allowing for no exceptions was challenged in the courts. The applicants fulfilled all eligibility criteria for long-term resident status established by national law.[105] However, due to their professional activities,

---

104 The Long-Term Residence Directive (LTR Directive) entered into force on 23 January 2006. The directive provides the EC right to a long-term residence permit for a third-country national. This right is granted to a third-country national who is residing on the territory of the MS for at least five years.

105 They have all presented documentary proof that their employment requires extensive travel. Therefore, their absence in total longer than ten months is conditioned by

they had failed to meet the requirement of less than ten months absence.[106] On this ground, their applications for long-term status were rejected. The applicants appealed the decisions through the pre-judicial administrative procedure and then in the national courts. The main argument of the applicants was that absence from the state due to employment obligations must be a legitimate exception to the general ten months rule (see Table 6.10).

Table 6.10 Long-term residence status – legal framework

Issue: Long-term residence directive – exceptions allowed in determination of acceptable periods of absence		
	EU level	National level
Rule	Article 4 (3) Long-term Residence Directive 2003/109/EC	Article 14 Aliens Act (Välismaalaste seadus)
Administrative Agency	Citizenship and Migration Board	
Application (main problem)	Incoherence between national provisions and the objectives of the Long-term Residence Directive	

The applicants argued that refusal to grant long-term residence status violates the requirements of Estonian legislation as well as the aims of the LTR Directive.[107] First, the applicants argued that the national implementing legislation, the Aliens Act, must be interpreted in the light of the purpose of the LTR Directive.

Section 6 of the Preamble to the LTR Directive reads:

> The main criterion for acquiring the status of long-term resident should be the duration of residence in the territory of a Member State. Residence should be both legal and continuous in order to show that the person has put down roots in the country. Provision should be made for a degree of flexibility so that account can be taken of circumstances in which a person might have to leave the territory on a temporary basis.

their professional activities. Equally, it was not contested that all applicants have resided legally on the territory of Estonia, that they have legal income and have a stable and permanent connection to the Estonian state.

106 See for example, cases 3-07-1417 and 3-08-614 where applicants had been employed as seaman.

107 See for example, para 14.

On the basis of the Preamble to the LTR Directive, which calls for a degree of flexibility in determining circumstances that justify temporary absence from the territory of the state, the applicants attempted to develop a contextual-harmonization argument: national law allowing no exceptions to the ten months rules must be read in the context of the purpose and aims of the LTR Directive.

Secondly, the applicants claimed that the directive allows exceptions to the general ten months rule. The general rule on determination of duration of residence is established in Article 4 (1) of the LTR Directive. This is five years of continuous and uninterrupted residency in a MS. Article 4 (3) states that periods of absence shorter than six consecutive months and not exceeding in total ten months within five years do not interrupt the eligible period and must be taken into account. However, in the second paragraph of Article 4 (3), the directive also provides in that in case of specific or exceptional reasons of a temporary nature and in accordance with their national law, MSs may accept that a longer period of absence does not interrupt the five-year period. The applicants argued that their absence from the territory of the state falls within the scope of specific reasons of a temporary nature.

Next, the applicants presented arguments why in their opinion a stay abroad for employment-related duties must be considered as an exceptional reason within the meaning of the second paragraph of Article 4 (3). The applicants claimed that they are well integrated and have permanent residence in Estonia. The only reason for their stay abroad longer than ten months is their professional activity:

> The applicant has been forced to stay abroad for work and the work is his only source of income, so that he cannot refuse the job. In the given situation, the right of the Applicant to pursue the profession of a seaman depends on whether CMB will take into account his specific situation and allow him to obtain long-term resident status, or prevents the appellant from receiving a long-term residence permit and seriously restricts the right to receive long term-resident status in the state where he was born and lived all his life.[108]

Further, the applicants argued that the provision of national law that allows no exceptions to the ten months general rule violates the principle of proportionality:

> The applicant has resided permanently and legally in Estonia for the past 15 years, and he finds that his right to obtain a permanent residence permit may not be restricted only because as a result of the activities of a state body the Aliens Act does not provide a possibility to take into consideration specific or exceptional circumstances in deciding on long term residence status. The Aliens Act provides that granting a long-term residence permit is conditioned on legal residence on the basis of a temporary residence permit under stable and growing presence in the country over the last five years. However, the applicant believes

108 3-07-1417 of 29 May 2008, para 16.

> that residence in Estonia should be assessed on an individual basis and the provisions of the Aliens Act must be extended to take into account the provisions of the Directive. Based on general principles of law in application of the Aliens Act it is necessary to accept that absence from the state for longer that 10 months due to work related obligations shall not interrupt the five-year period. There is no public interest consideration that would preclude the applicant's request for long-term resident status and refusal of a permit may lead to disproportionate consequences.[109]

Furthermore, the applicant relied on the case law of the Supreme Court that imposes an obligation on national authorities to harmonize national law with EC law and apply to the extent possible the principle of conforming interpretation:[110]

> Based on the principle of direct effect, foreigners have acquired the right to directly refer to the provisions of the Directive as if it were a local law. This right follows from ECJ case law. The fact that the Parliament did not timely and properly align the Aliens Act with the Directive does not give a right to the CMB not to review the applicant's application in accordance with Directive 2003/109/EC that has already entered into force. Given the fact that the requirements of the Directive are mandatory and the Estonian Supreme Court have confirmed the principle of primacy of EU law, the applicant submits that he is entitled to a permanent residence permit in Estonia.[111]

The CMB did not agree with the applicants. The CMB pointed out that according to national law that is in accordance with the directive, the applicant must permanently reside on the territory of the state at least for five years and his period of absence in total must not exceed ten months. Permanent residence as a central criterion in determination of a residence permit was also confirmed in the decision of the Tallinn Circuit Court in case 3-06-2058.[112] According to national law, the CMB has a right to reject an application for long-term residence status if one of the eligibility criteria is not met. The applicant failed to meet the ten months criterion.[113] The provisions of national law do not violate the provisions of the directive:

> The directive requires that EU member states, including Estonia, implement the principles of the Directive though their own rules. Unlike European Union regulations, which are directly applicable in all Member States after their entry into force and create direct rights and obligations to citizens, the Directive is not directly applicable and in principle requires implementation into national

109 Ibid., para 18.

110 3-3-1-29-06 of 11 April 2006, Supreme Court Constitutional Review Chamber.

111 3-07-1417 of 29 May 2008, para 19.

112 Ibid., paras 20–23.

113 Ibid., paras 24–5.

> law. MSs are left with decision making discretion on how to regulate principles established in a Directive or the Directive establishes general principles from which EU MSs base their national legislation. CMB considers it is important to note that directives are binding only as to the results to be achieved, and MSs can determine the means, forms and methods for harmonizing national law and implementing the directive; for that reason the directive as a rule does not provide additional rights or obligations to individuals. Thus, the Directive is not directly applicable, and thus the Directive does not provide rights and obligations to the Applicant; the conditions for obtaining a residence permit are set in national law applicable to foreigners. National law unequivocally states that a person must, immediately prior to requesting a residence permit, have resided in Estonia permanently for five years.[114]

The CMB further points out that in accordance with the interpretation of the appeal court in case 3-06-2058, Article 4 (3) of the directive does not have direct effect, because it leaves MSs a discretion to decide whether to provide exceptions to a general rule. Based on the above, the CMB argued that an obligation does not follow from the directive to include in the length of residence absence of the applicant from the state for work-related duties.

The courts of first and second instance in general agreed with the position of the CMB and rejected both the reading of national law in the light of the purpose of the directive and the proportionality arguments.

After restating the provisions of national law regulating the conditions and eligibility for a long-term residence permit, the court recalled Article 249 of the EC Treaty (now 288 TFEU). Additionally, the court pointed out that, according to Article 26 of the directive, the MSs are the addressees of the directive, not individuals. The Court then restated the provisions of Articles 4 (1) and 4 (3) of the directive.

Supporting the argument of the CMB, the court stated that 4 (3) does not have direct effect. This provision leaves discretion to a MS and therefore national law, so that rejection of the applicant's application is not contrary to the directive.[115] Rejection of the application on the same grounds was also considered as legitimate and not contrary to EC law by the appeal court, for example, in decision 3-06-2510. Residence cases have not been discussed by the Supreme Court.

Whilst it is correct that Article 4 (3) of the LTR Directive gives exclusive discretion to MSs on whether to allow an extension to the ten months rule and this provision of the directive has no direct effect, it is difficult to understand why national courts do not take up the proportionality argument. Even if the ten month rule is in compliance with the LTR Directive Article 4 (3), the 'legitimate aim' and 'proportionality' tests of the national provision allowing no exception to the ten months rule is expected both under national law and EU law principles.

114 Ibid., para 26.

115 Ibid., paras 33, 35.

The main criterion of the LTR Directive, according to section 6 of the Preamble, is length of residence. Although it is a matter of discretion for MSs, it is difficult to believe that absence from the territory of Estonia for employment reasons indicates a loss of attachment of the individual to the state. Interpreting national law narrowly, it is possible that a person who has lived for twenty years in a country but has a profession requiring frequent travel – for example, a seaman – may never have a right to long-term resident status. Thus, although a restriction under national law that does not allow to take into consideration the personal circumstances of the applicant in determining the length of residence is a matter of discretion for the MS and not in violation of Article 4 (3) of the LTR Directive, it is doubtful whether such a strict requirement providing for no exception is proportionate in accordance with the aim of the LTR Directive.

The restrictions imposed by national law on the right to receive a residence permit do not restrict the applicant's right to freely choose a profession or the possibility to work abroad, nor does it leave the applicant without a legal basis for residence in Estonia. The applicants have legally valid temporary residence permits in Estonia that they can prolong and they have a right to apply for a permanent residence permit if they meet all the necessary conditions.[116]

In contrast to the law regulating entitlement to long-term residence of third-country nationals discussed above, national law regulating eligibility for long-term residence status of EU citizens explicitly provides that prolonged absence from the territory of Estonia due to work-related duties, that is, not longer that one consecutive year, does not interrupt the five-year period.[117] The new Aliens Act that entered into force on 1 October 2010 also provides for a more flexible regulation.[118] Thus, according to Article 233 (3), if a third-country national before going abroad registers their intended absence from the country with the CMB or the Police and Border Guard authority, then this period of absence will be considered as founded. However, the five-year period obligation will be extended by the amount of months spent abroad (see Table 6.11).

Other Estonian Cases

Late payments in commercial transactions

Notably, among the four county courts, only Harju County Court has relied on Article 3 (1) Directive 2000/35 to stress MSs' obligation to ensure the legal right for a claim to penalty interest due for late payments. Case 2-06-29923 involved a dispute between two commercial companies over the basis for calculating penalty

116 Ibid., paras 36, 37.

117 Euroopa Liidu kodaniku seadus (EU Citizens Act), Article 5 (2) 2).

118 Välismaalaste seadus (Aliens Act) RT I 2010, 3, 4, adopted on 9 December 2009, entered into force on 1 October 2010.

Table 6.11 Residence rights of third-country nationals – summary and conclusions

Coherence Dimension	
Substantive	SINC 1 – conflict between national norms and EU norm Incoherence is not addressed by the court through EU law analysis
Institutional	Preliminary reference was not requested
Argumentative	Types of argument: *(c) Linguistic: ordinary meaning of EC law provisions* *(d) Linguistic: technical meaning*

interest due for late payment. The applicant claimed that penalty interest must be calculated on the basis of the interest rate included in the invoice (0.2 per cent per day) whereas the defendant claimed that interest payment must be calculated on the basis of Article 3 (1) d of Directive 2000/35.[119] The court dismissed the positions of the applicant and the defendant. In relation to the applicant's claim, the court found that the unilateral inclusion of an interest rate in an invoice cannot be considered a provision mutually agreed by the parties and therefore cannot be used for calculating the amount of the interest rate. The court also dismissed the claim of the defendant to base calculation of the interest rate on Article 3 of the 2000/35 Directive on the basis of inapplicability of the directive at the time of the dispute. Thus, the directive was not applied to the facts of the case.

In cases 2-05-1962, 2-06-28366 and 2-06-29923 involving disputes over payment of contractual obligations plus interest rate due for late payment in case of breach of contractual obligations, the parties did not rely directly on the 2000/35 Directive. The court on its own initiative in justifying the right of the applicant to claim penalty interest due for late payment relied, in addition to the provisions of the Law on Obligations Articles 94 and 113 (1), on Article 3 (c) (ii) of Directive 2000/35, and stated that MSs must ensure that a creditor is entitled to interest for late payment to the extent that he has not received the amount due on time, unless the debtor is not responsible for the delay.[120]

In case 2-06-3291, the defendant relied on Article 3 (3) to claim that an interest rate for late payment in the amount of 36.5 per cent yearly provided in the contract is grossly unfair to the debtor.[121] The court dismissed the argument by the

119 Differences approx. ten times.

120 In both cases, the penalty rate was high. In case 2-06-2836, the applicant claimed debt payment in the amount of 81,216,40 EEK and a penalty payment in the amount of 80,000 EEK.

121 According to Article 3 (1) (d) of the directive 'the level of interest for late payment ("the statutory rate"), which the debtor is obliged to pay shall be the sum of the interest rate applied by the European Central Bank to its most recent main refinancing operation carried

defendant. The court stated that the defendant pointed to Directive 2000/35/EC but did not show on what grounds determination of the interest rate for late payment is grossly unfair.

All in all, cases in national courts involving penalties for breach of contractual obligations are common. These cases as a common rule are adjudicated solely on the basis of Article 94 (1) and Article 113 (1) of the Law on Obligations. In this context, it is interesting, for example, why the court on its own initiative in cases 2-05-1962, 2-06-28366 and 2-06-29923 referred to the provisions of Directive 2000/35/EC to strengthen its argumentation strategy for the conclusion reached on the basis of the provisions of national law.

Intellectual property

The second category of cases involves disputes related to intellectual property rights. The intellectual property cases, two adjudicated by Harju County Court and one by Tartu County Court, involved the provisions of Directive 89/104 and Regulation 40/94. In case 2-04-71, the applicant relied on ECJ jurisprudence, Directive 89/104 and Regulation 40/94 to claim that in interpreting an obligation of clear distinction of business name, EU law regulating trade mark registration should be applied by analogy. The defendant disagreed. The court did not refer to EU law but found that the facts of the case indicate that the disputed business name is in fact in breach of the obligation of clear distinction provided in the Commercial Code. The court supported its conclusion by the expert opinion of senior experts of the trade mark expertise department of the Patent Office.

Article 7 (2) of Directive 89/104 was also relied on in case 2-04-474. The case was referred back to Harju County Court for adjudication by the Civil Chamber of the Supreme Court. The Supreme Court in its judgment of 3-2-1-4-06 explained in detail how the County Court should interpret Article 7 (2) of Directive 89/104/EC *vis-à-vis* the more limited provisions of Article 16 (3) of the Trade Marks Act:

> Since the Republic of Estonia is a member of the EU in trade mark disputes and interpretation and application of national law it is necessary to take into consideration also EU norms protecting intellectual property rights. More specifically the rights of the trademark owner are regulated by Council Directive 89/104/EEC of 21 December 1988 to approximate the laws of the Member States relating to trade marks. Article 5 provides exclusive rights of the registered trade mark proprietor. Restrictions to this exclusive rights are provided in Articles 6

---

out before the first calendar day of the half-year in question ("the reference rate"), plus at least seven percentage points ("the margin"), unless otherwise specified in the contract. For a Member State which is not participating in the third stage of economic and monetary union, the reference rate referred to above shall be the equivalent rate set by its national central bank. In both cases, the reference rate in force on the first calendar day of the half-year in question shall apply for the following six months.'

> and 7 of the Directive. Article 7 regulates the principle of exhaustion of rights conferred by a trade mark. According to Article 7 (2) principle of exhaustion of rights does not apply where there exist legitimate reasons for the proprietor to oppose further commercialization of the good, especially where the condition of the goods is changed or impaired after they have been put on the market. In addition to Directive 89/104/EEC the protection of rights of the trademark owner also follows from Directive 2004/48/EC of the European Parliament and of the Council of 29 April 2004 on the enforcement of intellectual property rights. According to Article 3 (1) MSs shall provide for the measures, procedures and remedies necessary to ensure the enforcement of the intellectual property rights. Misleading advertising is regulated by the Council Directive 84/450/EEC of 10 September 1984 relating to the approximation of the laws, regulations and administrative provisions of the Member States concerning misleading advertising.[122]

Therefore the Harju County Court was faced with the task of applying the interpretation of the Supreme Court to the facts of the case. Following the judgment of the Supreme Court, the defendant in the County Court litigation nevertheless argued that Article 7 (2) of Directive 89/104/EC is not horizontally applicable. Thus, an individual cannot rely on the provisions of the directive *vis-à-vis* another individual. However, the County Court followed the Supreme Court interpretation and, in reply to the arguments of the defendant, stated that the fact that the directive does not have direct effect does not imply that the court must not interpret provision 16(3) of the Trade Marks Act in the light of the provisions of the Directive. In accordance with Article 7 (2) of Directive 89/104/EC the proprietor of a trade mark may have additional grounds for prohibition of commercial use of goods protected by trade mark than provided in Article 16 (3) of the Trade Marks Act. The ECJ in the Dior case interpreting Article 7 (2) of the Directive defined the concept of 'legitimate reasons' broadly.[123]

In case 2-05-21745 involving a dispute over grounds for refusal of registration of a trade mark, the defendant extensively relied on the provisions of Regulation 40/94 as well as CFI and ECJ jurisprudence. The applicant tried to dismiss the EU law provisions and jurisprudence as not relevant to the facts of the case. The court disagreed with this submission by the applicant and stated that it is groundless to claim that judgments of the ECJ should be ignored. The general principle of legal uniformity follows from Article 142a of the Regulation.[124] According to the opinion of the court, it is also grounded to follow positions included in ECJ

122 3-2-1-4-06.

123 C-337/97 Parfums Christian Dior SA and Parfums Christian Dior BV v Evora BV. [1997] ECR I-6013. On interpretation of Article 7(2) and the concept of 'legitimate reasons' see also for example, C-558/08 Portakabin Ltd and Portakabin BV v Primakabin BV. [2010] ECR I-0000.

124 The text of the judgment does not include the number of the regulation.

judgments because the court cannot render a judgment that is contrary to general principles of EU law. The decision of the County Court was appealed by the applicant to the Regional Court; however, the Regional Court upheld the decision and reasoning of the County Court.

Insolvency

The category of cases involving insolvency proceedings was mostly adjudicated by the Viru County Court. The cases referred to Article 3 (1) of Regulation 1346/2000 as a ground for initiation of insolvency proceedings.[125] The cases did not involve substantive discussion of the regulation. The only case that referred to Regulation 1346/2000 in the text of the judgment was a dispute over the state of insolvency of a commercial entity where one of the members of the board was an individual whose main place of residence was in Finland. The court stated that the legal consequences of the judgment on opening insolvency proceedings rendered by an Estonian court have extraterritorial reach. The court explained that in insolvency proceedings initiated within the meaning of Regulation 1346/2000 then judgment on opening, carrying out and closing insolvency proceedings is automatically recognized in all EU MSs and its legal consequences reach all MSs.

125 Article 3(1) of the Regulation 1346/2000: 'The courts of the Member State within the territory of which the centre of a debtor's main interests is situated shall have jurisdiction to open insolvency proceedings. In the case of a company or legal person, the place of the registered office shall be presumed to be the centre of its main interests in the absence of proof to the contrary.'

Chapter 7

Jurisprudence of Latvian Courts

Tax and VAT cases

The largest group of 'economic' cases that emerged in Latvia concerns reimbursement of input value-added tax (VAT).[1] Harmonization of national legislation and practice with the Sixth Council Directive 77/388/EEC[2] and then Directive 2006/112/EC[3] triggered a substantial amount of litigation in national courts.[4] Two main groups of legal situations contested in national courts related to EU law provisions include (1) VAT deductibility in relation to alleged VAT fraud scheme cases and (2) VAT deductibility (VAT refund) in relation to taxable supplies (services or goods) situations.

VAT deductibility in relation to alleged VAT fraud scheme cases

In numerous cases of alleged VAT fraud schemes, the applicants were required to pay additional VAT and fines for overclaiming the amount of input VAT. After conducting an audit, the Latvian tax office (SRS) took the view that certain sales and purchases by the applicant were based on unduly signed contracts and invoices, devoid of economic substance and thus did not constitute eligible activity for the

---

1 Latvian administrative courts traditionally deal with a large number of tax-related disputes. In such disputes, taxpayers appeal decisions of the Latvian tax authorities. Latvia has not established specifically designed courts for hearing tax disputes. As a result, tax cases are settled by administrative courts.

2 Sixth Council Directive of 17 May 1977 on the harmonization of the laws of the Member States relating to turnover taxes – Common system of value added tax: uniform basis of assessment (77/388/EEC) (Sixth Directive).

3 Since 1 January 2007, the Sixth Directive was transformed into Council directive 2006/112/EC of 28 November 2006 on the common system of value added tax (VAT directive).

4 See for example, cases of the Administrative Regional Court AA43-0023-06, AA43-0079-08, AA43-0205-06, AA43-0292-08, A42-0112-06, A42-0112-06, A42-0237-07, A42-0237-07, A42-0 602-06, A42-0631-08, A42-0672-08, A42-0712-06, A42-0742-08, A42-4349-08, A42-4349-08, A42-6466-08, AA43-0023-06, AA43-0039-07, AA43-0079-08, AA43-0082-08, AA43-0205-06, AA43-0292-08, AA43-0537-07, AA43-0920-07, AA43-0928-07, AA43-0928-07, AA43-0928-07, AA43-0928-07; cases of the Supreme Court SKA-0136-08, SKA-0144-08, SKA-0276-08, SKA-0276-08, SKA-0276-08, SKA-0363-07, SKA-0397-07, SKA-0422-06, SKA-0441-06, SKA-0441-06.

Table 7.1 Latvia: Value-added tax cases – legal framework

Issue: Value-added tax deductibility and refund		
	EU level	National level
Rule	VAT Directive ECJ case law Optigen and Halifax	VAT Law
Administrative agency	National Tax Authority	
Application (main problem)	Incoherence between national provisions and ECJ jurisprudence	

purpose of VAT.[5] According to national law and established administrative and court practice,[6] a taxable entity has a right to deduct input VAT from the amount of tax payable to the state budget only if deductible amounts are supported by reliable documents (that is, invoices) addressed to a taxable person from another taxable entity for actual provision of goods and services.[7]

The applicant contested the decision of the tax authorities in pre-judicial administrative proceedings and then in the national administrative courts.[8] Challenging the decision of the administrative agency through all levels of the judicial system, the applicant argued that the contested transactions had actually taken place, served *bona fide* business purposes and the applicant was not aware that actions or documents of business partners were possibly vitiated by fraud.[9] Relying on the *Optigen* doctrine[10] developed by the ECJ, the applicant claimed that

5 A typical 'VAT fraud scheme and VAT deductibility' case relates to a situation where companies are involved in doing business with alleged VAT fraud scheme entities. By fraud schemes are meant purposefully created chains of companies involved in mutual transactions with the ultimate goal of evading payment of VAT to the treasury and usually cashing it out. The tax authorities normally attempt to demonstrate that fraudulent business partners are not actually existent and functional and for that reason are not able to provide actual services or goods.

6 See for example, for interpretation of article 10 (1) of the Law on Value Added Tax Supreme Court Senate judgments of 10 August 2004 case Nr.SKA-85 para 19.3; 11 January 2007 case Nr.SKA-22/2007 para 9, 3 October 2008 case Nr. SKA-0496/2008 para 8.

7 Article 10 (1) of the Law on Value Added Tax

8 See n. 4, for full list of cases refer to Annex 2 Latvia: List of Supreme Court Cases and Latvia: List of Regional Administrative Court Cases.

9 See for example, arguments of the applicant in Supreme Court case SKA-0397/2007 judgment of 25 June 2007, para 14.

10 In *Optigen*, the ECJ found that a right to deduct input VAT cannot be affected by the fact that in the chain of supply of which those transactions form part, another prior, or

in a supply chain each transaction must be considered on its merits as a separate economic activity. The right of a company to deduct VAT cannot be affected by the fact that, without it knowing or having any means of knowing, another transaction in the chain is vitiated by fraud:[11]

> The European Court of Justice in its 12 January 2006 decision in joined Cases C-354/03, C-355/03 and C-484/03 has indicated that it is not allowed that an honest taxpayer is punished for fraudulent transaction of which it was unaware or without any means of knowing. The European Court of Justice has also indicated that a taxpayer may not be held liable to the state treasury for damage caused without that taxable person knowing or having any means of knowing. The Regional Court of Administrative Cases has not found that the claimant knew or had any means of knowing about the fraudulent actions of its business partners.[12]

The courts of first and second instance denied the arguments by the applicant related to ECJ jurisprudence. Thus, for example, the Regional Court of Administrative Cases, denying the right of the applicant to deduct input VAT, concluded:

> The Regional Court of Administrative Cases is of the opinion that from the facts of the case, especially from the decision 12 April 2007 of the Riga Regional Court of Criminal Cases imposing criminal liability on ... is a proved fact that the claimant's business partners SIA 'V un J', SIA 'Unda RR' and SIA 'Imerlan' were not involved in real business activities and that real supplies from these companies were not made. Therefore, the condition provided by the case law of the European Court of Justice that the supply of goods is made and that the claimant in appropriate timing fulfils the set norms of VAT.[13]

---

subsequent transaction is vitiated by VAT fraud provided that the entity requesting a VAT refund did not know or did not have any means of knowing of the fraudulent behaviour.

11 'Carousel fraud' consists of chains of supplies of goods in which a defaulting company is involved. This company, liable to VAT, does not account for VAT to the tax authorities, or, for example, a defaulting company is using a hijacked VAT number. This type of fraud represents a major concern for tax authorities of MSs. As Advocate General Poiares Maduro observed in his Opinion in Joined Cases C-354/03, C-355/03 & C-484/03 (Optigen Ltd (C-354/03), Fulcrum Electronics Ltd (C-355/03) and Bond House Systems Ltd (C-484/03) v. Commissioners of Customs & Excise) delivered on 16 February 2005 although the exact amount of money involved is difficult to quantify, it clearly causes a considerable loss of national revenue (point 9 of the Opinion – ref. the Report from the Commission to the Council and the European Parliament on the use of administrative cooperation arrangements in the fight against VAT fraud, 16 April 2004, COM(2004) 260 final).

12 Paragraph 6.4 of SKA-144/2008.

13 A42411406; a similar line of argumentation is followed in other cases heard by the Regional Court of Administrative Cases see for example, SKA-496/2008, SKA-62/2009, SKA-166/2010.

Although the applicant *expressis verbis* did not claim a conflict between national and EU norms, in its substance the type of incoherence disputed in this series of cases involves provisions of the VAT Directive as interpreted by the ECJ in the *Optigen* and *Halifax* cases and national norms and practice on anti-abusive behaviour in reimbursement of input VAT. The applicant essentially maintained that the evaluation criteria adopted by the national authorities to limit the right to VAT deductibility is contrary to the right of good-faith traders to deduct input VAT, *inter alia*, protected by the VAT Directive.

Table 7.2 Incoherence between national norm and EU norm – VAT fraud cases

National Law	EU Law
Article 10 para 1 Law on Value Added Tax	EU VAT Directive
National case law establishing four cumulative conditions that need to be met in order to claim input VAT deduction (para 9)[14]	*Optigen* (relied on by applicants) *Halifax* (relied on by court)

The Latvian 'VAT fraud cases' are a litmus test for national courts to navigate in the most vividly ongoing developments in indirect taxation at the European level related to interpretation and application of the VAT Directive that, on the one hand, aims to protect the rights of traders acting in good faith and, on the other hand, to avoid abuse of tax schemes. As one commentator put it following the ECJ judgments in *Optigen* and *Halifax*, the task of national courts is not an easy one:

> It is for the courts to sail between the Scylla of abuse of law principle and the Charybdis of protecting good-faith traders. Finding a precarious balance between the legitimate interests of the Treasuries in protection against loss of revenue through applying the abuse of law rule (*Halifax*) and of legal certainty for third party traders acting in good faith (*Optigen*) will turn out to be quite an acrobatic *tour de force* and it is my prediction that we will witness a number of legal *saltos mortales*.[15]

A number of disputes reached the Supreme Court,[16] which, after establishing the facts related to the disputed transactions and citing relevant national practice,

14 See for example, SKA-114/2004, SKA-23/2005, SKA-472/2005, SKA-14/2006, SKA-154/2007, SKA-296/2007, SKA-46/2008.

15 Brederode 2008.

16 See for example, SKA-397/2007, SKA-496/2008, SKA-90/2009. One of the arguments of the applicants in the cassation appeal was that the courts at lower levels did

addressed the arguments of the applicant related to EU law and ECJ practice. First, the Supreme Court indicated that it is aware of the ECJ *Optigen* doctrine on carousel fraud transactions and reimbursement of VAT to companies that are not themselves vitiated by VAT fraud:

> The European Court of Justice in its 12 January 2006 decision in joined Cases C-354/03, C-355/03 and C-484/03 to which the applicant refers has indicated that each transaction must therefore be regarded on its own merits and the character of a particular transaction in the chain cannot be altered by earlier or subsequent events. The right to deduct input VAT of a taxable person who carries out such transactions cannot be affected by the fact that in the chain of supply of which those transactions form part another prior or subsequent transaction is vitiated by VAT fraud, without that taxable person knowing or having any means of knowing.[17]

However, the Supreme Court continued to point out that, according to the ECJ *Halifax* doctrine,[18] the parties cannot rely on EU law for abusive or fraudulent ends:

> The application of EC legislation cannot be extended to include business malpractice, meaning transactions that are carried out not in the context of a normal commercial framework but solely for the purpose of wrongfully obtaining advantages provided by law. The principle of prohibiting abusive practices also applies to the sphere of VAT. The ECJ stated that the right to deduct remains only if there is not fraud or abuse. The Sixth Directive must be interpreted as meaning that it precludes the rights of taxpayers to deduct if the transactions on which that right is based constitute an abusive practice.[19]

In an attempt to balance the *Optigen* and *Halifax* doctrines of the ECJ, the Supreme Court distinguished the facts of the case under adjudication from the factual circumstances of the *Optigen* case. The Supreme Court pointed out that, in *Optigen*, companies that were denied a VAT refund actually participated in economic activity but had no dealings with the defaulting trader. In the case of the Latvian taxpayer, the courts of lower instance determined that no real business activity took place between the applicant and other taxable entities:[20]

---

not discuss and apply ECJ case law, see for example, para 21 of SKA-144/2008 where the applicant claimed that the lower courts failed correctly to apply *Optigen*.

17 Para 21.3.

18 European Court of Justice, 21 February 2006, cited Nr.C-255/02 for a preliminary ruling in the proceedings Halifax plc, Leeds Permanent Development Services Ltd., County Wide Property Investments Ltd. and Commissioners of Customs & Excise.

19 Para 21.3

20 Para 21.4.

> The Senate admits that the factual circumstances in the present case do not correspond to the factual circumstances in Cases C-354/03, C-355/03 and C-484/03 reviewed by the European Court of Justice ... On the contrary in this case the Regional Court of Administrative Cases found that transactions between the applicant and SIA 'Beatta', SIA 'Spīdveja lokomotīve' and SIA 'Moduss LTD' had not taken the place, namely, the aforesaid companies have not been real business partners of the claimant.

The court then continued with analysis of the criteria established in *Halifax* to determine whether in fact abusive practice actually took place:

> In order to establish whether an abusive practice exists, it is necessary to establish that the transaction concerned, notwithstanding application of the Sixth Directive and national transposition law, results in obtaining a tax advantage the grant of which would be contrary to the purpose of those provisions. Secondly, it must also be apparent from a number of objective factors that the essential aim of the transactions concerned is to obtain a tax advantage.[21]

Considering that the business activity on the basis of which the applicant claimed input VAT had actually not taken place, the Supreme Court concluded that the applicant cannot rely on the protection of the *bona fide* trader principle established in *Optigen*. Thus, the administrative agency as well as the lower courts had correctly established that the applicant cannot claim input VAT on the basis of a nonexistent business transaction:

> The Administrative Regional Court did not conclude that the applicant's transactions had actually occurred in a chain of transactions [that is, a carousel fraud chain as in *Optigen*] but all together did not actually take place. Therefore cassation that is based on the assumption that the applicant's right to deduct input tax is not recognized in another chain of transactions [as in *Optigen*] is rejected.[22]

Consequently, the Supreme Court, as well as the appeal courts, assessed alleged incoherence between the provisions of national and European law relying on the principle of harmonious interpretation. The courts found that national law and practice do not conflict with EU law and ECJ practice. For example, in relation to compliance of Article 10 (1) of the Value Added Tax Law providing that input VAT may be claimed on the basis of relevant documents that clearly identify the taxable person, the amount of payment and services or goods provided is not in conflict with the VAT Directive's principles and ECJ case law:

---

21 Para 21.2., the Supreme Court directly cites provision 86 of the *Halifax* case.

22 SKA-0496/2008 para 11.

> The Senate interpreting Article 10 (1) of the Value Added Tax Law recognized that one of the prerequisites of the right to deduct input tax is the fact that a person has actually received an invoice that indicates taxable goods or services. Also the ECJ has consistently held that a transaction must actually take place. Taking account of the economic reality constitutes a fundamental criterion for applying a VAT system. [reference to C-260/95 para 23 and C-73/06 para 43]. The Regional Administrative Court found that the applicant had no actual transaction with X and thus the right to deduct input tax for this transaction was denied. Thus, the Regional Administrative Court interpreted and applied Article 10 (1) of the VAT law in accordance with the established practice of the Senate and in accordance with ECJ practice.[23]

On an institutional level, national courts of all instances in numerous VAT fraud cases have interpreted the relevant provisions of the VAT Directive and ECJ practice consistently. Although the applicants in cassation proceedings argued that the lower courts misunderstood and misapplied ECJ case law, specifically, the *Optigen* doctrine, the Senate of the Supreme Court consistently dismissed this claim and upheld the reasoning and findings of the lower courts.

Comparing the argumentative patterns adopted by the lower and Supreme Courts, it is evident that although the courts follow the same line of reasoning the appeal courts and the Supreme Court discuss ECJ case law in more detail. Thus, if lower courts just mention that ECJ case law cannot be applied to the circumstances of the case without providing any additional explanatory arguments, then the Supreme Court develops these arguments more intensively. The appeal courts and Supreme Court rely on two types of arguments: linguistic and systemic.

Table 7.3 Latvia VAT fraud cases – summary and conclusions

Coherence Dimension	
Substantive	SINC 1 – Conflict between national and EU law Resolved through principle of 'harmonious' interpretation
Institutional	Uniform practice of application of EU law provisions Preliminary reference was not requested
Argumentative	Types of argument: *(a) Linguistic (direct references and citations of EU law and ECJ case law)* *(b) Systemic (references and assessment of national provisions vis-à-vis ECJ jurisprudence; reference, application and balancing of competing ECJ doctrines)*

23 SKA-0496/2008 para 8.

VAT deductibility (VAT refund) in relation to taxable supplies (services or goods) situations

The second group of VAT-related cases contest the scope of definition of 'economic activity' that should be considered as an eligible transaction for input VAT deduction. Similarly to the VAT fraud cases, the applicants in this group of cases contest an administrative decision of the SRS that obligates the applicant to pay additional VAT and a fine.[24] Here, however, focus is not on the fraudulent or non-existent nature of the business transaction but rather on the definition of what constitutes an 'economic activity' for the purposes of input VAT deduction.

The applicants challenged the decision of the SRS first in pre-judicial administrative proceedings and then in the administrative courts.[25] The SRS through cassation appeal challenged the decision of the Regional Administrative Court in the Supreme Court Senate.[26] The applicants argued that they have a right to deduct input VAT charged on VAT-taxable service purchases (for example, fee for valuation of real estate property) for an envisaged project even if the project (purchase of real estate property) never took place due to business reasons. Therefore, the applicants claimed that they should not be denied entitlement to deduct VAT even if the economic activity envisaged does not give rise to a taxable transaction.[27]

For example, in case SKA-46/08 the applicant stated that its primary activity is real estate transactions. In order to decide whether to purchase a property, it needs professional expertise in the shape of a property valuation. In some cases, following property evaluation, the applicant decided not to acquire the property.

24 Apart from VAT fraud, the deductibility (VAT refund) cases appear in situations where the tax authorities question whether services or goods purchased are intended for creating other VAT-taxable supplies (services or goods). This issue is crucial because of the VAT neutrality principle implemented via the VAT deduction mechanism. In brief, it can be characterized that only the end-consumer pays VAT but for most businesses VAT is neutral. A business buys VAT-taxable services or supplies to create a value in its own services or supplies. This means that for a business to determine how much VAT it has to pay to the treasury it must deduct the input VAT (VAT paid for different supplies) from the output VAT (VAT collected on its sales). Thus a business ultimately pays to the treasury only the difference and effectively avoids VAT as a real business cost. If the business is oriented towards export activities, then its input VAT is normally much higher than output VAT and the treasury always owes VAT to a business and refunds it to a business. Also in the early stages of a business it is quite usual that input VAT exceeds output VAT (due to slow sales) and a business regularly requests a VAT refund from the treasury.

25 See for example, C39130603-166/04, A42088904.

26 See for example, SKA-23/2007, SKA-46/08, SKA-241/2008, SKA-46/2008, SKA-62/2009.

27 This has become especially important in the wake of the real estate crisis where a substantial number of projects were initiated but due to the crisis were postponed or cancelled.

Although the property was not purchased, the applicant incurred expenditure (on property valuation) that is directly related to its economic activity.[28]

The tax authorities, relying on Article 10 (1) of the VAT law, took the view that if a preparatory act does not lead to a taxable transaction then it cannot be considered an economic activity for the purposes of input VAT deduction:

> In order to claim input tax deduction there must be a direct and immediate link between the input and a taxable transaction. It is also essential that VAT would be paid for goods and services that are truly necessary for economic activity and ensure a taxable transaction. It is necessary to distinguish cases where VAT on property valuation can be deducted from cases where it cannot be deducted. One situation is that there is a voluntary choice not to purchase property, but another case where there are independent reasons leading to declining to purchase property or unpredictable obstacles to purchasing property. This means that in the prior case unlike in the latter case the cost cannot be used to provide a taxable transaction. Consequently, it was wrong to conclude that taxable supply expenditure [of the applicant] necessary to ensure selection of the goods is directly related to taxable transactions.

Thus, the alleged incoherence between provisions of national and EU law concerned the understanding of economic activity as provided by national law and administrative practice. The applicants, claiming unconformity with ECJ jurisprudence, challenged established administrative practice of the tax office.

Table 7.4 Incoherence between national norm/practice and EU norm – VAT refund cases

National Law	EU Law
Article 10 para 1 Law on Value-Added Tax	EU VAT Directive
Understanding of an 'economic activity' – National practice on deductibility of input VAT borne before and/or not leading to a taxable transaction	Understanding of an 'economic activity' VAT neutrality principle *Rompelman* *INZO*

The Regional Court of Administrative Cases relying, *inter alia,* on the provisions of the VAT Directive agreed with the arguments of the applicant and dismissed the position of the tax authorities. First, the court pointed out that national legal norms on VAT must be interpreted taking into consideration ECJ case law: '... [court] is of the opinion that the views expressed in the decisions of the European Court of

28 SKA-46/2008 para 3.

Justice regarding application of legal principles should be taken into consideration in the application of Latvian legal acts.'[29]

Then, the court specifically addressed the conflicting positions of the parties regarding interpretation of national law in the light of ECJ jurisprudence:

> The State Revenue Service has interpreted Article 10.1.1 in an unjustifiably narrow manner. For use of input VAT deduction rights provided in the aforesaid legal norm, in order to determine the use of the services to support one's VAT taxable services, the importance lies with the intent to receive such services for further use in its commercial activity.[30]

The SRS lodged a cassation complaint, though this was unsuccessful. The Supreme Court confirmed the decision of the Administrative Regional Court and therefore supported the position of the applicant. The Senate of the Supreme Court Department of Administrative Cases first explained how concepts such as 'economic activity' defined both by national and EU law should be interpreted in national administrative and judicial practice:

> Similarly to the Law on VAT the concept of 'economic activity' is also referred to in the Sixth Council Directive of 17 May 1977 (77/388/EEC) that provides rules on harmonization of turnover taxes. In this case, to clarify the concept of 'economic activity' provided in the Law on VAT it is also necessary to use the case law of the European Court of Justice.[31]

Assessing the jurisprudence of the ECJ on the concept of economic activity within the meaning of the VAT Directive, the Senate of the Supreme Court stated:

> … the ECJ in its *Rompelman* judgment [reference] admitted that the concept of 'economic activity' should be interpreted broadly and that it includes preparatory acts for taxable activities. In this case the purchase of not yet built housing for future use in economic activity was considered as preparatory. In its *INZO* judgment the ECJ reached the conclusion that a preparatory act also includes a profitability study in respect of an envisaged activity.[32]

Thus, the Supreme Court applying ECJ jurisprudence concluded that the understanding of the concept of economic activity adopted by the national tax authorities denying a VAT refund in cases where economic activity of the taxable person does not necessarily lead to a taxable transaction is contrary to EU law and practice:

---

29 Para 16 of A42088904.

30 Para 5.3.

31 Para 11, SKA-46/2008.

32 Para 12; Case 268/83, Rompelman vs. Netherlands; C-110/94 Intercommunale voor zeewaterontzilting (INZO) v Belgium.

Table 7.5 Latvia VAT cases – summary and conclusions

Coherence Dimension	
Substantive	SINC 1 – Conflict between national and EU law Resolved through indirect reliance on the principle of supremacy and application of the principle of 'harmonious' interpretation
Institutional	Conflicting understanding of EU law provisions by national administrative agency and national judicial system Uniform practice of understanding of EU law provisions by national courts Preliminary reference was not requested
Argumentative	Types of arguments: • *linguistic (direct references to ECJ case law)* • *systemic (references and assessment of national provisions vis-à-vis ECJ jurisprudence)*

> The cassation complaint provides that there is a need to differentiate between cases where the choice not to purchase property is made voluntarily from cases where reasons are beyond the parties' control. The SRS takes the view that in the first case but not in the latter case the cost cannot be used to constitute a taxable transaction. The Senate recognizes this argument to be unfounded since, as noted above, the reasons why preparation made for economic activity is not followed by a taxable transaction are only of legal importance when a person is acting in bad faith.[33]

Notably, in this series of cases, the Latvian courts convincingly demonstrated that they are able to overrule long-established administrative practice of national tax authorities. They have done so through indirectly relying on the principle of supremacy of EU law and applying the principle of harmonious interpretation. The national lower courts, including courts of first instance, showed legal craft in interpreting provisions of national law taking into consideration the practice of the ECJ. Finally, litigants must be credited for contesting decisions of national tax authorities in courts through an argumentative strategy built on the provisions of EU law.

33 SKA-46/2008, para 15.

Competition Law

Another large group of 'economic cases' in Latvia concerns competition law-related disputes.[34] Competition cases and more generally competition law in Latvia is strongly based on EU competition law practice. Indeed, the practice of the Latvian Competition Council (an administrative agency) is an example of where EU competition rules and practices of the European Commission form an integral part.[35] This applies especially in cases related to abuse of a dominant position and concerted practices.[36] The Latvian Competition Council supports its EU law-integrated interpretation as follows: 'Latvian Competition Law has been harmonized with EU competition law. Consequently, in assessment of the case, the Competition Council took into account European Commission practice in similar cases.'[37]

In practical terms, this approach was adopted due to absence of national regulation and practice, for example, on what is to be taken into account in establishing market dominance or establishing a concerted practice. In this context, the Competition Council and courts have as a general rule relied on well-established EU law and practice (Gailis and Maskalans 2009, Azanda 2009). This explains a large number of cases that actually intensively refer to EU law provisions and ECJ jurisprudence but do not substantively discuss or display any kind of incoherence between national and EU law. Consequently, in this series of cases, EU law is predominantly used not to confront national law or practice but to fill the lacuna of undeveloped national regulations.

Equally, undertakings generally do not challenge the application of EU law but rather dispute the applicable facts. The exception here is 'transition period' cases where the disputed facts took place before 1 May 2004 but the administrative authority nevertheless applied EU law criteria. The applicants argued that EU law should not apply to facts before accession. The courts rejected this position with an argument of harmonization of national law with EU law obligations under the Europe Agreement that already existed before formal accession to the EU.[38] Therefore, the court found that EU law can be used for teleological and historical interpretation, because disputed Latvian law, although adopted before formal

34 Most cases in this group are litigated in the courts of first and second instance and only a few in the Supreme Court.

35 Practice of the Competition Council is available publicly, free of charge at http://www.kp.gov.lv/ (in Latvian).

36 See for example, decisions of the Regional Administrative Court judgment A43-0018-09-2.

37 See for example, decisions of the Competition Council Nr.E02-60 of 28 May 2008; Nr. 10 of 23 January 2008.

38 See for example, AA43-850-08/2 where the Court stated 'In accordance with the Europe Agreement establishing an association between the European Communities and their Member States, of the one part, and the Republic of Latvia, of the other part (1995), Latvia has agreed to approximate its laws. Consequently national competition law should be read in conformity with EU law.'

accession, was specifically aimed at implementation of EU law. Accordingly, in the 'transition period' courts intensively applied EU law. The courts, for example, refer to ECJ case law in order to define the concept of dominant position (Case 27/76 United Brands Company and United Brands Continental BV v. Commission [1978], ECR 207, 322/81 Michelin v. Commission [1983] ECR 3461, paras 32–4) and unfair selling prices (Case 27/76 United Brands v. Commission [1978] ECR 207, paras 250–53).[39]

Even as concerns the 'transition period', for example, the Regional Court of Administrative Cases argued that Art. 17 of CL (1997) is analogous to Art. 82 (a) EC. This makes an impression that the existence of analogous norms automatically means that EU law can be applicable even to pre-accession facts: 'The court holds the view that although the decision of the Competition Council was adopted before Latvia became a member state of the EU, the interpretation of particular articles established by ECJ case-law must be considered when interpreting Competition law.'[40]

In support of its position the Regional Court also refers to the ECJ case *Beck Liegenschaftsverwaltung* (C-355/97, para. 22), where the ECJ held that ECJ case law can be used as a source of historical and theological interpretation. The Regional Court finds it justified to apply this reasoning to a case that deals with events taking place prior to a MS's accession to the EU.

The claimant brought an action to the Supreme Court arguing that both the Competition Council and the Regional Court unjustifiably referred to EU law which was not in force at the time when a possible breach of law was committed.[41] The Senate of the Supreme Court Department of Administrative Cases dismissed the cassation application and upheld the reasoning of the Regional Court. Additionally the Senate underlined: 'Albeit that EU law is not directly applicable to issues related to administrative acts issued prior to 1 May 2004, ECJ case law should be used as a means of historical and theological interpretation for norms that derive from EU law.'[42]

In contrast to the above mentioned case, in the *Kempmayer Media Limited* case, an undertaking argued that the Competition Council was obliged to apply EU law to facts which took place prior to 1 May 2004. The applicant argued:

> In accordance with the Europe Agreement establishing an association between the European Communities and their Member States, of the one part, and the Republic of Latvia, of the other part (Art. 64), the Competition Council was

39 AA43-850-08/2; SKA-0308-07, para; AA43-687-07/8, A43-0009-09-11, para 10; quite often the Competition Council and courts do not give any reason for using EU law or even do not analyse it in connection with a particular case, but only cite the legal norms, for example, Art. 81ECT.

40 AA43-0087-07/9, para 13.

41 SKA-0284-07, para 2.4.

42 SKA-0284-07, para 6.

> obliged to issue an administrative act based on criteria defined by Art. 81 of ECT. [43] Although the facts of the case took place before 1 May 2004, the challenged administrative act was issued after accession and after Regulation 1/2003 came into force. Consequently, the Competition Council was obliged to apply Art. 3 of the Regulation.[44]

The Regional Court first analysed the concept of 'trade between member states' in accordance with criteria stated in the Commission's *Guidelines on the effect on trade concept contained in Articles 81 and 82 of the Treaty* and concluded that that particular agreement did not fulfil the criteria defined in the *Guidelines*. Thus, the dispute must be resolved on the basis of national law.[45] Next, the Regional Court analysed whether Regulation 1/2003 can be applied:

> The Competition law was adopted on 4 October 2001 and came into force on 1 January 2002. There was adopted a law on 22 April 2004 'Amendments to the Competition law', which came into force on 1 May 2004 … the amendments ensured the application of Council Regulation No 1/2003 (16 December 2002). In accordance with Art. 45 of … regulation this is applicable since 1 May 2004. The law does not provide for retroactive application of the regulation. In a letter from DG Competition dated July 20, 2004, which is a part of the case file, it is indicated that Article 81 TEC was not yet in force as to the infringements that occurred till April 30, 2004 in the member states which acceded to the European Union on May 1, 2004, and for that reason review of such cases after accession is continued only in accordance with national legislation and they are not subject to the conditions of regulation (EC) no.1/2003. Therefore, CC (*Competition Council*) would have been entitled to exercise the authority stipulated in regulation (EC) no.1/2003 if the infringement of competition law had occurred or continued after May 1, 2004. CC found that occurrence of the infringement was from November 14, 2002 until September 10, 2003, namely, a period from the conclusion of the Contract until the moment AS 'DLRTC' announced to the applicant regarding stopping fulfilment of obligations.[46]

The Regional Court concluded that there is no legal basis for direct application of EU law; however, the court relied on ECJ case law to interpret the provisions of national competition law.

Similarly to the practice of the Competition Council and the 'transition period' cases, it seems to be a well-established general practice of national courts straightforwardly to acknowledge that national competition law must be applied based on analogy with EU competition law:

---

43 AA1221-05/8, para 4.2.

44 AA1221-05/8, para 4.4.

45 Ibid., para 19.

46 Ibid., para 20.

> Article 13 of the Competition Law is analogous to Article 82 EC Treaty, that among other things prohibits a dominant undertaking, without objective reasons, from refusing to enter into a transaction agreement with downstream market participants, if such action results in reduced competition in a downstream market. Accordingly, the present case, *inter alia*, can also be attributed to ECJ jurisprudence.[47]

In most cases, reliance on EU law directly or by analogy is central. This is specifically true of the definition and determining of the concept's dominant position,[48] relevant market, abuse of market power, and concerted practice. The definition of national concepts in the light of EU law-developed jurisprudence is justified by the courts as 'analogous legal norm' argument. Thus, the courts often state that a substantial part of Latvian competition law was adopted on the basis of EU law.[49] Thus, national legal norms that are considered as analogous to a particular EU law should be interpreted in conformity with EU law. Furthermore, the courts point out that EU competition rules can be used as useful interpretation tools of national competition law as they are similar legal regulations.[50]

The advanced reasoning of the national courts on the relationship between national and EU competition rules is illustrated in the *Lattelecom* case:[51]

> In the case law it has been recognized that with the Accession Treaty between the European Union and its member states and the Republic of Latvia dated June 12, 1995 (in force since February 1, 1998) Latvia has undertaken to harmonize its legislation with EC law. Article 82 TEC provides that any abuse by one or more undertakings of a dominant position within the common market or in a substantial part of it shall be prohibited as incompatible with the common market insofar as it may affect trade between Member States. Such abuse may, in particular, consist in directly or indirectly imposing unfair purchase or selling prices or other unfair trading conditions. From the aforesaid the Regional Court of Administrative Cases concludes that the Competition Law provides an identical norm to Article 82 of TEC. Therefore, in the opinion of the Regional Court of Administrative Cases, although the factual circumstances of the case occurred prior to the accession of Latvia to the European Union, the case law of the European Court of Justice (hereinafter – ECJ) is applicable for hearing the present case.[52]

---

47 AA43-0300-08/10, para. 11.

48 A43-0018-09-2, para 15.

49 SKA-0284-07.

50 SKA-0096-08.

51 The case was heard in all three instances.

52 AA43-850-08/2, para 17.

In addition to references to primary law and intensive references to ECJ case law, courts also rely on Commission Notices. For example, in determining the relevant market in the territory of Latvia, the Competition Council refers to the Commission Notice on the Definition of Relevant Market for the Purposes of EU Law.[53] The undertaking, a company that organizes exhibitions, argued that the relevant market is broader than the territory of Latvia.[54] However, the court followed and further developed the Competition Council argumentation. In addition to national law and the Commission Notice, the court also discussed ECJ case 22/78 Hugin Kassaregister AB and Hugin Cash Registers Ltd. v. Commisssion [1973] ECR 1869 paras 5–8.[55]

The undertaking appealed the position of the Competition Council and of the lower courts to the Supreme Court. However, the Senate of the Supreme Court found that the national lower courts had correctly determined the relevant market: 'The mere fact that there were participants from other countries at the exhibition does not lead to extension of a particular geographical market.'[56] The Supreme Court also upheld the practice of applying EU law by analogy to national cases that are subject to national competition rules rather than to EU competition rules. This includes cases that formally do not distort EU competition but rather competition in the national market.

Nevertheless, in a few cases the parties attempted to challenge this general approach by interpreting even a purely national situation with EU competition-law rules and principles. An example is a case where the national courts applied principles included in Regulation 2988/74 concerning limitation periods in proceedings and enforcement of sanctions. In contrast to the regulation, Latvian competition law did not provide time limits on Competition Council powers to fine undertakings in breach of competition law. The court found that applying by analogy the rules regulating actions of the European Commission to the national Competition Council lies within the field of competition control. In determining the limitation period, the courts indirectly relied on Regulation 2988/74.[57]

The applicant objected:

> ... application of the Regulation was unjustified. In the applicant's view the deadline of 3–5 years given by the court relates to cases heard on grounds of EU competition law. The legislator in Latvian Company Law did not provide any time limits. For that reason the fact that the institution has issued an unfavourable

53 97/C 372/03, case AA43-0300-08/10, para 5.3.

54 They argued that participants of other states were taking part in its organized exhibition (Finland, Iceland, Estonia). Also Latvian entities are participating in events beyond the borders of Latvia. As a result, competition conditions are similar throughout the EU. So, the particular geographical market could be extended.

55 AA43-0300-08/10, para 13.1.

56 AA43-1516-09-18, para 13.3.4.

57 AA43-0463-09-13, para 6.8.

> decision must be taken into account. The less harmful interpretation for the individual must be followed.[58]

However, the Regional Court dismissed this argument and upheld the position of the court of the first instance.

Labour Law

Labour law cases involve cases challenging grounds for dismissal[59] and non-competition obligation following dismissal.

There are two related cases where non-competition clauses stipulated in employment contracts are analysed against provisions on free movement of workers following from Article 39 ECT. According to the employment contract, for two years after termination of the employment relationship, the applicants were prohibited from working for an employer who can be regarded as a competitor of the current employer within the territories of Latvia, Estonia and Lithuania. In both cases, the applicants had violated this clause of the employment contract by working for a competitor of the previous employer (in the sphere of commercial auto trading). The crucial difference between both employees concerned the job position they held at their previous workplace.

In the first case, the applicant was the wholesale manager. He argued that:

> … limits of competition [established by the non-competition clause in the agreement] have to be necessary and proportionate, because too wide limitations of fundamental rights are regarded as unlawful, and contradict the principle of free movement of workers stipulated in Art. 39 ECT. Limitations must be precisely defined, reasonable and fair.[60]

The applicant argued that prohibition of exercising professional activity in Lithuania and Estonia is contrary to Article 39 EC because the respondent does not carry on business in those countries.

The Senate dismissed this argument, stating that in the three mentioned countries:

> … competition conditions of particular goods are similar enough for all market participants. Besides, this restriction does not preclude the claimant as a worker from exercising his rights to free movement according to Article 39 ECT. Prohibition is limited within both the time and the particular sphere of activity.

---

58 Ibid., para 7.6.

59 SKC-437/2008, SKC-88/2009; for discussion, see above under Preliminary reference procedure – Latvia; see also SKC-196/2009, SKC-187/2009, SKC-500/2009.

60 SKC-576/2009.

The court added that EU law 'defines only the main direction concerning free movement of workers. Member States then individually implement directives within national law. The Labour Law is drafted in accordance with EU law and principles.' The court further continued 'In the court's view, the particular non-competition clause is not considered as violating the principle of free movement of workers, because within a free market it is acceptable and reasonable.'

Interestingly, the court did not refer to any ECJ case law while discussing the issue of the EC right to free movement of workers.[61]

In contrast to the above-mentioned case, in the second case the applicant had held the position of secretary. In this case, the court found that the prohibition clause was too vague with regard to the duties that a secretary had. However, the Senate did not pay attention to the fact that the Court of Appeal directly applied Article 39 ECT and did not discuss it, but focused only on some aspects of national employment law. In this way, the Senate upheld the conclusions by the Court of Appeal that a prohibition on working in Lithuania and Estonia contradicted Article 39 ECT.[62]

Consumer Protection

An extensive number of cases[63] deal with arbitration clauses and their enforcement in the relationship between corporate service providers, such as banks and insurance businesses, and their clients, namely, ordinary individual customers. It is a standard Latvian practice that businesses include in their standard retail contracts arbitration clauses appointing arbitration courts as a dispute-resolution forum. The main reason for this is that arbitration courts are a significantly more effective dispute-resolution fora in comparison with ordinary courts and allow faster hearings of disputes which, on their face, might seem rather trivial – for example, when a customer fails to pay monthly mortgage payments to a bank. Moreover, there is also a perception that at least several arbitration courts are significantly pro-industry (for example, banking or insurance) oriented and that customers' chances of succeeding in these arbitration courts are fairly low.

Thus the traditional scenario of an 'arbitration' dispute would be that a corporate entity brings a claim against its customer in an arbitration court and succeeds there. The next step then is to obtain a receiving order from an ordinary state court to execute the arbitral award. Customers put their efforts into questioning these receiving orders.

61 SKC-576/2009.

62 SKC-0006/2008.

63 SPC-0013/2007, SPC-82/2008, SPC-81/2008, SPC-83/2008, SPC-17/2009, SPC-32/2009, SPC-45/2009, SPC-122/2009, SPC-118/2009, SPC-123/2009, SKC-113/2009, SKC-478/2010.

The Senate of the Supreme Court Department of Civil Cases in the 'arbitration' cases provided a non-explanatory model for introducing EU law and basically concurred with the Chamber of Civil Cases:

> The Chamber of the Civil Cases department, taking into consideration Council Directive 93/13/EEC of 5 April 1993 on unfair terms in consumer contracts, Directive 98/27/EC of the European Parliament and of the Council of 19 May 1998 on injunctions for the protection of consumers' interests and Article 5 and Article 6 section 3 and 8 and 6 Consumers' Rights Protection Act, has found that clause 11.3 of the Insurance contract ... is to be considered unfair ... .[64]

Consumer contracts often provide that the only option for dispute resolution is an arbitration court. Latvian consumer protection legislation fairly clearly indicates that these conditions constitute unfair terms for a consumer. It is interesting to note that the District (City) Courts fairly easily issue receiving orders enabling execution of arbitral awards.[65] Thus the case law in the Senate of the Supreme Court Department of Civil Cases concerning 'arbitration' cases mostly arises due to proceedings brought to reverse receiving orders issued by the District (City) Courts which are not effective in considering consumer protections aspects in relation to arbitral proceedings.[66]

Therefore, there is no direct conflict involving EU vs Latvian law, despite the strong EU flavour in the background of most of the judgments. In fact, Latvian consumer protection legislation has allegedly adopted EU consumer protection legislation and there is not an obvious need to refer to EU legislation. In principle, EU law is referred to as a legal source that enhances national law-based argumentation.

Other cases involve the right of an applicant to terminate a purchase contract. For example, one applicant requested termination of a purchase contract because the mobile phone set that he had purchased was defective and repair by the seller lasted more than two weeks. The Senate of the Supreme Court Department of Civil Cases analysing the case did not provide explanations as to why EU consumer protection law should be applied and went straight to EU law interpretation issues:

> According to Article 28.2 of the Consumers' Rights Protection Act, goods which do not correspond to consumer contract characteristics should be repaired free of charge within a reasonable term without inconvenience to the consumer. The aforesaid norm implements Article 3.3 section 3 of Directive

64 Page 2 of SKC-478/2010.

65 ECJ in case C-168/05 Elisa v Centro Movil Milenium [2006] ECR I-10421 ruled that the national court, in an action for annulment of an arbitration award against a consumer, can of its own motion determine the unfairness of the arbitration clause. For discussion see Reich 2007.

66 For example, SKC-113/2009, SPC-123/2009.

> 1999/44/EC of the European Parliament and of the Council of 25 May 1999 on certain aspects of the sale of consumer goods and associated guarantees: Any repair or replacement shall be completed within a reasonable time and without any significant inconvenience to the consumer, taking account of the nature of the goods and the purpose for which the consumer required the goods. The court makes a conclusion that Latvian law sets a higher standard: without inconvenience vs any significant inconvenience. The aforesaid directive clearly indicates that if the repair does not take place within a reasonable time and without any significant inconvenience to the consumer it is entitled to ask for termination of the purchase agreement.

However, the Senate found that the applicant's reference to Directive 2005/29/EC of the European Parliament and of the Council of 11 May 2005 (the 'Unfair Commercial Practices Directive'), was not grounded because at the time of application in 2006 the implementation period for this directive had still not expired (12 December 2007).

Conclusions on Jurisprudence of Ordinary Courts in Estonia and Latvia

Analysis of the general principles of European law and jurisprudence of the Supreme Court has highlighted general tendencies and understanding of EU law at the highest level of the judicial system. The jurisprudence of the ordinary courts is a more nuanced reflection of application of EU law in national legal systems. Highest courts primarily define the operational system for resolving legal conflicts and incoherencies between national and EU law and apply it to the most complex cases. Ordinary courts must apply this system to all cases that reach the court.

The negative predictions related to the ability of lower courts to apply EU law beyond the textual positivist approach – that is, the argument by Kuhn – in general are not confirmed either in the Estonian or the Latvian courts. The overall conclusion on jurisprudence of Estonian and Latvian courts is rather positive. First experiences with the EU mandate of ordinary courts were, however, different in Estonia and Latvia. The central differences are in the type of cases adjudicated, initial engagement with EU law arguments and institutional intra-court cooperation. Especially in the initial post-accession period, there was a clear correlation between coherence of national constitutional structures defining application of EU law as discussed in Part II and practice of ordinary courts.

Estonian constitutional structures and judicial institutions being more coherent resulted in a faster, better-argued and more dynamic engagement of ordinary courts with EU law application. Constitutional structures on application of EU law, well defined both in Estonia and in Latvia, were central. However, what was even more important at the initial stage is the institutional coherence and discursive-dialogic style of the Estonian Supreme Court in explaining EU legal principles and applying EU law. Those were clearly a pivotal factor facilitating the activism of Estonian ordinary courts.

Estonian ordinary courts, already starting from early 2005 in surplus stock and structural fund cases, have extremely actively engaged with discussion of EU law principles and application of EU law. Latvian lower courts initially took a more cautious approach to engaging with EU law arguments: 'no resistance but also no warm welcome'. In some instances, main EU law principles have been clearly misunderstood (for example, the *OCMA* case). The VAT cases, however, positively suggest that ordinary courts are becoming increasingly active and able to resolve complex EU law-related disputes. Thus, perhaps with a somewhat slower start, the Latvian ordinary courts are learning the craft of applying EU law.

Paradoxically, the institutionally more centralized Estonian court system in practice resulted in a more decentralized and dynamic application of EU law by national courts at all instances. Estonian courts of all levels immediately after accession actively engaged with EU law. Following procedural guidance from the Supreme Court on preliminary rulings, ordinary courts submitted a number of references to the ECJ on points of EU law. Moreover, as a result of the ECJ judgment, for example, in the *Balbiino* case, ordinary courts did not hesitate to decline the Supreme Court and applied ECJ reasoning. This is a healthy indicator of the maturity and independence of the national judicial system.

The Latvian judicial system, institutionally more decentralized than the Estonian, produced a more restrained and rather 'top-down' application of EU law. Especially during the initial post-accession years, it was often not until the case reached the Supreme or Constitutional Court that EU law rights were fully enforced. Thus, national ordinary courts did not feel comfortable in justifying and explaining application of EU law and often left it to the Supreme Court to settle difficult EU law-related questions. The preliminary reference procedure still remains a tool to be discovered by national ordinary courts.

Table 7.6 Jurisprudence of ordinary courts in Estonia and Latvia – conclusions

Factors	Estonia		Latvia	
Application of main EU law principles by national ordinary courts	Accepted and applied consistently Resolution	+++	Terminological inconsistencies Some (limited) instances of misapplication by lower courts	++
Substantive adjudication of EU law disputes	There are some differences in '*effet utile*' application of EU law in economic and non-economic cases	++	No differences in application of EU between economic and non-economic cases	+++
Intra-court cooperation	No conflict or resistance between national ordinary courts and the Supreme Court Active role of the Supreme Court in ongoing discursive dialogue through jurisprudence with national ordinary courts	+++	No conflict or resistance between national ordinary courts and the Supreme Court Supreme Court is magisterial and authoritative. Weak dialogue with national ordinary courts	++
Preliminary reference procedure	Requested by all court levels	+++	In all cases but one requested by the Supreme Court. No references from the courts of the first instance. Courts are hesitant and passive in referring to the ECJ.	+
Style of the opinions	Opinions extended and elaborate	+++	EU law applied but not always explained and justified.	++
Legal methodology	Model of rationality – discursive, that is, choices supported by arguments Points of EU law well-explained and justified, especially in economic cases with higher proportion of substantive rather than formal reasons However, in non-economic cases higher proportion of formal than substantive reasons In addition to linguistic references, systemic and teleological arguments are common	++	Model of rationality – deductive Higher proportion of formal than substantive reasons	+

Note: Impact on coherence: '+++' = strongly positive; '++' = positive; '+' = rather positive (but with important constraints); '---' = strongly negative; '--' = negative; '-' = rather negative.

Synthesis and Conclusion

Chapter 8
Domestic Courts and the Application of EU Law: Sources and Methods of Coherence

Analysis of national adjudication of European Union law is by now a classical play of EU legal scholarship. As a contribution to this classical scholarship, this book provides a comparative case study on adjudication of EU law in two post-Communist Member States, Estonia and Latvia. Effectiveness of application of EU law and ultimately the direction of European integration depends crucially on cooperation with national courts. Denied direct legal access to European courts, individuals turn to '*National-European judges*' to enforce their EU law-based rights. Thus, national courts' understanding of what EU law is indeed becomes a prism through which the practical meaning of EU law is projected to citizens. Adjudication is also a reflection of the process of Europeanization: a process involving not only adoption and institutionalization of legal rules, procedures, values and methods, but also the socio-political dynamics of the national polity.

New MSs upon accession have been faced with the task of integrating the EU legal system into their national legal order and applying EU law thereto. This means that an adolescent, post-Communist national judiciary has to understand and navigate through a pluralism of legal authorities and institutional mechanisms of a novel supranational legal regime. Moreover, this mandate is to be fulfilled without infringing EU law or undermining national legal doctrine, and in the context of a still ongoing process of formation of the judicial branch. To comparatively assess the mechanisms though which this mandate is fulfilled and the degree of national courts' success, this book relies on the concept of coherence (Part I of the book).

Coherence of the judicial system of application of EU law means that a national legal order that is based on respect for fundamental democratic values has in place a functioning system of rules, procedures, institutions and methods to resolve normative legal conflicts and enforce supranational legal norms. Comparative assessment of the degree of coherence of the Estonian and Latvian legal systems in the judicial application of EU law is structured along three interrelated but analytically independent dimensions: substantive, institutional and argumentative. In addition, this assessment has two levels. The first level, analysed in Part II of this book, centres on the constitutional structures and jurisprudence of the national highest courts. The second level focuses on the ordinary courts, discussed in Part III.

Bringing the analysis together, it is argued that neither strongly sceptical nor miraculous accounts of applications of EU law by national courts of new

MSs, voiced in the literature, are correct. The disability hypothesis, as it relates to adjudication of substantive supranational norms, fails remarkably. Judges of higher and ordinary courts in both jurisdictions have showed legal craft and ability in applying and resolving complex EU law-related disputes. However, a more nuanced assessment of national adjudication through three dimensions of coherence reveals that Estonian and Latvian cases on many accounts differ in the extent and degree of this generally positive assessment.

The *substantive dimension of coherence* focuses on the understanding of legal rules and principles structuring application of EU law by national higher courts and their application by ordinary courts.

The Estonian Supreme Court has developed a doctrine of interpretation of national law that permits unconditional acceptance of EU law supremacy. This position was not *expressis verbis* formulated by the legislator. The court, relying on the understanding of supremacy as developed through the process of European integration, convincingly has elaborated and developed this position through a series of cases. The Latvian Constitutional Court approaches the supremacy doctrine through the international law angle. By adopting the EU Accession Treaty, Latvia assumed international law obligations. Those international law obligations take priority over national law based on Latvian constitutional theory of international law primacy. EU law supremacy is limited by national constitutional principles protecting the sovereignty and democratic order of the state. Regrettably, Latvian national procedural codes have conflicting and not always clear provisions regulating the hierarchy of legal norms. However, this seems to have little impact in the practice of national courts.

The understanding and application of the principle of direct effect is unproblematic in Estonia. The Supreme Court has clearly explained and applied this principle against conflicting national law provisions, a practice equally well-followed by ordinary courts. This is less so in Latvia. On a terminological level, there is still no consistent practice as to how to refer to the principle of direct effect in the Latvian language. This is true for both legal scholarship and jurisprudence. In scholarship, this is more of a linguistic than a substantive shortcoming. However, especially in the early practice of the lower courts, there is evidence of confusion and misunderstanding on both linguistic and substantive levels, particularly as applies to the distinction between the notion of immediate (direct) applicability and the principle of direct effect. Following a number of Supreme Court judgments, the most recent practice of ordinary courts discussing direct effect suggests a gradual improvement in the understanding of this fundamental principle of EU law.

Most EU law-related legal disputes adjudicated in Estonian courts did not include a direct clash between national and EU norms. This specifically applies to structural fund and surplus stock fee cases. These two groups of economic cases generated a substantial amount of national litigation. Courts were faced with technically nuanced assessments of national rules implementing EU norms. Judges relied on a variety of legal arguments and justifications to assess compliance of national rules with EU norms. Preliminary rulings were requested from the ECJ both concerning the method of calculating the surplus stock fee and national rules limiting the class of eligible applicants for structural fund subsidies. A sharply different approach was adopted by national courts in the more complex and politically sensitive residence permit and pension cases. National courts dismissed EU law arguments of the applicants as ungrounded and refused to submit requests for preliminary rulings.

Latvian courts have been mostly concerned with disputes related to value-added tax, competition law and consumer protection. In the VAT cases, challenging national administrative practice against EU law and ECJ jurisprudence, national courts were most vividly confronted with ongoing EU law developments in the field of direct taxation. Notably, in this series of cases, the Latvian courts convincingly demonstrated that they are able to overrule the long-established administrative practice of national tax authorities. They have done so through indirectly relying on the principle of supremacy of EU law and applying the principle of harmonious interpretation. VAT cases underline the importance and professionalism of the Latvian Constitutional Court. The Constitutional Court has developed a persuasive legal argumentation style to overrule the position of the Supreme Court and apply ECJ preliminary rulings.

The *institutional dimension* of coherence concentrates on institutional cooperation mechanisms and constraints on national judicial systems. The Estonian judicial system is organizationally highly centralized. This, however, does not apply to the application of EU law by national courts. The Supreme Court has explicitly set guidelines for lower courts, encouraging their direct engagement with EU law adjudication. These include an obligation to review the conformity of national law with EU law provisions and a right to directly request a preliminary reference from the ECJ in cases of doubt. Both obligations are to be fulfilled by ordinary courts without necessary involvement of the Supreme Court. Indeed, the national ordinary judiciary has understood this obligation well. This is demonstrated by the involvement of ordinary courts with EU law matters and the fact that requests for preliminary rulings have been submitted from all levels of national courts.

The Latvian judicial system is organizationally less centralized. Immediately following accession, there was a degree of reluctance or uncertainty by national ordinary courts in their discussion and application of EU law. This resulted in a situation where, to enforce EU law, rights cases had to be appealed up to the Supreme Court. The Supreme Court finally applies EU law but often provides little or no guidance to the ordinary courts on general principles of institutional delimitation of competences within the national judicial system and in relation to the Court of Justice of the European Union. Thus, the practice of EU law application is somewhat more centralized. This is evidenced by a heavy reliance on the Supreme Court in resolving EU law-related disputes and the national courts' record in submission of preliminary references. All but one request for a preliminary ruling have been submitted by the Senate of the Supreme Court.

The Estonian judicial system through modern information technologies guarantees free public access to legal information including jurisprudence that importantly contributes to the accessibility and transparency of the legal process. National legal scholarship both in Estonian and English is relatively well-developed. This is not the case in Latvia. Access to national jurisprudence, except for the case law of the Constitutional Court, until most recently was available only through subscription to the privately owned, expensive, case law database. Alternatively, case law is only available in paper form at the court register or as an annual publication of the most important court judgments, for example, of the Supreme Court. Moreover, the electronic database, *inter alia* due to issues related to personal data protection rules, was not available at all during certain periods. Notwithstanding substantial improvements from 2009, full access to court cases in Latvia remains problematic. Public, no-fee access is partial and highly selective, while full access is still expensive and thus generally remains unavailable to the public and academic researchers.

Formation of the judicial system in Estonia proceeded without major problems. The period analysed witnessed no major difficulties or public debates concerning the independence or professionalism of judges. Issues of concern raised by the courts themselves included extremely high state fees, costs of legal proceedings, and limited access to legal aid. At the same time, transformation of the judicial system in Latvia faced major complications. These included: public scandals related to corruption of the judicial branch, allegedly politically motivated nominations of the highest judicial personnel and substantial reduction of judicial remuneration by the legislator that, according to the Constitutional Court, infringed the principle of division of powers.

The practice of an institutionally more centralized system of adjudication of EU law in conjunction with a number of substantial incoherencies of the judicial system in the Latvian case partly confirms the 'Slow Starter' hypothesis. In the Estonian case, the 'Slow Starter' hypothesis is not confirmed.

Intra-court cooperation between national courts in both countries has developed undisturbed: that is, without conflicts over competences or normative positions within the national court system. Equally, there is no evidence of an unreceptive position towards cooperation with the European courts. On the contrary, references to the jurisprudence of the ECJ are frequent. This is especially so in the jurisprudence of the Latvian judiciary. National ordinary courts and equally the highest courts have a generally welcoming and cooperative attitude towards the ECJ. Thus, national courts regard European courts as partners rather than threats to institutional powers or national sovereignty. The 'Conflict' hypothesis is not confirmed.

The *argumentative dimension of coherence* discusses the methods of interpretation applied by national courts in EU law-related cases.

The Estonian Supreme Court started to refer to EU law and ECJ case law long before formal accession to the EU. In the pre-accession period, EU law played two main functions: as a persuasive, additional supporting authority and as a 'gap-filling' tool in the rapidly developing national legal doctrine. The legal bases for references to EU law were the general openness of Estonian constitutional doctrine to international law and at a later stage the harmonization obligation following from the Europe Agreement. The material content of EU law arguments included mostly references to general principles of EU law as developed by the ECJ. The forms of EU law-related arguments invoked were simple: often it was a sub-argument in the chain of a complex justification pattern.

The Latvian Constitutional Court also first referred to EU law before formal accession. The European Charter of Fundamental Rights, at the time a non-binding legal instrument, was the most frequently cited source of persuasive legal authority in pre-accession cases. This reference to the charter may be explained by the prominence of the international human rights law approach in Constitutional Court jurisprudence. Linguistic, simple arguments were the most common. However, shortly before formal accession, the Constitutional Court in invoking EU law and principles also relied on complex contextual harmonization arguments.

In the post-accession transitional period, judges generally have applied the following rule. In cases of direct conflict between pre-accession national law and EU law, national law was applied to facts that took place before formal accession. In cases of minor inconsistencies, harmonious interpretation with EU law was preferred. Some inconsistencies have been noted in the practice of the Latvian Supreme Court that in similar transition cases invoked EU law-related arguments differently.

Interpretation methods in EU law-related jurisprudence in the post-accession period include all the classical methods of interpretation. That is, linguistic, systemic, teleological and transcategorical arguments are used. This applies both to Estonian and Latvian courts.

Estonian courts refer to a variety of EU legal materials, authoritative and non-authoritative, to support their argumentative strategy. Courts most often rely on primary authoritative sources. These include EU legal texts and jurisprudence of the Court of Justice of the European Union. Additionally, legal materials and interpretation techniques include comparison of linguistic versions of legal texts in different EU languages, references to policy documents and secondary literature. Admittedly, in cases where EU law arguments are dismissed, courts tend to rely predominantly, if not exclusively, on technical linguistic arguments. An example is the series of pension discrimination cases. In other cases, systemic arguments are also often invoked. Teleological and transcategorical arguments are less common. Decisions of the Estonian Supreme Court are often more extensive and discursive. At the same time, there is no large gap between highest and ordinary courts. Judges of some ordinary courts in EU law cases have remarkably developed complex justifications, actively and extensively engaging not only with EU legal texts and case law but also with fundamental principles.

Recent judgments of the Latvian Constitutional Court are examples of argumentative excellence. Relying on a variety of national, EU and international legal sources, the Constitutional Court has developed a unique style of interpretation. This includes systemic and teleological interpretations of national and EU legal norms in their broader international law context with special focus on individual human rights. Opinions of the Senate of the Latvian Supreme Court have a high proportion of formal rather than substantive reasons. The Supreme Court refers to and cites a variety of legal sources but does not always discursively engage with the materials of the argument. The Senate classifies the facts, applies legal rules and then makes a conclusion stating the correct solution. In this sense, the Senate frequently makes insufficient efforts to develop a learning dialogue with national lower courts. Dialogue may take place, for instance, through extended discussion explaining why national lower courts misapplied EU law provisions or misunderstood legal principles. Further development of this discursive justificatory style is necessary. Specifically, this can facilitate more active, direct engagement of Latvian lower courts with EU law.

Linguistic arguments are conventionally a starting-point of legal analysis. They are central to adjudication and cannot be ignored or excluded. At the same time, linguistic arguments are only the first step. The appeal to coherence often requires going beyond a narrow linguistic reading of a legal text. This is particularly true in EU law-related cases involving a multitude of legal sources and underlying values. Applying this yardstick, judicial opinions of the Estonian courts generally have a lower proportion of legalistic and technical language and a lower proportion of formal rather substantive reasons than the Latvian courts. Thus the overall justification style of Estonian courts is more argumentative and dialogic. In contrast, the style of Latvian courts, with the exception of the Constitutional Court, tends to be relatively more magisterial and authoritative.

The 'disability hypothesis', suggesting heavy reliance on textual positivism and lack of argumentative skills by national judges generally, is not confirmed. However, important exceptions are the 'selective disability' of Estonian courts in certain politically sensitive policy areas and some opinions of Latvian ordinary courts.

The cumulative force of the findings discussed under three dimensions of coherence suggest that overall the Estonian system of application of EU law is relatively more coherent than the Latvian.

The Estonian judicial system has developed a relatively coherent *modus operandi* for application of EU law. This system, tested through the jurisprudence of highest and ordinary courts, has proved a strong capacity to generate well-argued, justified and reason-based solutions of EU law-related disputes. Factors that have contributed to the high degree of coherence include the pro-active legal-communicative role of the Supreme Court, the dynamic role of lower courts, open access to legal information and jurisprudence, intra-institutional judicial organization as well as intensive use of modern e-technologies. Considering 'economic' cases, the Estonian system is an extremely positive example of intra-system coherence of application of EU law that resolves inconsistencies between legal norms without either undermining EU or national norms and principles. Notably, this coherent 'operation system' fails in non-economic 'citizenship' cases of ethnic discrimination on pension and residence entitlements.

The Latvian judicial system and adjudication is more complex and less coherent in terms of institutional arrangements and argumentative patterns. However, it is more coherent in terms of substantive adjudication of both strictly economic and non-economic cases. The national legal order generally provides a relatively well-functioning adjudication system of cases concerning EU law. However, recent problems related to the Latvian judicial system triggering public outrage and constitutional disputes between judicial and legislative branches, as well as a tendency of national courts to be not always comfortable with a discursive-dialogical justification style leading to limited involvement of the lower courts, contribute to institutional and argumentative incoherencies of the system. Moreover, difficult access to national case law and still not fully and consistently developed EU law terminology in the Latvian language constitute further impediments to the coherence and ultimately the effective application of EU law.

Arguably, differences in the degree of coherence of the legal systems may be explained by and rationally grounded in three main factors. First, there are differences in the institutional organization and the role of courts *vis-à-vis* other political actors. The Latvian judiciary tends to be more often subject to indirect political intrusion. Latvian courts also still considerably lag behind in the degree of technical modernization and use of e-technologies in the judicial process.

A second, closely related aspect is differences between judicial personnel. The position of the judge in Latvia is less stable and thus less attractive. The judicial reform announced by the government in the final pre-accession round in 2003 has still not been fully implemented.

Finally, there are differences of conceptual frameworks, underlying values and assumptions on the relationship between national and EU legal orders. The Estonian system generally seems to rely more on the values discourse. The underlying assumption is that the EU legal system is a positive and integral part of the Estonian legal system and thus an important value in itself. Under this understanding, the hierarchical nature of claims to final binding authority is less important. The Latvian system relies on a rights/obligations discourse. EU law is a *lex specialis* of international law, an international treaty-based source of rights and obligations.

Returning to the models of normative conflict solutions by national courts in the EU legal system outlined in Table 1.1., the Estonian case is a strong candidate towards a post-sovereign model of conflict solution with a discursive/persuasive justification style. The post-sovereign approach suggests that a focus on sovereignty is not necessary and should be replaced by a heterarchical system of authority that goes beyond state-centred understandings. This model of reasoning is advanced through discursive rationality. The Latvian case is moving away from a sovereign-pluralistic model based on legalistic/mechanical justifications towards a sovereign-pluralistic model increasingly based on discursive/persuasive justifications. The pluralist approach builds on the logic of sovereignty and respect for plurality of sovereign authorities.

Table 8.1 Synthesis and conclusions on the jurisprudence of the national higher and ordinary courts

		Estonia				Latvia			
		Higher Courts		*Ordinary Courts*		*Higher Courts*		*Ordinary Courts*	
Substantive	Legal principles	Unconditional acceptance and application of main EU law doctrines.	+++	Acceptance and application of EU law provisions, case law and principles.	++	Not clearly regulated but applied without problems.	++	Some terminological confusion and limited instances of misapplication.	++
	Areas of law			Structural Funds Surplus Stock Pension Residence	+++ ++ +/- +			VAT Competition Consumer Labour	+++ +++ ++ ++
Institutional		Active and open cooperation between national higher and EU courts. No major institutional problems. Open and free access to legal information and jurisprudence.	++ +	Active and open cooperation between national higher and ordinary courts. Preliminary references submitted by all court levels.	++ +	Open cooperation between LSC and EU courts. A number of institutional difficulties related to independence and functioning of the court system. Access to legal information and jurisprudence difficult and expensive.	+	Weaker inter-court cooperation with ECJ. Only one preliminary reference submitted by appeal court, no preliminary references from courts of first level.	+
Argumentative		Discursive rationality based on extensive justifications and reasoning. High proportion of substantive reasons.	+++	Points of EU law acknowledged, discussed and applied. Justifications based on variety of legal sources and methods.	++	LCC – discursive rationality based on extensive justifications and reasoning. LSC – often deductive rationality. Proportion of formal reasons high..	++	Points of EU law acknowledged and applied but not always discussed. Higher proportion of formal than substantive reasons.	+

Table 8.2 Models of conflict solution by Estonian and Latvian courts in the EU legal system

Locus of final authority/ mechanism of justification	**Hierarchical**		**Non-hierarchical**
	'Westphalian' (sovereign-pluralist)	'Regulatory' (complex unity)	Post-sovereign (synthesis)
Legalistic/ mechanical	LV		
Discursive/ Persuasive	LV EST		EST

Certain factors of Latvian system incoherence identified in this research are becoming less prominent. For example, there is a considerable difference between the argumentative strategies of the national courts in the first few years after accession and more recent cases. There is a clearly observable learning pattern in judicial opinions of all levels. Certainly positive is the attempt to provide no-fee electronic access to national case law. Those factors if further developed, *inter alia*, through a more dialogic style of the Senate of the Supreme Court, further continuous training in EU law of judges and legal practitioners, and a commitment to transparency and access to information, could even in the short term positively contribute to the coherence of the system. However, other factors connected to reforms of the judicial branch and its relationship with other branches of power are less predictable and will most likely take longer to change.

By way of a final comment and perhaps a direction for further research: a short reflection on the consequences of the conclusions drawn from this book for the project of European legal integration. I argue that both cases bring new dynamics and fresh air to the project of European legal integration. On many accounts, the Estonian case, albeit with some important drawbacks indicated by discrimination cases, presents an example of legal conceptual and methodological modernity. This is particularly so through its understanding of the supremacy and role of EU law in the national legal system as well as accessibility of legal and judicial materials through e-technologies. The Latvian case is an interesting methodological example where international and EU law norms and principles are successfully synthesized by national courts to resolve complex legal issues. Thus, the Latvian Constitutional Court seems to be developing a methodology that suggests a special kind of conforming interpretation where national, EU and international norms have to be substantively balanced and reconciled with each other.

Bibliography

Aarnio, A (1997), *Reason and Authority. A Treatise on the Dynamic Paradigm of Legal Dogmatics* (Aldershot, Dartmouth).

—— (1998), 'Why Coherence – A Philosophical Point of View', in A Aarnio (ed.), *On Coherence Theory of Law* (Lund, Juristfoerlaget).

——, Alexy, R and Peczenik, A (1981), 'The Foundation of Legal Reasoning', 2 *Rechtstheorie* 133.

Aigars G (2001), *Latvian judicial system*, (Riga, Tiesu Namu Aģentūra).

Ajani, G (1995), 'By Chance and Prestige: Legal Transplants in Russia and Eastern Europe', 43 *The American Journal of Comparative Law*, 93.

Albers, M (2012), 'Höchstrichterliche Rechtsfindung und Auslegung gerichtlicher Entscheidungen, in: Grundsatzfragen der Rechtsetzung und Rechtsfindung', 71 Veröffentlichungen der Vereinigung der Deutschen Staatsrechtslehrer 257.

Albi, A (2001), 'Europe Agreements in the Light of Sovereignty and Legitimacy', in Kellermann, AE, Zwaan, JW, and Czuczai, J (eds), *EU Enlargement: The Constitutional Impact at EU and National Levels* (The Hague, TMC Asser Press).

—— (2002), 'Estonia's Constitution and the EU: How and to What Extent to Amend It?', VII *Juridica International*.

—— (2005a), *EU Enlargement and the Constitutions of the Central and Eastern Europe* (Cambridge, Cambridge University Press).

—— (2005b), '"Europe" Articles in the Constitutions of the Central and Eastern European Countries', 42 *Common Market Law Review*, 399–423.

—— (2010), 'From the Banana Saga to a Sugar Saga and Beyond: Could the Post-communist Constitutional Courts Teach the EU a Lesson in the Rule of Law?', 47 *Common Market Law Review*, 791–829.

—— and Ziller, J (2007), *The European Constitution and National Constitutions: Ratification and Beyond* (The Hague, Kluwer).

Alexy, R (1998), 'Coherence and Argumentation or the Genuine Twin Criterialess Super Criterion', in A Aarnio, R Alexy, A Peczenik, W Rabinowicz and J Wolenski (eds), *On Coherence Theory of Law* (Lund, Juristfoerlaget)

—— (2010), *A Theory of Legal Argumentation: The Theory of Rational Discourse as Theory of Legal Justification* (Oxford, Oxford University Press).

Alter, KJ (1996), 'The European Court's political power', 19(3) *West European Politics* 458.

—— (1998), 'Who are the "masters of the Treaty"? European governments and the European Court of Justice', 52 (1) *International Organisation* 121.

—— (2000), 'The European Union's legal system and domestic policy: spillover or backlash?', 54(3) *International Organization* 489.

—— (2001), *Establishing the Supremacy of European Law: The Making of an International Rule of Law for Europe* (Oxford, Oxford University Press).

—— (2006), 'Private Litigants and the New International Courts', 39(1) *Comparative Political Studies* 22.

—— (2009), *The European Court's Political Power: Selected Essays* (Oxford, Oxford University Press).

Amichai, M (2006), 'The Shadow of Enlargement: Can the European Neighbourhood Policy Achieve Compliance?', 12(2) *The Columbia Journal of European Law*.

Annus, T and Taavits, M (2004), 'Judicial Behaviour After a Change of Regime', 38 *Law and Society Review* 716.

Azanda, I (2008), Dominējošā stāvokļa ļaunprātīgas izmantošanas aizliegums, Research paper, available at www.borenius.lv.

Bankowski, Z and MacCormick, N (eds) (1992), *The Judicial Application of Law* (Dordrecht, Kluwer).

—— and Scott, A (eds) (2000), *The European Union and its Order: The Legal Theory of European Integration* (Oxford, Blackwell).

Barents, R (2004), *The Autonomy of Community Law* (The Hague, Kluwer).

Beaulac, S (2000), 'The Westphalian Legal Orthodoxy – Myth or Reality?', 2 *Journal of the History of International Law* 148.

—— (2004), 'The Westphalian Model in Defining International Law: Challenging the Myth', 8 *Australian Journal of Legal History* 181.

Bertea, S (2005), 'Looking for Coherence within the European Community', 11(2) *European Law Journal* 154.

Bobek, M (2007), 'On the Application of European Law in (Not Only) the Courts of the New Member States: "Don't Do as I Say"?', 10 *Cambridge Yearbook of European Legal Studies*.

—— (2008), 'The Fortress of Judicial Independence and the Mental Transitions of the Central European Judiciaries', 14(1) *Europan European Public Law*.

—— (2010), 'The Administration of Courts in the Czech Republic: In Search of a Constitutional Balance', 16(2) *European Public Law* 251.

Bogdandy, A von (2000), 'The European Union as a Supranational Federation: A Conceptual Attempt in the Light of the Treaty of Amsterdam', 6 *Columbia Journal of International Law* 27.

Borkoveca, M (2010), 'Eiropas Savienības tiesību sistēmas mijiedarbība ar dalībvalstu tiesību sistēmām', 13 *Jurista Vārds* 608.

Börzel, T (2006), 'Empowering Citizens in Post-Decisional Politics?', 39 (1) *Comparative Political Studies* 128.

Brederode, RF van (2008), 'Third-Party Risks and Liabilities in Case of VAT Fraud in the EU', *International Tax Journal*, January–February.

Brūklenis, J and Lapsa, L. (2007), Tiesāšanās kā ķēķis : advokāta Gūtupa "sakārtošanas" receptes, (Rīga: Mantojums)

Buckel, S, Christensen, R, and Fischer-Lescano, A, (eds) (2009), *Neue Theorien des Rechts*, 2nd edn (Stuttgart, Lucius & Lucius).

Burley, AM and Mattli, W (1993), 'Europe before the Court: A Political Theory of Legal Integration', 47 *International Organization* 41.

Čakste, E (2000), 'Par Eiropas Savienības tiesību īstenošanas principiem', 35 *Jurista Vārds* 188.

Capeta, T (2005), 'Courts, Legal Culture and EU Enlargement', 1 *Croatian Yearbook of European Law and Policy*.

Cappeletti, M, Seccombe, M and Weiler, JHH (eds) (1985), *Integration Through Law: European and the American Federal Experience* (Florence, EUI), Band 1.

Carrubba, CJ and Murrah, L (2005), 'Legal integration and the use of the preliminary ruling process in the European Union', 59 *International Organization* 399.

Cichowski, R and Stone Sweet, A (2003), 'Participation, Representative Democracy, and the Courts', in B Cain, R Dalton and S Scarrow (eds), *Democracy Transformed?*, (Oxford: Oxford University Press).

Chalmers, D, Davies, G and Monti, G (eds) (2010), *European Union Law. Text and Materials*, 2nd edn (Cambridge, Cambridge University Press).

Claes, M (2005), 'Constitutionalising Europe at its Source: The "European Clauses" in the National Constitutions: Evolution and Typology', 24 *Yearbook of European Law* 81.

—— (2006), *The National Courts Mandate in the European Constitution* (Oxford, Hart).

Closa, C (2009), 'From Constitution to Treaty: democratic paradoxes and clandestine constitutional politics in the EU', in Cruz, JB and Closa C (eds), *European integration from Rome to Berlin: History, Law and Politics*, (London: Peter Lang).

—— (2012), 'National Courts and Ratification of the EU Treaties: Assessing the Impact of Political Contexts in Judicial Decisions', in Evas, T, Liebert, U and Lord, C (eds), *Multilayered Representation in the European Union: Parliaments, Courts, Civil Society and the Public Sphere, (*Baden-Baden. Nomos).

—— and Fossum, JE (2005), 'Deliberative Constitutional Politics', 11 *European Law Journal*.

Connant, L (2001), 'Europeanization and the Courts: Variable Patterns of Adaptation Among National Judiciaries', in MG Cowles, JA Caporaso and T Risse (eds), *Transforming Europe: Europeanization and Domestic Change* (Ithaca, NY, Cornell University Press).

—— (2002), *Justice Contained: Law and Politics in the European Union* (Ithaca, NY, Cornell University Press).

—— (2006), 'Individuals, courts, and the development of European social rights', 39 (1) *Comparative Political Studies* 76.

Craig, P (2003), 'The ECJ National Courts and the Supremacy of Community Law', in I Pernice and R Miccù (eds), *The European Constitution in the Making* (Baden-Baden, Nomos).

—— and de Burca, G (2008), *EU Law. Text, Cases and Materials*, 4th ed., (Oxford, Oxford University Press).

Cutler, AC (2001), 'Critical Reflections on the Westphalian Assumptions of International Law and Organization: A Crisis of Legitimacy', 27 *Review of International Studies* 133.

Dworkin, R (1986), *Law's Empire* (London, Fontana Press).

Eleftheriadis, P (1996), 'The Direct Effect of Community Law: Conceptual Issues', 16 *Yearbook of European Law* 205.

Emmert, F (2003), Administrative and Court Reform in Central and Eastern Europe, 9 (3) *European Law Journal*.

Endzinš, A (2004), 'The Position of the Constitutional Court of the Republic of Latvia Following Integration into the European Union.', Conference paper presented at the international conference "The Position of Constitutional Courts following Integration into the European Union", Bled, Constitutional Court of the Republic of Slovenia September 30 to October 2, 2004 available at http://www.us-rs.si/en/about-the-court/conferences/pcceu-bled-30-september-2-october-2004/presentation-by-dr-aivars-endzins-chairman-of-the/ [last accessed on 1 December 2011] paras 2 and 3.

Eriksen, EO (ed.) (2007), 'How to Reconstitute Democracy in Europe?', *RECON Report* No 3.

—— and Fossum, JE (eds) (2009), 'Theory in Practice', *RECON Report* No 8.

European Commission (2003 a), Comprehensive Monitoring Report on Estonia's Preparations for Membership, available at http://ec.europa.eu/enlargement/archives/pdf/key_documents/2003/cmr_ee_final_en.pdf [last accessed 01.07.2012]

—— (2003 b), Comprehensive Monitoring Report on Latvia's Preparations for Membership, available at http://ec.europa.eu/enlargement/archives/pdf/key_documents/2003/cmr_lv_final_en.pdf [last accessed 01.07.2012]

European Parliament (2007), 'The relationship between national courts and the European Court of Justice in the European Union judicial system - preliminary ruling regimes under Articles 234 EC, 68 EC, and 35 EU', DG Internal Policies, available at http://www.europarl.europa.eu/comparl/juri/study/courts_en.pdf [last accessed 01.09.2011].

Evas, T (2005), 'Access to Justice in Estonia', Open Society Institute, Second Access to Justice Forum, Budapest.

—— (2007), 'Elitist with a Russian twist: Mass media discourses on European constitutional ratification in Estonia and Latvia', 8 (3) *Perspectives on European Politics and Society* 373.

—— (2009), ', Distributive conflict, social justice and rule of law in ethnically diverse post-communist democracies in the EU: A case study of the jurisprudence of Estonian courts', European Consortium for Political Research General Conference, Potsdam, Germany, 9.-12.9.2009

—— (2010), 'Integration and Ethnic Cohesion of the Estonian Society', in Käsper, K and Marianne Meiorg, M (eds), *Human Rights in Estonia* (Tallinn, Human Rights Institute).

—— (2011), '*Domestic Courts, National Political Actors and European Judiciary: New Forms of Political Participation*, RECON Workshop "Strengthening Democracy in the EU – Alternative Forms of Representation", Bremen RECON Conference, 14-15.07.2011.

—— (2012), *Integration and Ethnic cohesion of the Estonian society, 6 L'Europe unie/United Europe* (forthcoming).

—— and Liebert, U (2009), *Turning Aliens into Members: Globalisation, Immigration, and Citizenship in the Union of States*, 21st World Congress of Political Science, IPSA, Santiago de Chile, 12–16.7.2009.

—— and Liebert, U (2010), 'Enhancing Democracy Through Constitutional Pluralism? The Czech, German and Latvian Lisbon Ruling in Dialogue', Conference paper presented at the Fifth Pan-European Conference on EU Politics, Porto, Portugal.

——, Liebert, U and Lord, C (2012), 'Multilayered representation across the European Union in dialogue: Introduction', in Evas, T, Liebert, U and Lord, C (eds), *Multilayered Representation in the European Union: Parliaments, Courts, Civil Society and the Public Sphere, (*Baden-Baden. Nomos).

—— and Liebert, U (2013, forthcoming), 'Still 'between Eros and civilisation'? Citizens, courts and constructing European Citizenship', in U Liebert, A Gattig and T Evas (eds), *Democratizing the European Union from Below: Citizenship, Civil Society and the Public Sphere in Making Europe's Order*, (Farnham, Ashgate).

Febbrajo, A, and Sadurski, W, (eds) (2010), *Central and Eastern Europe After Transition: Towards a New Socio-Legal Semantics* (Aldershot, Ashgate).

Fischer-Lescano, A, and Teubner, G (2006), *Regime-Kollisionen. Zur Fragmentierung des globalen Rechts* (Frankfurt, Suhrkamp).

Fossum, JE, and Menendez, AJ (2010a), *The Constitution's Gift: A Constitutional Theory for a Democratic European Union* (Lanham, MD, Rowman & Littlefield).

—— (2010b), 'The Theory of Constitutional Synthesis. A Constitutional Theory for a Democratic European Union', *RECON Online Working Paper* 25/2010.

Gailis, M and Maskalans, I (2009), 'Latvia', in *International Comparative Legal Guide to Dominance*, (London, Global Legal Group).

Galligan, DJ and Matczak, M (2007), 'Formalism in Post-Communist Courts: Empirical Study on Judicial Discretion in Polish Administrative Law', in Coman, R and de Waele, JM, *Judicial Reforms in Central and Eastern European Countries* (Bruges, Vanden Broele).

Gerstenberg, O and Sabel, CF (2002), 'Directly-Deliberative Polyarchy: An Institutional Ideal for Europe?', in C Joerges and R Dehousse (eds), *Good Governance in Europe's Integrated Market* (Oxford, Oxford University Press).

Ginter, C (2007), 'Procedural Issues Relating to EU law in the Estonian Supreme Court', XII *Juridica International.*

—— (2008), *Application of Principles of European Law in the Supreme Court of Estonia* (Tartu, Tartu University Press).

Golub, G (1996), 'The Politics of Judicial Discretion: Rethinking the Interaction Between National Courts and the European Court of Justice', 19 *West European Politics* 360.

Guild, E (2000), 'European Developments. The EC Directive on Race Discrimination: Surprises, Possibilities and Limitation', 29(4) *Industrial Law Journal.*

Guļāns, A (2005), 'History and development of the Supreme Court: revolution, evolution or a fate pre-set by legal norms?', Chief Justice of the Supreme Court of Latvia, Conference Report, October 7, 2005,

Habermas, J (1997), *Between Facts and Norms: Contribution to a Discourse Theory of Law and Democracy*, English edn (Cambridge, Polity Press).

Hage, JC (2004), 'Law and Coherence', 17(1) *Ratio Juris* 87.

Haltern, U (2004), 'Integration Through Law', in A Wiener and T Diez (eds), *European Integration Theory* (Oxford, Oxford University Press).

Hart, HLA (1994), *The Concept of Law*, 2nd edn (Oxford, Clarendon Press).

Hendley, K (1996), *Trying to Make Law Matter* (Ann Arbor, University of Michigan Press).

Hoecke, M van (2001), 'Judicial Review and Deliberative Democracy: A Circular Model of Law Creation and Legitimation', 4 *Ratio Juris.*

Jupille, J and Caporaso, JA (2009), 'Domesticating Discourses: European Law, English Judges and Political Institutions', 1 *European Political Science Review* 205.

Kanger, L (2007), 'Euroopa Liidu õiguse kohaldamine Eesti halduskohtute praktikas: põllumajandustoetuste ja üleliigse laovaru tasu kaasuste näitel', Supreme Court of Estonia legal analysis of the case law, available at http://www.riigikohus.ee/vfs/776/Analyys%20EL%20oiguse%20kohaldamine%20HK%20praktikas%20%28L_Kanger%29.pdf [last accessed on 01.07.2012]

Kellermann AE, Czuczai, J, Blockmans, S, Albi, A and Douma, WT (eds) (2006), *The Impact of EU Accession on the Legal Orders of New EU Member States and (Pre)Candidate Countries – Hopes and Fears* (The Hague, TMC Asser Press).

Kelsen, H (1967), *The Pure Theory of Law*, 2nd edn (Berkeley, University of California Press).

Kerikmäe, T (2009), *Estonia in the European Legal System: Protection of the Rule of Law through Constitutional Dialogue* (Tallinn, Tallinn University).

Ketelhut, J (2010), *Der EuGH und die deutschen Arbeitsgerichte – Strategische Interaktionen in komplexen Entscheidungskontexten. Eine politikwissenschaftliche Analyse judizieller Governance im EU-Mehrebenensystem* (Baden-Baden, Nomos).

Komárek, J (2005), 'European Constitutional Pluralism and the European Arrest Warrant: Contrapunctual Principles in Disharmony', 10 *Jean Monnet Working Paper*.

Kress, K (1999), 'Coherence', in D Patterson (ed.), *A Companion to Philosophy of Law and Legal Theory* (Oxford, Blackwell).

Kühn, Z (2004), 'Worlds Apart: Western and Central European Judicial Culture at the Onset of the European Enlargement', 52 *The American Journal of Comparative Law*.

—— (2005), 'The Application of European Union Law in the New Member States: Several Early Predictions', *German Law Journal* 564.

—— (2006), 'The Authoritarian Legal Culture at Work: The Passivity of Parties and the Interpretation Statements of Supreme Courts', *Croatian Yearbook of European Law and Policy*.

Kumm, M (1999), 'Who is the Final Arbiter of Constitutionality in Europe?: Three Conceptions of the Relationship Between the German Federal Constitutional Court and the European Court of Justice', 36 *Common Market Law Review*, 351.

La Torre, M (1999), 'Legal Pluralism as an Evolutionary Achievement of Community Law', 12 *Ratio Juris* 182.

Laffranque, J (2000), 'Estonia's association agreement with the European Union: legal and constitutional aspects', IV *Juridica*.

—— (2001), 'Constitution of the Republic of Estonia in the Light of Accession to the European Union', VI *Juridica International* 207.

—— (2002), 'Co-existence of the Estonian Constitution and European Law', VII *Juridica International*.

—— (2005), 'The Judicial System of Estonian and European Union Law', 33 *International Journal of Legal Information*, 224–39.

—— (2009), 'Sõltumatu ja demokraatlik õigusriik Riigikohtu praktikas', 8 *Juridica International*, 483–99.

Liebert, U (2005), 'Der Verfassungsvertrag: Ein Fortschritt für die demokratische Legitimität in der Europäischen Union?', in M Jopp and S Matl (eds), *Der Vertrag über eine Verfassung für Europa. Analysen zur Konstitutionalisierung der EU*, (Baden-Baden, NOMOS).

—— (2006), 'Democracy Beyond the State: Assessing European Constitutionalisation', in U Liebert, J Falke and A Maurer (eds), *Postnational Constitutionalisation in the New Europe*, (Baden-Baden, Nomos).

—— (2007a), 'Europe in Contention: Debating the Constitutional Treaty', 8 (3) *Perspectives on European Politics and Society*.

—— (2007b), 'The European Citizenship Paradox: Renegotiating Equality and Diversity in the New Europe', 10 (4) *Critical Review of International Social and Political Philosophy* 417.

—— (2007c), 'The Politics for a Social Europe and the Lisbon Process', in L Magnusson and B Strath (eds), *European Solidarities. Tensions and Contentions of a Concept* (Brussels, Peter Lang).

—— and Trenz, HJ, (2008), 'Mass media and contested meanings: EU constitutional politics after popular rejection", 28 *RSCAS Working Paper*, European University Institute, Florence.

—— (2009), 'Civil society and the reconstitution of democracy in Europe: Introducing a new research field', in U Liebert and HJ Trenz (eds), New Approaches to Civil Society in Europe, 28 *Policy and Society 1*.

—— (2010), 'Contentious European Democracy: National Intellectuals in Transnational Debate', in J Lacroix and K Nicolaïdis (eds), *European Stories Intellectual Debates on Europe in National Contexts*, (Oxford, Oxford University Press).

—— (2012a), 'European democracy and identity constructions: Framework and measurement', in O Brzezinska, E Kurucz, U Liebert and R Sackmann, R (eds), *Identity and Democracy in the New Europe, The Next Generation Finds Its Ways*, ARENA Report No 2/12, RECON Report No 18, (Oslo, ARENA).

—— (2012b), 'Rethinking the "No European Demos" Thesis: Transnational Discursive Representation as a Prerequisite of EU Democracy', in T Evas, U Liebert and C Lord (eds) (2012), *Multilayered Representation in the European Union: Parliaments, Courts and the Public Sphere*, ZERP Schriftenreihe No. 64, (Baden-Baden, Nomos).

Lieven, A (1993), *The Baltic Revolution: Estonia, Latvia, Lithuania and the Path to Independence* (New Haven, CT, Yale University Press).

Lindahl, H (2003), 'Sovereignty and Representation in the European Union', in N Walker (ed.), *Sovereignty in Transition* (Oxford, Hart).

Linntam, M (2002), 'Building a Just Society: the Role of the Constitutional Jude', VII *Juridica International.*

Lõhmus, U (2007), 'Kuidas liikmesriigi kohtusüsteem tagab Euroopa Liidu õiguse tõhusa toime', III *Juridica.*

—— (2010), 'Põhiõiguste kaitse kolmnurgas riik – Euroopa Nõukogu – Euroopa Liit (Protection of Fundamental Rights in the Triangle State – Council of Europe – European Union)', V *Juridica* 354.

Määlksoo, L (2003), *Illegal Annexation and State Continuity: The Case of the Incorporation of the Baltic States by the USSR* (Leiden, Martinus Nijhoff Publishers).

MacCormick, DN and Summers, RS (eds) (1991), *Interpreting Statutes* (Aldershot and Dartmouth, NH, Ashgate).

MacCormick, N (1978), *Legal Reasoning and Legal Theory* (Oxford, Clarendon Press).

—— (1984), 'Coherence in Legal Justification', in A Peczenik et al. (eds), *Theory of Legal Science* (Dordrech, D. Reidel Publishing).

—— (1993), 'Beyond the Sovereign State', 56 *Modern Law Review* 1.

—— (1999), *Questioning Sovereignty: Law, State and Practical Reason* (Oxford, Oxford University Press).

—— (2007), *Institutions of Law. An Essay in Legal Theory* (Oxford, Oxford University Press).

Maduro, MP (2000), 'Europe and the Constitution: What if this is as good as it gets?', in JHH Weiler and M Wind (eds), *European Constitutionalism beyond the State* (Cambridge, Cambridge University Press).

—— (2003), 'Contrapunctual Law: Europe's Constitutional Pluralism in Action', in N Walker (ed.), *Sovereignty in Transition* (Oxford, Hart).

—— (2008), 'Interpreting European Law – Judicial Adjudication in a Context of Constitutional Pluralism', Working paper IE Law School, WPLS08-02.

—— and Azoulai, LM (2010), *The Past and Future of EU Law: The Classics of EU Law Revisited on the 50th Anniversary of the Rome Treaty* (Oxford, Hart Publishing).

Mattli, W and Slaughter, AM (1989), 'The Role of National Courts in the Process of European Integration: Accounting for Judicial Preferences and Constraints', in AM Slaughter, AC Sweet and JHH Weiler (eds), *The European Courts and National Courts: Doctrine and Jurisprudence* (Oxford, Hart Publishing).

Mayer, FC (2005), 'Supremacy – Lost? – Comment on Roman Kwiecien', 6(11) *German Law Journal* 1497.

Menendez, AJ (2000), 'Complex Democracy and the Obligation to Obey the Law', *ARENA Working Paper* 00/25.

Micklitz, HW and Reich, N (eds) (1997), *Public Interest Litigation before European Courts*, (Baden-Baden: Nomos).

Mits, M (2010), *European Convention on Human Rights in Latvia: Impact on Legal Doctrine and Application of Legal Norms* (Lund, Media Tryck).

Moral, SL (2003), 'A Modest Notion of Coherence in Legal Reasoning. A Model for the European Court of Justice', 16(3) *Ratio Juris* 302.

Müllerson, R, Fitzmaurice, M and Andenas, M (eds) (1998), *Constitutional Reform and International Law in Central and Eastern Europe* (The Hague, Kluwer).

Narits, R (2002), 'The Republic of Estonia Constitution on the Concept and Value of Law', (2002) VII *Juridica International.*

—— (2008), 'Konstitutsioonikohtute tänapäevastest töömeetoditest mandrieuroopaliku õiguskultuuri ja common law kui mõtlemisviiside lähenemise tingimustes 17 *Riigikogu Toimetised* 85.

Nourse, V and Shaffer, G (2009), 'Varieties of New Legal Realism: Can A New World Order Prompt A New Legal Theory?', 96 *Cornell Law Review* 61.

Nyikos, S (2007), 'Courts', in P Graziano and MP Vink (eds), *Europeanization: New Research Agendas* (New York, Palgrave).

Palazzo, G (2002), *Die Mitte der Demoktratie* (Bade-Baden, Nomos).

Parfjonova, A (2002), 'Par Eiropas Kopienas asociācijas līgumiem', 14 *Jurista Vārds* 247.

Peczenik, A (1989), *On Law and Reason* (Dordrecht, Kluwer).

Pelša, I (2009), 'Eiropas Savienības konkurences tiesību piemērošana', 11 *Jurista Vārds* 564.

Pernice, I (2002), 'Multilevel Constitutionalism in the European Union', 27 *European Law Review* 51.

Pettai, V and Veebel, V (2005), 'Navigating between Policy and Populace: Estonia, its Accession Referendum & the EU Convention', 1 *Politique européenne* 113.

Prechal, S (2005), *Directives in EC law*, (Oxford, Oxford University Press).

—— and van Roermund B (eds) (2008), *The coherence of EU law: the search for unity in divergent concepts* (Oxford, Oxford University Press).

Rask, M (2010), 'Ülevaade Kohtukorralduse, õigusemõistmise ja seaduste ühetaolise kohaldamise kohta', transcript of the oral speech at the Estonian Parliament, spring session.

Raz, J (1994), 'The Relevance of Coherence', in J Raz (ed.), *Ethics in the Public Domain. Essays in the Morality of Law and Politics* (Oxford, Clarendon Press).

—— (2007), 'More Clarity after "Claro"? Arbitration Clauses in Consumer Contracts as an ADR (Alternative Dispute Resolution) Mechanism for Effective and Speedy Conflict Resolution, or as "deni de justice"?', 3(1) *European Review of Contract Law*.

Reich, N (1999), 'On National Courts, European Law and Constitutions: Dialogue and Conflict', 5 (2) *European Law Journal* 154.

—— (2005), *Understanding EU law, Sources and Methods of EU law*, 2nd edn (Antwerp, Intersentia Publishers).

—— (2007), 'More clarity after "Claro"? Arbitration Clauses in Consumer Contracts as an ADR (alternative dispute resolution) Mechanism for Effective and Speedy Conflict Resolution, or as "deni de justice"?', 3 (1) European Review of Contract Law 41.

—— (2009), '"Europarechtsfreundlichkeit" und "Integrationsverantwortung" – eine lettische Variante', *Europäische Zeitschrift für Wirtschaftsrecht* 713.

Richmond, C (1997), 'Preserving the Identity Crisis: Autonomy, System and Sovereignty in European Law', 16 *Law and Philosophy* 377.

Rodin, S (2005), 'Discourse and Authority in European and Post-Communist Legal Culture', 1 *Croatian Yearbook of European Law and Policy*.

Rodriguez-Blanco, V (2001), 'A Revision of the Constitutive and Epistemic Coherence Theories in Law', 14 *Ratio Juris* 212.

Roermund, van BC (1990), 'Narrative Coherence and the Guises of Legalism', in P Nerhot (ed.), *Law, Interpretation and Reality*. Essays in Epistemology, Hermeneutics and Jurisprudence, Law and Philosophy Library (Dordrecht, Kluwer).

Roger, S (2007), 'Human rights and access to justice', 14(3) *International Journal of the Legal Profession* 261.

Romans, A (2001), *The Baltic States at Historical Crossroads* (Riga, Latvian Academy of Sciences).

Sadurski, W (2005), *Rights Before Courts* (Dordrecht, Springer).

—— (2006), 'Solange, Chapter 3: Constitutional Courts in Central Europe, Democracy, European Union', *EUI Working Paper* 40.

——, Ziller, J and Zurek, K (2006), *Après Enlargement: Legal and Political Responses in Central and Eastern Europe* (Florence, Robert Schuman Centre).

Schiek, D (2010), 'Is there a Social ideal of the European Court of Justice?', in U Neergaard, R Nielsen L and Roseberry (eds), *The Role of Courts in Developing a European Social Model* (Copenhagen: DJØF Publishing).
—— (2012), 'Social Ideals of the Court of Justice of the European Union', in T Evas, U Liebert and C Lord (eds) (2012), *Multilayered Representation in the European Union: Parliaments, Courts and the Public Sphere*, ZERP Schriftenreihe No. 64, (Baden-Baden, Nomos).
Schilling, T (1996), 'The Autonomy of the Community Legal Order', 37 (2) *Harvard International Law Journal* 389.
Sikk, A (2009), 'Parties and Populism', University College London, School of Slavonic and Eastern European Studies Working Paper, 2009-02, available at http://www.ssees.ucl.ac.uk/PartiesandPopulism.pdf.
Sildam, T and Mattson, T (1997), 'Kohtunik seaduse ja väärtuse vahel', 21 *Luup* 10.
Škoba, L (2003), 'Par Eiropas Savienības direktīvu tiešo iedarbību', 42 *Jurista Vārds* 300.
Škutāns, D (2006), 'Valsts un privātā partnerība publiskā iepirkuma kontekstā', 34 *Jurista Vārds* 437.
Slaughter, AM (1995), 'International Law in a World of Liberal States', 6 *European Journal of International Law* 503.
—— (2003), 'A Global Community of Courts', 44(1) *Harvard International Law Journal* 191.
——, Stone Sweet, A and Weiler, JHH (eds) (1998), *The European Court and National Courts – Doctrine and Jurisprudence: Legal Change in its Social Context* (Oxford, Hart).
Stone Sweet, A (2004), *The Judicial Construction of Europe* (Oxford, Oxford University Press).
—— (2007), 'The Juridical Coup d'Etat and the Problem of Authority', VIII(10) *German Law Review*.
Teubner, G (1997), 'Altera Pars Audiatur: Law in the Collision of Discourses', in R Rawlings (ed.), *Law, Society and Economy* (Oxford, Oxford University Press).
—— and Fischer-Lescano, A (2004), 'Regime Collisions: The Vain Search for Legal Unity in the Fragmentation of Global Law', 25 *Michigan Journal of International Law*.
Uibopuu, HJ (2005), 'The European Convention on Human Rights as a Legal Source for the Courts', X *Juridica* 443.
Uitz, R (2007), 'Constitutional Courts in Central and Eastern Europe: What makes a Question too Political?', XIII *Juridica International* 47.
Vallikivi, H (1999a), 'Millal jõustus Eestis kehtiv põhiseadus?', 7 *Juridica* 348.
—— (1999b), 'Use of the European Convention on Human Rights in the Practice of the Supreme Court', VII *Juridica International* 399.
Vauchez, A (2008), 'Integration-through-law', Contribution to a Socio-history of EU Political Commonsense', *EUI Working Papers RSCAS* 2008/10.

Vink, M, Claes, M and Arnold, C (2009), Explaining the Use of Preliminary Reference by Domestic Courts in EU Member States: A Mixed – Method Comparative Analysis', EUSA Biennial Conference paper, available at www.euce.org/eusa2009/papers/vink_06B.pdf [last accessed 01.07.2012]

Vutt, M (2009), 'Kohtupraktika analüüs Riigikohtus', VIII *Juridica* 528.

Walker, N (2002), 'The Idea of Constitutional Pluralism', 65 Modern Law Review 317.

—— (2003), 'Late Sovereignty in the European Union', in N Walker, N (ed.), *Sovereignty in Transition* (Oxford, Hart).

—— (2005a), 'Legal Theory and the European Union: A 25th Anniversary Essay', 25 *Oxford Journal of Legal Studies* 581.

—— (2005b), 'Legal Theory and the European Union', *EUI Working Paper Law*, No. 2005/16.

—— (2008), 'Out of Place and Out of Time: Law's Fading Co-ordinates', University of Edinburgh School of Law Working papers Series, No. 2009/01.

Watson, A (1995), 'From Legal Transplants to Legal Formants', *American Journal of International and Comparative Law* 469.

—— (1996), 'Aspects of Reception of Law', *American Journal of International and Comparative Law* 333.

Weiler, JHH (1994), 'A quiet revolution: the European Court of Justice and its interlocutors', 26 (1) *Comparative Political Studies* 510.

—— and Haltern, UH (1996), 'The Autonomy of the Community Legal Order – Through the Looking Glass', 37(2) *Harvard International Law Journal* 411.

Winter, T (1972), 'Direct applicability and direct effect: two distinct and different concepts in Community law', 9 Common Market Law Review 425

Witte, B de (2010), 'European Union Law: How Autonomous is its Legal Order?', 65 *Zeitschrift für öffentliches Recht* 141.

Zemanek, J (2006), 'The Constitutional Courts in the New Member States and the Uniform Application of European Law', in I Pernice, J Kokott and C Saunders, (eds), *The Future of the European Judicial System in a Comparative Perspecive* (Baden-Baden, Nomos).

Ziemele, I (2005), *State Continuity and Nationality: Baltic States and Russia: Past, Present and Future as Defined by International Law* (Leiden, Martinus Nijhoff Publishers (Brill Publishers)).

Zigurds, GM (2002), *Expression of Constitutionalism in the Satversme: Problems of Transformation of Law in Connection with European Integration* (Riga, University of Latvia).

Zukova, G (2009), 'Eiropas Savienības tiesību piemērošana Latvijā', *Jurista Vārds* 51/52.

Index

www.ingramcontent.com/pod-product-compliance
Ingram Content Group UK Ltd.
Pitfield, Milton Keynes, MK11 3LW, UK
UKHW010959180926
475701UK00004B/470
* 9 7 8 1 1 3 8 2 7 9 1 1 7 *